Language Policy
in Higher Education

MULTILINGUAL MATTERS

Series Editor: John Edwards, *St. Francis Xavier University, Canada*

Multilingual Matters series publishes books on bilingualism, bilingual education, immersion education, second language learning, language policy, multiculturalism. The editor is particularly interested in 'macro' level studies of language policies, language maintenance, language shift, language revival and language planning. Books in the series discuss the relationship between language in a broad sense and larger cultural issues, particularly identity related ones.

Full details of all the books in this series and of all our other publications can be found on http://www.multilingual-matters.com, or by writing to Multilingual Matters, St Nicholas House, 31-34 High Street, Bristol BS1 2AW, UK.

MULTILINGUAL MATTERS: 158

Language Policy in Higher Education

The Case of Medium-Sized Languages

Edited by
F. Xavier Vila and Vanessa Bretxa

MULTILINGUAL MATTERS
Bristol • Buffalo • Toronto

Library of Congress Cataloging in Publication Data
A catalog record for this book is available from the Library of Congress.
Language Policy in Higher Education: The Case of Medium-Sized Languages/Edited by
F. Xavier Vila and Vanessa Bretxa.
Multilingual Matters: 158
Includes bibliographical references and index.
1. Native language and education—Cross-cultural studies. 2. Language policy—Cross-cultural studies. 3. Multilingualism—Cross-cultural studies. 4. Sociolinguistics—Cross-cultural studies. 5. Education, Higher—Cross-cultural studies. I. Vila, F. Xavier, editor of compilation. II. Bretxa, Vanessa, 1980- editor of compilation.
LC201.5.L37 2014
370.117'5-dc23 2014023726

British Library Cataloguing in Publication Data
A catalogue entry for this book is available from the British Library.

ISBN-13: 978-1-78309-275-8 (hbk)
ISBN-13: 978-1-78309-274-1 (pbk)

Multilingual Matters
UK: St Nicholas House, 31-34 High Street, Bristol BS1 2AW, UK.
USA: UTP, 2250 Military Road, Tonawanda, NY 14150, USA.
Canada: UTP, 5201 Dufferin Street, North York, Ontario M3H 5T8, Canada.

Website: www.multilingual-matters.com
Twitter: Multi_Ling_Mat
Facebook: https://www.facebook.com/multilingualmatters
Blog: www.channelviewpublications.wordpress.com

Copyright © 2015 F. Xavier Vila, Vanessa Bretxa and the authors of individual chapters.

All rights reserved. No part of this work may be reproduced in any form or by any means without permission in writing from the publisher.

The policy of Multilingual Matters/Channel View Publications is to use papers that are natural, renewable and recyclable products, made from wood grown in sustainable forests. In the manufacturing process of our books, and to further support our policy, preference is given to printers that have FSC and PEFC Chain of Custody certification. The FSC and/or PEFC logos will appear on those books where full certification has been granted to the printer concerned.

Typeset by Deanta Global Publishing Services Limited.

Contents

Tables and Figures — vii
Contributors — xi

1 Language Policy in Higher Education in Medium-Sized Language Communities: An Introduction — 1
   F. Xavier Vila

2 The Position of Danish, English and Other Languages at Danish Universities in the Context of Danish Society — 15
   Hartmut Haberland and Bent Preisler

3 The Position of Czech and Other Languages at Universities in the Czech Republic: Some Initial Observations — 43
   Tamah Sherman

4 The Position of Finnish and Swedish as well as Other Languages at Universities in Finland — 64
   Sabine Ylönen

5 Challenges for Hebrew in Higher Education and Research Environments — 103
   Drorit Ram

6 Challenges for South Africa's Medium-Sized Indigenous Languages in Higher Education and Research Environments — 132
   Anne-Marie Beukes

7 The Position of Catalan in Higher Education in Catalonia   153
   Eva Pons Parera

8 Medium-Sized Languages as Viable Linguae Academicae   181
   F. Xavier Vila

   Index   211

Tables and Figures

Tables

Table 1.1 Guidelines for the presentation of challenges for medium-sized language communities in higher education and research environments — 8

Table 2.1 Danish universities: Languages used and organizing principles — 27

Table 2.2 Students at Copenhagen Business School enrolled in English-medium and Danish-medium programmes — 29

Table 2.3 Academic publications in Denmark, 2009, by field of research — 34

Table 4.1 Language policies at Finnish universities (in January 2012 and August 2013) — 71

Table 4.2 Degree programmes in Finland taught in English by educational level for 2008 — 80

Table 4.3 Percentage of foreign degree students at Finnish universities 2007–2009 — 81

Table 4.4 Scientific publications at three Finnish universities for 1998–2005: Country and language of publication — 87

Table 5.1 Patterns of Hebrew and of English as mediums of university instruction — 126

Table 6.1 Choice of language(s) as medium of instruction in South African schools (2007) — 135

Table 6.2 Comparison of total number of students in 1993 and in 2004 indicating growth in higher education sector — 136

Table 6.3 Language dispensation at South African higher education institutions (1994) — 137

Table 6.4 Language dispensation at South African higher education institutions subsequent to a rationalisation process (2004) — 138

Table 6.5 Current dispensation regarding language of instruction at previously 'Afrikaans universities' — 140

Table 6.6 Enrolment of students at University of Johannesburg who chose Afrikaans as language of instruction (1999–2011) — 142

Table 6.7 Enrolment of Afrikaans students at UJ (2000–2009) — 142

Table 6.8 Student enrolment for BA CESMS degree at University of Limpopo (2003–2012). — 144

Table 6.9 Summary of current language practices at South African higher education institutions as regards languages used for teaching and learning — 146

Table 7.1 Proficiency in Catalan by population according to age groups. Catalonia 2008. — 155

Table 7.2 Language policies at Catalan universities — 163

Table 7.3 Language of the articles that appeared in Catalan scientific journals — 174

Figures

Figure 2.1 Research publications, Roskilde University, 1995–2008 — 34

Figure 4.1 Comparison of any language use between different personnel groups and students — 77

Figure 4.2 Language use at Finnish universities in terms of different skills 78

Figure 4.3 Foreign degree students in relation to the total number of students at Finnish universities (Yo) and universities of applied sciences (Amk) 81

Figure 4.4 Language of PhD dissertations from the 17th century to 2009 89

Figure 4.5 Language of PhD dissertations in the past 40 years 90

Figure 5.1 Lecturers' language preference 116

Figure 5.2 Lecturers' reasons for their language preference 117

Figure 5.3 The prevalence of English in reading and writing activities 122

Figure 5.4 Measures of reading in English among arts and sciences students 124

Picture 5.1 Example of a poster in Hebrew and English 128

Contributors

F. Xavier Vila is an associate professor at the University of Barcelona. He obtained an Extraordinary Degree Award in Catalan Philology from the University of Barcelona and a PhD in linguistics from the Vrije Universiteit Brussel. He was the first director of the CRUSCAT Research Network on sociolinguistics of the Institut d'Estudis Catalans, the Catalan National Academy of Sciences, and is the current director of the University Centre for Sociolinguistics and Communication at the University of Barcelona (CUSC-UB). He is also the director of the master's programme in language consultancy, multilingual language management and editorial services at the University of Barcelona's Catalan Philology Department. He has published a wide range of books and specialized articles in the areas of sociolinguistics, demolinguistics and language policy with reference to Catalan and other medium-sized and minority languages, among them *Survival and Development of Language Communities: Prospects and Challenges* (Multilingual Matters, 2013).

Vanessa Bretxa is a researcher in the sociology of language at the University Centre for Sociolinguistics and Communication (CUSC) at the Universitat de Barcelona and a part-time lecturer in the Department of Linguistics at the same university. She has participated in several large-scale sociolinguistic projects regarding language use and competence in the Catalan-speaking areas, and in the practices of cultural and media consumption of young speakers of Catalan and Spanish in the Barcelona metropolitan area. She was a visiting researcher at the Centre for Catalan Studies, – School of Modern Languages – Queen Mary, University of London in 2007 and CREFO – Centre de Recherches en Éducation Franco-Ontarienne, University of Toronto in 2008–2009. She is the co-editor of the academic journal *LSC* (Language, Society and Communication).

Hartmut Haberland is professor of German language and the sociolinguistics of globalization at Roskilde University, Denmark. With Jacob Mey, he founded the *Journal of Pragmatics* in 1977. He is a co-editor of *Pragmatics and Society* and of *Acta Linguistica Hafniensia* and is on the Editorial Boards of *Linguistik online* and *Language Problems and Language Planning*, as well as the books series *Studies in Pragmatics and Multilingual Education*. He is vice director of the CALPIU Research Centre in Roskilde and has been a senior external research fellow of RCLEAMS, Hong Kong. His research has been on the semantics, pragmatics and sociolinguistics of German, Danish, English and Greek.

Bent Preisler is Professor Emeritus of English Language and Sociolinguistics at Roskilde University. He holds a Dr.Phil. (Habilitation) from Aarhus University, 1987. He was a Visiting Professor/Scholar in the United States during 1984 (State University of New York, Binghamton) and 2000 (University of California, Santa Barbara). His research includes works on the structure and functions of English, including gender-based variation in the spoken language; the concept and functions of Standard English; English as an international language; and the influence of English on other languages. He was Associate Editor of English Studies from 2003 to 2012 and is the founder and former director of the international research center on "Cultural and Linguistic Practices in the International University" (CALPIU) funded by the Danish Research Council.

Drorit Ram is an Israeli (born and raised) with a global perspective who has mastered three languages (Hebrew, English and French) and is in favour of multilingualism. She is a graduate of Tel-Aviv University (MA in language arts) and Bar-Ilan University (PhD in sociolinguistics). She specializes in academic writing in Hebrew and English and in language policy in the Israeli context of tertiary education. She is an English teacher and teacher trainer in TESOL. She is currently engaged in teacher training and supervising action research of pre-service teachers, instruction of language arts, language policy and academic writing at Levinsky College, Tel-Aviv. Her main interests in research are language policy, languages in contact, TESOL, action research, academic writing and writing instruction.

Tamah Sherman is an assistant professor at the Institute of General Linguistics, Charles University, Prague. Her research focuses on interaction and meta-linguistic behaviour in general, using the frameworks of language management theory, ethnomethodology and conversation analysis, with a particular focus on situations of multiple language use in the Czech Republic after 1989. From 2006 to 2010, she worked for the EC 7th Framework Program project LINEE – Languages in a Network of European Excellence, leading a team of researchers dealing with communication in multinational companies in Central Europe and participating in research on English as a lingua franca in Europe.

Sabine Ylönen is a senior researcher at the Centre for Applied Language Studies, University of Jyväskylä (JyU), Finland. She received a Dr. Phil. in 1999, and she has been associate professor in German language and culture at JyU since 2001. Her research interests and publications are in the fields of text and discourse analysis (scientific writing, oral academic discourse, webvertising), German as a foreign language, multimodal language pedagogy and language policies. She is coordinator of the FinGer project (German as a vehicular language in academic and business contexts in Finland). She is co-author of numerous teaching materials of genre-oriented learning and with digital media (Webvertising 2001, Euromobil 2004). She is also co-editor of the *Journal of Applied Language Studies (Apples)*.

Anne-Marie Beukes is a professor in linguistics and is head of the Department of Linguistics at the University of Johannesburg, South Africa. She is also the chairperson of the South African Translators' Institute, a former vice president of the International Federation of Translators and a former member of the Pan South African Language Board. Her areas of specialization include language policy and planning, sociolinguistics and the sociology of translation. She is the author of some 37 scholarly articles and chapters in eight books and the co-editor of Veeltalige Vertaalterminologie/Multilingual Translation Terminology (2010), for which she (with co-editor Marné Pienaar) was conferred the PanSALB's 2010/2011 Multilingualism Awards.

Eva Pons is Associated Professor of Constitutional Law at the Faculty of Law, Universitat de Barcelona (UB), Barcelona. Her research focuses on public law, federalism, human rights and language rights. She is author of many contributions in the field of language rights in international, European and Spanish legal systems and the regulation of the Catalan language. She is member of the Board of Directors of the specialised journal Llengua i Dret, of the UB research institut CUSC and the Institut d'Estudis Catalans network in sociolinguistics CRUSCAT.

1 Language Policy in Higher Education in Medium-Sized Language Communities: An Introduction

F. Xavier Vila

The Challenge of Internationalisation for Linguae Academicae Other than English

The world of higher education is changing at a rapid pace. Universities all over the world are taking on the increasing pressures exerted by globalisation, the commodification of education and the economic crisis. As a result, in recent years, universities from both hemispheres and all continents are increasingly embarking upon the process of 'getting international', a process that, first and foremost, involves the irruption of English in contexts where it used to be absent (Arzoz, 2012a).

In truth, up to quite recently, language policy and language management issues in higher education had attracted relatively little interest from researchers. During the 19th and 20th centuries, universities abandoned Latin and transited towards the national university model (Haberland & Preisler, this volume; Mortensen & Haberland, 2012: 192), where the nation-state's language was adopted as the main medium of instruction. This was the case not only for the demographically major languages, but also for a remarkable number of medium-sized languages (Vila, 2013), especially in Europe and some central and eastern regions of Asia. Universities located in colonial and postcolonial countries followed a parallel path, except that they rarely substituted the colonial language for an indigenous one. All over the world, in fact, the lingua academica, i.e. the language used for most university functions, tended to coincide with the country's official language. It was only in very specific functions, in many ways oriented towards international diffusion, such as the production of written dissertations and the dissemination of science via scientific journals and books, that a handful of academic linguae francae competed for supremacy. Indeed, even at the beginning of the 21st century, it was the language of science, not the language of universities themselves, that was the main object of research for language policy researchers (Ammon, 2001).

But especially since the last decade of the 20th century, the ever ongoing upsurge of university internationalisation has led to the blossoming of English-medium courses in countries where this language had never been used (Brenn-White & van Rest, 2012; Wächter & Maiworm, 2008), and this development has spurred the research on multilingualism in higher education.[1] The orientation of these studies is, as expected, variegated: a significant percentage of these studies have adopted a pedagogical or applied linguistics stance and occupy themselves with applied linguistic issues (Björkman, 2012; Doiz *et al.*, 2013), including the development of content and language integrated learning (CLIL) methods (Fortanet-Gómez, 2013) or the introduction of bilingual education principles and techniques into higher education contexts (van der Walt, 2013). Others, like Preisler *et al.* (2011), have focused on the management of the learning processes in multilingual, international universities. It is impossible to summarise here the growing literature on multilingualism in higher education. But irrespective of whether it shows a more educational, pedagogical, anthropological or other approach, most research on language management in higher education puts only English at the centre of its attention (Söderlundh, 2012: 90).[2] And this is, without doubt, a serious limitation to our understanding not only of the internationalisation of higher education, but also of language policy in higher education. While English is without doubt the language most favoured by globalisation processes, it should not be forgotten that it is all languages that are being globalised (Blommaert, 2010). There is, therefore, a real need that the analysis of the internationalisation process does not restrict its attention to just the hypercentral language (de Swaan, 2001), at least for two reasons.

On the one hand, we know at least since Haugen's (1971) seminal work that any sociolinguistic approach should be ecosystematic. The spread of any given language in one particular sphere of life is deemed to have an impact on the other languages that used to occupy it, or might have occupied it. We still know very little about the actual consequences of the spread of English on other linguae academicae. Scandinavian societies, for instance, have discussed the risk of actual 'domain loss' (e.g. Haberland & Preisler, this volume; Kangas Christiansen, 2009;

Ljosland, 2007; Preisler, 2009), but it is not clear that internationalisation has actually led to the total relinquishment of any lingua academica. In fact, from the theoretical perspective of the political economy of languages, not only English, but also many other languages, could become valued linguistic capital (Heller & Duchêne, 2012). The loss of state control over education may favour access to higher education for historically minoritised languages, and higher facility for mobility and the enhanced use of information and communication technologies might, in fact, create opportunities for increased cooperation in language communities up to now separated by nation-state boundaries (Arzoz, 2012b: 230). But these prospects may be too optimistic. Not many languages seem to be enjoying the purported benefits of liberalisation and commodification. In fact, '[...], as regards traditional higher education (i.e. physical colleges and campuses), the trend appears to be rather the reduction, not the expansion, of languages of tuition' (Arzoz, 2012b: 231). Voices such as Robert Phillipson (2006, 2009) denounce the progress of English at the expense of other languages as a 'pandemic', and compare English as 'a cuckoo in the European higher education nest of languages'. In any case, too little is still known to evaluate properly the result of the process.

On the other hand, attention to the 'other' languages is also fully justifiable on a simple quantitative basis. It should never be overlooked, unless we want to fall into what we could describe as the 'English-only delusion', that, as Haberland and Mortensen (2012: 1) put it, 'English is *not* spoken in *every* corner of the world, just in more places than any other language ever before'. In the real world, dozens of other languages are vibrant mediums of instruction in higher education, hundreds of thousands of university professors develop most of their professional lives without much recourse to English, millions of students follow their courses in other languages, uncountable researchers all over the world generate knowledge and make discoveries in their own languages and the amount of scientific publications in languages other than English can be counted in the thousands – although many of them are not necessarily registered by English-medium agencies (Vivanco Cervero, 2010). The negative impacts derived from the biased perception that English is the 'only' language of science and knowledge have been repeatedly denounced from different perspectives (Gazzola, 2012; Hamel, 2013; Phillipson, 2006, 2009). Beyond the undesirable consequences of not taking into account the scientific results produced in languages other than English, it is clear that any theory of language policy in higher education should not be built exclusively on the basis of one single language, even if it is the major language of internationalisation.

The Goal of this Volume

This volume is designed to help answer some of the questions that surround the rapid changes that are taking place in universities around the world in non-English-dominant countries. The volume focuses its attention on medium-sized languages, i.e. all those placed between the biggest and the smallest languages (Vila & Bretxa, 2013). Whereas it is difficult to imagine that big languages like Chinese, Spanish or Russian might be massively abandoned as a medium of instruction in the next decades, the growing role of English in higher education may pose a realistic challenge for languages whose presence in higher education depends on their actual use in a small number of university centres. It should not be forgotten that, at the end of the day, it is only a very small percentage of the world's languages that have actually entered the field of higher education and science (Laponce, 2006). It is not at all inconceivable that, under the pressure of internationalisation, some of these may simply quit the club. Taking into account that university provides one of the highest levels – if not *the* highest level – of linguistic elaboration that a language can reach, it is not at all surprising that many decision-makers, linguistic activists and even plain scholars within the language communities whose language has entered this select club feel worried that it could lose such a status. What are the actual prospects for such a change? Is it really taking place? What would the social, political, economic, cultural and linguistic consequences of such a loss of status be? Simultaneously, all around the world there are a significant number of societies whose languages have not managed to penetrate the fortress of higher education, or have done it only partially, but have the potential – in demographic, economic and sociopolitical terms – to attempt it. In view of the predominant discourses insisting on the hegemony of English, they have good reasons to ask themselves whether the efforts needed to conquer such a status are (still) worth it and/or are realistic. Will it still pay off?

This volume is devoted to exploring the current situation and immediate prospects for a number of selected medium-sized languages in the sphere of higher education. The volume constitutes an effort to understand not only the actual situation of these languages in this sphere, but also the dynamics that are sustaining, promoting and/or reducing their use as linguae academicae in the current situation of the globalisation, internationalisation and commodification of higher education associated with the information society that has developed in this phase of late capitalism (Heller & Duchêne, 2012).

The roots of this volume are to be found in the Medium-Sized Language Communities Project, a project aimed at analysing the conditions for the sustainability of medium-sized languages and language communities (Milian-Massana, 2012; Vila, 2013).[3] The first conclusions of this project pointed out that the critical demographic mass for the complete development and comfortable sustainability of a language community may be well below one million speakers, i.e. that the number of speakers could not be argued as an ineluctable factor promoting a language shift in many communities around the world. The project also identified higher education and science as one of the fields, if not *the* field, where most medium-sized languages faced serious difficulties (Vila, 2013). Indeed, for many of these languages the crucial question was not one of internationalisation and anglicisation, but a more basic one: to what extent were medium-sized languages (still) viable as languages of university and research activities? Comparative research suggested that different strategies and different discourses were being developed to respond to these challenges (Arzoz, 2012a; Cots *et al.*, 2012). But irrespective of the particularities, two pieces of evidence were especially troublesome: on the one hand, most medium-sized languages around the world have so far not been developed as linguae academicae, i.e. they have virtually no presence in higher education. On the other hand, it is precisely among some of the medium-sized languages with an older and stronger position in higher universities, like the Nordic languages and Dutch, that the process of the anglicisation of higher education is apparently making more inroads. Once combined, these two facts seem to suggest that the age when medium-sized languages managed to occupy the sphere of higher education might be coming to an end. But is this really so? While some sources confirmed that English was replacing the local languages in some of the existing courses, quite often the courses where English was used were newly created and explicitly designed to attract foreign students, especially internationally oriented postgraduate courses. On the other hand, although diagnosing a global trend towards linguistic homogenisation and attributing it to globalisation in general terms was tempting, it was necessary not to overestimate partial evidence. National and regional factors might predominate over global trends. At the end of the day, previous research has shown that medium-sized languages are extremely sensitive to the legal and political factors of their nation states (Milian-Massana, 2012; Vila, 2013). The orientation adopted by each university is crucial to understanding the ultimate position of each language in its practices and discourses: universities that are primarily oriented to serve the needs of the immediate community and are less market oriented prove surprisingly able to function in local, demographically small languages, and they even manage to become *international* without becoming *globalised* (Bull, 2012).

In other words, empirical research showed different, even contradictory evolutions, with some languages retaining the upper hand in their universities or even gaining ground, whereas others were losing ground. It is within this context that the Medium-Sized Language Communities Research Team decided to focus its third round of conferences in Barcelona (Catalonia) to discuss the actual position of these languages in higher education. With this goal in mind, several scholars from three continents who had investigated the effects of globalisation and internationalisation on higher education language policies in higher education in medium-sized language communities were invited to present the results of their research and to discuss them from a comparative perspective in Barcelona in October 2011.

In order to enhance the comparative approach, the medium-sized languages selected for exploration had significantly different positions and histories in the field of higher education. In this respect, the lack of recent research substantially reduced the number of potential candidates. To carry out the selection, a number of criteria were taken into account to guarantee that a variety of experiences could be compared. To start with, the focus was placed on languages that already enjoyed the full status of lingua academica, assuming that these languages were the natural source of information on the challenges and opportunities generated by the internationalisation of higher education. Some of these languages had been linguae academicae for a long time, while others had achieved this status more recently. The different role of English in each society was also taken into consideration: in some of the societies selected for comparison, English enjoyed a wide currency, but its presence was much lower in others. A majority of the candidates came from Europe, which is not surprising considering that most medium-sized languages that have achieved the status of lingua academica are from this continent, but some medium-sized languages from two other continents were also included in the analysis. While a larger number of scholars were initially invited to the conference, in the end the number of cases presented was six. These were, in alphabetical order: Catalan in Catalonia, Czech in the Czech Republic, Danish in Denmark, Modern Hebrew in Israel, Finnish and Swedish in Finland, and South African medium-sized languages in South Africa. As is clear from the list, four of these case studies deal with a single, medium-sized language, while two deal with two or more medium-sized languages. It goes without saying that while our focus of interest was the respective medium-sized languages, the analysis of their reality had to be done necessarily in a holistic, ecological perspective, which means that several other languages – not only English of course but also Castilian/Spanish, Arabic, German, Russian, Slovak, etc. – entered once and again into the picture.

Like any other possible choice, our selection might have improved had other cases been included in the sample. To mention but a few factors, a wider representation of Asian medium-sized linguae academicae would have greatly enriched the possibility of comparison. The analysis would also have been enhanced by the presence of some smaller language communities, such as the Baltic countries or Iceland. Less-affluent countries might have offered a different picture in several respects, but it should not be forgotten that in a majority of these countries medium-sized languages are absent from higher education, which made them non-candidates for the sample. However, these and other considerations do not alter the fact that the selection of the cases presented here was variegated and highly illustrative, and allowed for much discussion and comparative analysis both during the conference and afterwards.

To facilitate comparison and discussion, participants were invited to organize their papers at their convenience, but they were asked to include in as much detail as possible the answers to the questions included in the guidelines presented in Table 1.1.

The speakers were invited to present publicly their cases and discuss them among themselves and with academics and researchers gathered for the sessions, so that a clearer understanding of the role and position of each language in each society could be adequately achieved. Subsequent to the discussion, a presentation of each case was developed in writing by the respective authors.[4]

The Contributions

The present volume includes the papers that were written after the presentation and the discussions. It should be taken into account that the chapters do not represent strictly the papers presented at the conference. On the contrary, the papers were written once the debates and discussions had concluded and, therefore, all were heavily reworked in comparison with the original presentations.

Chapter 2 is titled 'The Position of Danish, English and Other Languages at Danish Universities in the Context of Danish Society', written by Hartmut Haberland and Bent Preisler from the University of Roskilde, Denmark. In this chapter, it is argued that the sociolinguistic scenario of Danish universities, where English has made significant inroads during the

Table 1.1 Guidelines for the presentation of challenges for medium-sized language communities in higher education and research environments

- **Language policy at university level:** Are language practices somehow regulated in an explicit way? Are language competences somehow regulated in an explicit way? To what extent are universities autonomous in defining their language policy? In general terms, do different universities have different language policies? Are academic areas (natural sciences, humanities, etc.) relevant in order to define the university policies? Could we talk about a nationwide university language policy?
- **Language practices at university level (oracy/literacy/signacy):** What languages are used as means of instruction at degree level? At research master level? At professionalising masters and postgraduate courses? At postdoctoral courses? Continuous education (lifelong learning)? Other? What languages are used for PhD dissertations?
- **Language competence:** *Teaching staff*: What (national/foreign) language/s are teaching staff members expected to know? Is language competence officially verified in any way? *Students*: What (national/foreign) language/s are the students expected to know? Is language competence officially verified in any way? *Administrative staff*: What (national/foreign) language/s are administrative staff members expected to know? Is language competence officially verified in any way?
- **Language ideologies and discourses:** What are the main discourses about languages policies at university level? What social sectors are supporting each discourse?
- **Research:** To what extent is your medium-sized language used in scientific publications? To what extent is your medium-sized language used orally in research centres?

last decades, can only be understood in the frame of contemporary Danish society as a whole. As in the rest of Scandinavia, English in Denmark is being spread not only from above, i.e. institutional agents and the mass media, but also from below, as proved by its pervasive presence in youth culture. In this scenario, the wide presence of English in Danish higher education is by no means independent from its presence in many other social spheres. But this wide presence does not mean that Danish and other languages have disappeared from the stage. Following a diachronic review of language policies in higher education in Denmark, the authors argue that Danish universities have been multilingual for a long time, and that even today, the linguistic practices found in Danish universities comprise the use of several languages. Following their rejection of 'language domain' as an analytical tool, the authors show that the different activities developed in higher education institutions – namely instruction, administration, research production and research dissemination – often show different patterns of language use. The chapter concludes that, even in contexts such as Danish academia where English has made deep inroads, Danish remains solidly established as a language of higher education and that proficiency in more than one language is still necessary to function adequately in this environment.

'The Position of Czech and Other Languages at Universities in the Czech Republic: Some Initial Observations', by Tamah Sherman from Charles University, Prague, focuses on a demographically homogeneous country where the presence of English is much lower than in Scandinavia. The chapter reviews the problems that arise from the coexistence of Czech, a medium-sized language solidly established as a lingua academica, with other languages – especially Slovak, German and English – in higher education, which is one of the country's most multilingual spheres of life. The chapter pays specific attention to the issue of English and its role as an additional language of instruction, as a language of the universities' outward presentation, and as a language of international collaboration and research publications. The chapter identifies a number of areas in higher education in which observable language management occurs, with a focus on the specific situation of the humanities and social sciences, and discusses a number of instances of specific management collected by means of ethnographic procedures and long-time participant observation. Most of this management happens at the local level, since national or even university regulations tend to be rare. The author considers the pros and cons of several measures, highlighting the dubious, even contradictory effects of some of the measures adopted. On the whole, she concludes that, although perceived as a highly multilingual environment in comparison with the country as a whole, Czechs do not experience any domain loss in higher education. Rather, the main problem in the area is considered to be the lack of proficiency in foreign languages.

In 'The Position of Finnish and Swedish as well as Other Languages at Universities in Finland', Sabine Ylönen, from the University of Jyväskylä, Finland, takes us back to the Nordic countries. The chapter gives an overview of language policies and practices at Finnish universities at undergraduate and postgraduate levels, required language competences, discourses about languages and language use in research. Even though skills in foreign languages have traditionally been valued very highly in Finland, the role of English has increased rapidly in the last decades, which has resulted not only in the decreased use of other foreign languages but has also affected the use of the national languages for academic purposes. There is no governmental strategy for the status of foreign languages or the growing influence of English on language practices in Finnish higher education. The analysis of the existing language policies in Finnish universities shows that English is generally highlighted as the language of internationalisation, although the legislation about the national languages is not infringed.

Universities are encouraged to offer foreign language teaching to attract foreign students, and today a foreign language invariably means English. There are still no concrete measures to ascertain the language competence of the staff teaching in a foreign language. The use of English is also favoured in research.

The following chapter, 'Challenges for Hebrew in Higher Education and Research Environments', by Drorit Ram from the Levinsky College of Education, Israel, takes the reader away from Europe and plunges him or her into an analysis of language management, language ideologies and actual language practices in Israeli universities. The chapter combines a general view of the situation with on-the-ground research of language management in five departments at three universities in Israel, including an analysis of documents, interviews with lecturers and academic staff as well as questionnaire data from students. The results reveal that a multiplicity of actors takes part in the definition of actual policies, among which Ram selects the most important four: the Ministry of Education, the Hebrew Language Academy, university senates and individual professors. The results show a distance between the country's official language policy– Hebrew is *the* language of instruction in Israeli universities – and a reality that appears to be more nuanced, for not all agents share the same views, and some degree of dissent is also present among lecturers with regard to relaxing this official policy. On the ground, policies are also more complex than official statements. Hebrew is clearly the predominant language of oral instruction, but English is widely present as a written language – especially as far as reading materials are concerned – and significant as a means of oral instruction, in particular when foreign students and/or lecturers are involved. In fact, English turns out to be the most common language in activities connected with the dissemination of science among researchers. Interestingly enough, the preference for Hebrew is widely spread among lecturers for pragmatic reasons, which leads Ram, together with some of her interviewees, to question the need for a tough top-down policy.

The next chapter leads the reader to a third continent and to a country where language policies have been deeply modified during the last decades, following the fall of the ominous apartheid regime. In 'Challenges for South Africa's Medium-Sized Indigenous Languages in Higher Education and Research Environments', Anne-Marie Beukes from the University of Johannesburg, South Africa, provides an overview of the political, economic and even demographic dilemmas of these languages in higher education in post-apartheid South Africa, which in many respects are representative of those faced by many other medium-sized languages all over the world. At the end of the racist regime, and with the exception of Afrikaans, a language that has been used for most formal functions including higher education for a long period, the other South African indigenous languages had a precarious sociopolitical status. Regarded as an instrument to perpetuate racial segregation, the post-apartheid authorities replaced language-based universities with integrated centres which were supposed to promote multilingualism. But the sociolinguistic metamorphosis of South African universities has not been beneficial for medium-sized languages. On the one hand, in spite of lip service to linguistic equality, multilingualism and theoretical promotion of all languages, and with the exception of some groundbreaking activities, African languages have remained basically absent from higher education. On the other hand, the position of Afrikaans both as a language of learning and teaching and as a language of scholarship and science is deteriorating rapidly. On the whole, this chapter presents a complex and fascinating instance of the difficulties involved in implementing multilingualism in the absence of monolingual institutions.

The following chapter, and the last case study, takes the reader back to Europe and offers the story of a medium-sized language that has (re-)conquered the field of higher education in the last decades. In 'The Position of Catalan in Higher Education in Catalonia', Eva Pons Parera from the University of Barcelona, Catalonia, explores the position of Catalan in universities, the policies implemented in recent years to promote its use and the challenges now being faced as a consequence of globalisation and European integration. Although the author stresses the legal aspects of language policy, she also presents a detailed account of the major language management actions adopted, and offers an overview of the quantitative evolution of the languages in contact. References are also made to the scarce use of Catalan in postgraduate courses and as the language of scientific publication, and of the growing, although still minor, role of English as a lingua academica.

To conclude, the last chapter includes a comparative perspective on the viability of medium-sized languages as linguae academicae by the editor of the volume. This chapter underlines the view that, in spite of some appearances, medium-sized languages remain viable vehicles of teaching and research, although in a pattern of specialised distribution with academic linguae francae. The author reviews some of the main areas of language policy as described in the case studies, and identifies a number of paradoxes connected with the management of English and other languages in these communities. The chapter, and the volume as a whole, closes with a number of reflections about the future of medium-sized languages as linguae academicae.

Acknowledgements

This book benefited from support provided by the Ministerio de Economía y Competitividad, Gobierno de España (FFI2012-39285-C02-01), Linguamón – Casa de les Llengües, the Grup d'Estudi de la Variació (2009 SGR 521) and the Catalan Agency for University and Research Funds (AGAUR).

Notes

(1) Between April 2012 and 2013, the following meetings were announced on the web: Multilingualism in Society, the World of Work, and Politics. New Challenges for Teaching at Institutes of Higher Education/Universities (Freiburg, April 2012); Higher Education Across Borders: Transcultural Interaction and Linguistic Diversity (Roskilde, April 2012); Language Futures: Languages in Higher Education Conference 2012 (Edinburgh, July 2012), International Conference on Multilingualism and Language Studies in Higher Education (Paris, August 2012); a panel on language policies in higher education organised at the Sociolinguistics Symposium SS19 (Berlin, August 2012); Integrating Content and Language in Higher Education (Maastricht, April 2013); The English Language in Teaching in Higher European Education (Copenhagen, April 2013); and the Nitobe Symposium on Languages and Internationalization in Higher Education: Ideologies, Practices, Alternatives (Reykjavik, July 2013); Multilingualism at Work: Language Interactions at the University (Copenhagen, October 2013). The number of specialised publications is also rapidly growing. In fact, even more structured initiatives, such as the creation of the Integration of Content and Language in Higher Education Association, with its three consecutive conferences, and the recent launch of the journal *Language Learning in Higher Education* (Mouton de Gruyter), are speeding up research on this field.
(2) For alternative views, see Arzoz, X. (ed.) (2012) or Haberland, H. and Mortensen, J. (ed.) (2012).
(3) See http://www.ub.edu/cusc/llenguesmitjanes/?lang=en.
(4) For additional information about the symposium, including the possibility to watch the lectures online, see http://www.ub.edu/cusc/llenguesmitjanes/?page_id=730&lang=en.

References

Ammon, U. (ed.) (2001) *The Dominance of English As a Language of Science*. Berlin: Mouton de Gruyter.
Arzoz, X. (2012a) Legal education in bilingual contexts: A conceptual, historical and comparative introduction. In X. Arzoz (ed.) *Bilingual Education in the Legal Context. Group Rights, State Policies and Globalisation* (pp. 3–34). Leiden/Boston: Martinus Neijhoff.

Arzoz, X. (2012b) The transformation of higher education and medium-sized language communities. In A. Milian-Massana (ed.) *Language Law and Legal Challenges in Medium-Sized Language Communities: A Comparative Perspective* (pp. 219-252). Barcelona: Institut d'Estudis Autonòmics.
Arzoz, X. (ed.) (2012) *Bilingual Education in the Legal Context. Group Rights, State Policies and Globalisation.* Leiden/Boston: Martinus Neijhoff.
Björkman, B. (2012) *English as an Academic Lingua Franca. An Investigation of Form and Communicative Effectiveness.* Berlin: Mouton de Gruyter.
Blommaert, J. (2010) *The Sociolinguistics of Globalisation.* Cambridge: Cambridge University Press.
Brenn-White, M. and van Rest, E. (2012) *English-Taught Master's Programs in Europe: New Findings on Supply and Demand.* New York: Institute of International Education. See http://www.iie.org/Research-and-Publications/Publications-and-Reports/IIE-Bookstore/English-Language-Masters-Briefing-Paper (accessed 27 July 2014).
Bull, T. (2012) Against the mainstream: Universities with an alternative language policy. *International Journal of the Sociology of Language* 216, 55-73.
Cots, J.M., Lasagabaster, D. and Garrett, P. (2012) Multilingual policies and practices of universities in three bilingual regions in Europe. *International Journal of the Sociology of Language* 216, 7-32.
de Swaan, A. (2001) *Words of the World. The Global Language System.* Malden, MA: Polity Press.
Doiz, A., Lasagabaster, D. and Sierra, J.M. (eds) (2013) *English-Medium Instruction at Universities: Global Challenges.* Bristol: Multilingual Matters.
Fortanet-Gómez, I. (ed.) (2013) *CLIL in Higher Education: Towards a Multilingual Language Policy.* Bristol: Multilingual Matters.
Gazzola, M. (2012) The linguistic implications of academic performance indicators: General trends and case study. *International Journal of the Sociology of Language* 216, 131-156.
Haberland, H. and Mortensen, J. (eds) (2012) Language and the international university monograph. *International Journal of the Sociology of Language* 216, 1-204.
Haberland, H. and Mortensen, J. (2012) Language variety, language hierarchy and language choice in the international university. *International Journal of the Sociology of Language* 216, 1-16.
Hamel, R.E. (2013) El campo de las ciencias y la educación superior entre el monopolio del inglés y el plurilingüismo: Elementos para una política del lenguaje en América Latina. *Trabalhos em Linguística Aplicada* 52 (2), 321-384.
Haugen, E. (1971) The ecology of language. *The Linguistics Reporter* Supplement 25 winter, 19-26. Reprinted in Haugen, E. (1972) *The Ecology of Language. Essays by Einar Haugen* (pp. 325-339). Selected and introduced by A.S. Dil. Stanford, CA: Stanford University.
Heller, M. and Duchêne, A. (eds) (2012). *Language in Late Capitalism: Pride and Profit.* New York: Routledge.
Kangas Christiansen, M. (2009) The language of instruction at Danish universities. *Angles on the English Speaking World* 9, 58-67.
Laponce, J. (2006) *Loi de Babel et autres régularités des rapports entre langue et politique.* Lévis, Québec: Presses de l'Université Laval.
Ljosland, R. (2007) English in Norwegian academica: A step towards diglossia? *World Englishes* 26 (4), 395-410.

Milian-Massana, A. (ed.) (2012) *Language Law and Legal Challenges in Medium Sized Language Communities: A Comparative Perspective*. Barcelona: Institut d'Estudis Autonòmics.

Mortensen, J. and Haberland, H. (2012) English – the new Latin of academia? Danish universities as a case. *International Journal of the Sociology of Language* 216, 175–197.

Phillipson, R. (2006) English, a cuckoo in the European higher education nest of languages? *European Journal of English Studies* 10 (1), 13–32.

Phillipson, R. (2009) English in higher education: Panacea or pandemic? In P. Harder (ed.) *Angles on the English Speaking World. English in Denmark: Language Policy, Internationalization and University Teaching* (pp. 29–54). Copenhagen: Museum Tusculanum Press; University of Copenhagen.

Preisler, B. (2009) Complementary languages: The national language and English as working languages in European universities. *Angles on the English Speaking World* 9, 10–28.

Preisler, B., Klitgård, I. and Fabricius, A. (2011) *Language and Learning in the International University From English Uniformity to Diversity and Hybridity*. Clevedon: Multilingual Matters.

Söderlundh, H. (2012) Global policies and local norms: Sociolinguistic awareness and language choice at an international university. *International Journal of the Sociology of Language* 216, 87–109.

Vila, F.X. (2013) Challenges and opportunities for MSLCs in the 21st century: A (preliminary) synthesis. In F.X. Vila (ed.) *Survival and Development of Language Communities: Prospects and Challenges* (pp. 179–200). Bristol: Multilingual Matters.

Vila, F.X. (ed.) (2013) *Survival and Development of Language Communities: Prospects and Challenges*. Bristol: Multilingual Matters.

Vila, F.X. and Bretxa, V. (2013) The analysis of medium-sized language communities. In F.X. Vila (ed.) *Survival and Development of Language Communities: Prospects and Challenges* (pp. 1–17). Bristol: Multilingual Matters.

Vivanco Cervero, V. (2010) Proyección internacional de la producción científica en español. *Anales de Documentación* 13, 275–284.

Wächter, B. and Maiworm, F. (2008) *English-Taught Programs in European Higher Education. The Picture in 2007*. Bonn: Lemmens.

van der Walt, C. (2013) *Multilingual Higher Education: Beyond English Medium Orientations*. Bristol: Multilingual Matters.

2 The Position of Danish, English and Other Languages at Danish Universities in the Context of Danish Society

Hartmut Haberland and Bent Preisler

The Danish Language Community as a Medium-Sized Language Community

Ranked lists (Wee, 2011) and language hierarchies (Risager, 2012) are in vogue. De Swaan's (2001) hierarchy of one hypercentral language (English), 12 supercentral languages (Arabic, Chinese, English, French, German, Hindi, Japanese, Malay, Portuguese, Russian, Spanish and Swahili), about 100 central languages and a great many peripheral languages (the rest) is well known. Danish fits the description of a central language given by de Swaan: it is used in elementary as well as secondary and tertiary education, and it appears in newspapers, textbooks and fiction, as well as on radio and television (de Swaan, 2001: 4f). Actually, it fits the description of a central language better than many of the others (it is not essential for a central language to have television programmes). But it is important to note that de Swaan's hierarchy is neither impressionistic nor based solely on qualitative criteria; rather, it is closely linked to his quantitative concept of 'communicative potential' (see below).

In 2007, there were a total of 5,581,690 speakers of Danish, of which 5,450,000 lived in Denmark, 21,000 in Germany (2000) and 7,830 in Greenland (1986) (source: Ethnologue (2013), www.ethnologue.com.). However, less than 1% of the European Union (EU) population speaks Danish as a first language; even fewer speak it as a foreign or second language (source: Eurobarometer 2006: questions 48a and 48b), and many Danes speak languages other than Danish.

There have been several attempts to set up hierarchies of languages (quantifiable and non-quantifiable, linear and non-linear). Concepts such as the following abound: languages with small numbers of speakers (demographic factors being considered 'first order' or *'erstrangig'* [Kloss, 1974: 14]); specifically small languages, defined as languages with less than 4.5 million speakers (Haarmann, 1973: 19); lesser-used languages (see the former European Bureau for Lesser-Used Languages [EBLUL 2010]); less-widely taught languages (Mac Mathúna *et al.*, 1988); languages with restricted official national or international status (Peeters, 1988); languages with a low gross national product (or low contribution to the gross national product) (Ammon, 1991: 245); and, of course, minority languages (for an overview, see Ammon, 2010).

Haberland attempts to provide a *functional* definition of a 'lesser-than-some-other language':

Wenn wir uns zunächst auf die rein repertoirebedingten Kriterien konzentrieren, können wir [sagen], dass kleine Sprachen öfter dominiert werden als dominieren und selten als *lingua franca* verwendet werden. (Haberland, 1993: 99)[1]

The technical sense of *dominiert* (i.e. 'dominated') for the 'not preferred' choice in multilanguage encounters is taken from Ammon (1991: 61; see also Ammon, 2003: 232).

Similarly, de Swaan (2001, 2007) has tried to quantify the communicative potential of a language in a way that basically measures its usefulness as a lingua franca, on the basis of the two concepts of prevalence and centrality. Both can be measured, and their product $Q_i = p_i \cdot c_i$ is a measure of the communication potential of a language. Explained by a simple example: English has a higher communicative potential than that of Chinese in spite of the higher prevalence of Chinese (there are more speakers of Chinese than of English) because English is a far more central language than Chinese: there are more multilingual speakers of English than multilingual speakers of Chinese. English is simply better connected than Chinese.

The communicative potential of Danish, according to de Swaan, is small. Not so much because there are few Danish speakers, but because there are even fewer speakers of other languages who learn Danish. Many Danes are multilingual speakers of Danish, English, German, French, Arabic or other languages, but very few others are multilingual speakers of Danish. Hence, the Q-value of Danish is negligible, like that of other lesser-taught (and lesser-learned) European languages, such as Finnish, Swedish and Greek (de Swaan, 2001: 158).

What is left out of the picture here is that in calculating the Q-value of a language, only 'speakers' are taken into consideration, including multilingual speakers. But in Scandinavia, widespread receptive multilingualism enhances the communicative potential of Danish, Norwegian and Swedish, i.e. there are many more 'readers' and 'listeners' of Danish than 'speakers' and 'writers' (on unidirectional receptive multilingualism in Scandinavia, see Zeevaert, 2007). The Q-value of Danish even for Scandinavia does not reflect this, since many Icelanders, Norwegians and Swedes cannot be counted as 'speakers' of Danish, while being receptive users of Danish. Therefore, the actual connectedness of Danish in Scandinavia is far higher in Scandinavia than its Q-value would indicate, and it is certainly not negligible. Hilmarsson-Dunn (2006) has even suggested that Danish is a 'supracentral' language in the Nordic area (a term inspired, but not used, by de Swaan).

So, the speakers of Danish constitute a group that can be characterised as a medium-sized language community. Danish does not belong to the big languages, not so much due to its low number of speakers but because so few people outside Scandinavia can use it. But it is not a small community, since its language has a high vitality with a book market, television and radio programmes, and theatre and film productions in Danish. In Denmark, there are also several universities and other institutions of higher learning, which until about 30 years ago were functioning largely in Danish. Today, they are among the places where languages other than Danish are most often heard. In the following sections, we will be focusing on them, after first giving an overview of the language ecology of Danish society (with special respect to English) and of the language ideologies prevalent in this society.

The Incomplete Vernacularisation of English in Denmark

Blommaert's (2009: 561) juxtaposition of 'a "world language" – English – and local speech repertoires or speech communities' would be misinterpreted if seen as just another global/local distinction. Not only does English permeate local speech habits and form part of some local speech repertoires – as Blommaert points out – but it is also a 'world language' in very different ways in different countries. In a country like Hungary, where only 20% of the population state that they are able to have a conversation in English (as opposed to 86% in Denmark; Eurobarometer, 2012: 23), English is much less of a 'world language' than in Denmark.

In Denmark, English has become a language that large segments of the population, especially the younger generation, are quite familiar with (Haberland & Mortensen, 2009; Lønsmann, 2009; Preisler, 1999a, 1999b). Thus, one could talk about a tendency towards the vernacularisation of English in Denmark (Anne Fabricius, personal communication). However, not everyone in Denmark speaks or can function in English. A recent study of language choice and language repertoires in a Danish multilingual workplace has shown that the 'English-have-nots' still constitute a significant part of the workforce (Lønsmann, 2011). Another case study showed that fears of exclusive use of English, e.g. in natural science research departments – with ensuing 'domain loss' for Danish – are exaggerated (Madsen, 2008). In general, the term 'domain loss', which is often heard in the public debate, is considered theoretically weak and empirically inadequate by Danish sociolinguists (Preisler, 2008, 2010: 165; also see Li, 2012). The discussion of 'domain loss' seems to belong to the domain of language ideology (see below).

Denmark taken as a whole is not a stable multilingual speech community. Of the sample for the Eurobarometer (2006: 7) survey for 2005 published in 2006, 97% stated that Danish is their first language and only 4% mentioned other first languages (multiple answers were possible). It is an exaggeration, at least for Denmark, when de Swaan (2001: 56) claims that 'some European countries, like the Netherlands, Luxembourg and Denmark, are rapidly approaching a state of universal multilingualism and pervasive diglossia: up to 80% of the population is more or less competent in English'. The catch is that 'universal multilingualism and pervasive diglossia' and 'more or less competent in English' are not necessarily the same thing. The latter is certainly the case; in 2005, 76% chose English in response to the question: 'Which languages do you speak well enough to be able to have a conversation, excluding your mother tongue?' (Eurobarometer, 2006: question D48b); in 2012, it was 86% (Eurobarometer, 2012: 23). This is certainly much higher than the EU average of 38% (Eurobarometer, 2012: 23), and tallies with Preisler's (1999a) finding that (only) as many as 20% of the Danish adults population were 'English-have-nots'. But this is a far cry from 'universal multilingualism and pervasive diglossia'.

It should be added, though, that this situation is quite different from the situation that prevailed immediately after World War II. Sevaldsen reports a study from 1945, according to which 9% of the adult population could speak English, as opposed to 14% who could speak German (Sevaldsen, 1992: 12). In a later study by Bacher et al. (1992), 57% claimed to be able to have a conversation in English and 33% in German. In

2012, the figures for English were 86% (as mentioned above) and 47% for German (as against an EU average of 11%). These figures may not be completely comparable, but the trend is clear: a steady increase in the self-perceived ability to communicate not only in English, but also in German – although the figures are much more dramatic for English than for German.

Though it is relatively – but only relatively, i.e. in comparison with other countries – unproblematic to implement language policies focused on English at Danish universities, it should be noted that the foundation for such a language policy at Danish universities has already been laid in high school and before, and cannot be regarded independently as an issue of higher education; it is supported by strong motivation to learn and use English, even among those who never see a university from the inside as students or teachers. In other words, the extensive use of English as an international academic contact language and the second most important language of teaching, after Danish, at Danish universities today has been made possible by the role that English plays in Danish society *outside* universities. The role of English at universities has to be seen against the background of the processes by which the use of English is integrated into the practices of the Danish language community.

The media – unidirectional as well as interactive – play an important part in these processes, but their role is a complex one. On television and in the cinema, only preschool children's programmes (of non-Danish origin) are dubbed in Danish[2] – all other foreign programmes and films are shown in the original language with Danish subtitles. The vast majority of these programmes and films are in English, which means that the adult and teenage population's exposure to English is massive. However, being exposed to a language is not necessarily the same as being influenced by it, e.g. in the sense of code-switching to English in informal speech (inserting shorter or larger chunks of English into Danish utterances). This only happens if the foreign language (*in casu* English) is felt to carry prestige. The target groups of many of the media texts in Denmark which use (code-switching to) English are obviously the younger generations and, as we will make a point of showing below, use of English is a value symbol among young Danes. The majority of media programmes targeting young people are usually *produced* by young people, and specialised products such as computer magazines and radio programmes hosted by famous DJs etc. may reinforce the tendency for young people to code-switch between Danish and English. The same is true of the language of the latest American action movie hero. However, as far as media programmes and films produced in Denmark for young

Danes are concerned, the use of English primarily echoes a development that has already taken place in the spoken language of young Danes (see further below).

The social history of the personal computer, furthermore, is an example of how the pressure from English becomes particularly strong when the medium is the object of one of the most popular youth cultures *at the same time* as being intensely promoted by the dominant society, where computer expertise is associated with job status, and where a knowledge of English is therefore not just a tool but a value symbol. That does not mean that the use of computers always and for all implies the use of English. From 1 November 2014, all Danish citizens will be required to have email access to receive documents from the authorities; English will not play any role in that for most people. Likewise, it is not necessary to know any English to use social media, since they all have Danish interfaces. Still, on Facebook, many Danes use Danish for specifically reaching their local friends, and English for reaching a wider audience (*including* their local, usually Danish-speaking friends). Switching to English is a way of prestige-enhancing 'doing being international'. English is the language chosen most often, by far, for 'doing being international' – since so many, especially younger, Danes have access to English – though it is far from the only language for doing this.

We can, thus, distinguish between *English from above* and *English from below* (Preisler, 1999a). By English 'from above', we mean the skills and attitudes relating to the use of English which are due to English being promoted by the institutions of the dominant society – the educational system and various official and semi-official agencies involved in international communication (e.g. foreign trade and tourism). In the school system, English as a Foreign Language has, since 2002, been a compulsory subject from Year 3, with most schools allotting two 45-minute periods (i.e. a total of 90 minutes) a week to the subject in both Year 3 and Year 4. So far, educational policies have resulted in roughly 80% of the adult population having had some English in primary school; the figure is almost 100% for those under 40. In primary school, they have been taught English for an average of close to five years. And more than half of the adult population have had English in their post-primary education. *As a general rule*, the language of teaching is Danish throughout primary and secondary school. The Ministry of Children and Education may, on application, allow individual schools to offer tracks taught in English, German or French, and some high schools (*gymnasier*) offer one year of 'Pre-IB' taught in English, qualifying students for the 'International Baccalaureate', a two-year programme for students with a special background in languages. However, these programmes are the exceptions to the rule. (See the Ministry of Children and Education, 2005, 2006, 2012.)

English is promoted not only by the institutions of the dominant society, i.e. 'from above', but also by the many Anglo-American-inspired youth cultures (especially hip hop), which began as underground cultures, but which have, for decades, been disseminated to mainstream society, more or less successfully, through the audiovisual media, and for which the use of English – mostly through code-switching – is a (life)style marker and value symbol. This spontaneous use of English, introduced by Anglo-American-inspired Danish youth, is what we referred to above as *English from below*. More to the point, it is from among this youth population that universities recruit their students.

Having a student population that has been heavily influenced by (and contributing to) *English from below* during adolescence and later may be the decisive difference between universities in Denmark (possibly the Nordic countries in general) and much of the rest of Europe. English, particularly *mastery* of English, is certainly a status symbol in Denmark, but it is no longer restricted to an educational elite, as the figures mentioned above indicate.

The following is an example of how Danish interactional language among a group of young computer enthusiasts employs elements of English as a natural aspect of interaction – a true example of *English from below*.[3] Many computer 'freaks' (their own term) go to computer parties, an underground culture they used to call 'copy parties' until that term began to arouse the interest of the police. Computer parties may have from ten to several thousand participants and last for several days. They may take place in private homes (when the parents are out) or in buildings rented for the purpose, e.g. schools. In the present example, the party was held in a vast hall, with rows of tables from one end to the other, all filled with computer equipment. Activities are non-stop; people sleep as little as possible and drink coffee or Coke to stay awake (no beer or alcohol, as such beverages are considered detrimental to one's powers of concentration). The example represents the interaction of a group of five male computer 'freaks' – without the researcher being present – as they were experimenting with their computers. Their language is best characterised as an insider jargon which is largely incomprehensible to outsiders (including native speakers), partly because it is full of English specialised and technical terms, acronyms and other expressions and partly because it is completely dependent on a knowledge of the participants' immediate and shared context for its comprehensibility. For this reason, there is no point in attempting to translate it; it is interesting primarily because of the insight it gives us into the role of the English language in Danish youth-cultural usage. Influence from English, mainly in the form of code-switching and borrowings, has been highlighted:

B: [throws a diskette after A] **Attack of the Killer Disk**!
A: Årh! Du kaster værre end min mor! (...)
A: **Hey, wow**! Hvor er kassen henne?
C: Jah, det er sådan en øh ... **Pepsi**-kasse der ... der ikke virker som den burde.
A: Du har ikke lagt mærke til, Jesper, øh ... altså den er **major bug**, den ... den der øh ... **Size Won't Fit**, den er der ikke (...)
B: Hvadfor en version af **Scorched** har vi? (...)
B: Sikke noget **fuck**! (...)
A: Hvad, **World Construction**, kan jeg ikke lige øh ... hvordan får jeg hurtigt det? (...)
B: Se en **Game Boy Simulator** vi har gang i!
A: Hvem fanden i helvede [...?]?
D: Nå, der er da gået et eller andet **seriøst** i kage her! Øh ... længe leve en **PC**-diskette!
B: Øh ... en **PFS**-formateret 1,6 **Megabyte** ... (...)
B: Det bliver bare mere og mere perverst [...?] eller hvad?
A: Ja, ja, mand [...?]
C: **Return of the Killer Disk**!
D: **Dammit**!

We note, of course, a number of technical terms – terms that the computer was 'born with', so to speak – but we also see a number of English expressions which are not technical: interjections, slang usage, obscenities, swear words and intertextual style emulations based on action films or computer games. The word *seriøst* (cp. English 'seriously'), when used as an adverb, is usually one of *manner* in Danish, and whereas the English word can also function as a *degree* adverb in standard English, *seriøst* cannot function as a degree adverb in standard Danish. To this extent, the two words are *faux amis* ('false friends'), and the function of *seriøst* as a degree adverb in the above text must be regarded as an Anglicism (cp. 'something is seriously wrong') on a par with the other Anglicisms used in the text, i.e. as a style feature that contributes to the construction of a youth cultural identity.

Code-switching to English is an aspect of the linguistic style that underpins various Anglo-American youth culture practices, such as, as we see in this example, underground computer practices. It positions speakers socially and culturally in relation to other social groups and lifestyles. It often symbolises the *rejection* of the values of the dominant (mainstream) culture and *identification* with alternative values (*English from below*) that young people come into contact with, often through the audiovisual media. It is a common belief inside and outside Denmark that English is learnt as a result of the efficiency of our internationally oriented educational and business institutions (what we have called *English from above*). This is correct, as far as it goes, but it is not the whole story. Code-switching to English in everyday Danish contexts is *enabled*, but not *motivated*, by the educational system; it is motivated by social needs and pressures. However, it helps to lay the foundation for the way in which English can be further used and developed within higher education.

Some Remarks about Language Ideologies and Discourses in Denmark

The use of, and ideas about, languages at the university have to be seen in the wider context of language ideologies prevalent in Danish society at large. In her analysis of the dominant discourses about languages in Denmark, Daryai-Hansen (2010a) concludes that there are three relevant categories of languages in these discourses: first, Danish and English (as languages of parallel use), then 'other relevant languages' and finally, the languages of 'the bilinguals', i.e. immigrant languages. In discussions of the 'parallel language use' of English and Danish, English is simultaneously categorised as a competitor of Danish (a threat) *and* promoted as the most relevant other language in Denmark (a necessity). The 'other relevant languages' are seen as competing more with English than with Danish, i.e. in the end mostly relevant in connection with fighting the 'threat' of English. Finally, not only are immigrant languages regarded as non-Danish; they are not even counted as proper foreign languages, and therefore they are considered irrelevant or even illegitimate in the context of Danish society (Daryai-Hansen, 2010a, 2010b: 100–101). A consequence of this is also that discourses on language at Danish universities (which this contribution tries to report on while being part of them itself) focus on the relationship between Danish and English, while occasionally referring to the role that other languages have, could have or should have at Danish universities, and largely ignoring immigrant languages.

In her study of language use and language ideologies in a major international corporation in Denmark, Lønsmann (2011) identified the following as important language ideologies: (1) we speak 'Danish because we are in Denmark'; (2) 'using the mother tongue is natural'; (3) 'English is the international language' (excluding Danish, other Scandinavian languages and non-Scandinavian languages that used to be widely learnt); and finally (4) 'English is the future'. These ideologies are partly contradictory, but are still thriving, although the common conception, not least among foreign knowledge workers, is that people who do not know Danish do not have much of a chance in the Danish labour market, as a recent study confirmed: 'Good Danish language skills drastically improve the feeling of being integrated' (Mahncke & Nymark, 2010: 10).

The common belief about English in Denmark we referred to above, namely that English is learnt as a result of the efficiency of Denmark's internationally oriented educational and business institutions – what we called *English from above* – leads to another belief, namely that the influence of English on Danish can be regulated and controlled by the same institutions through language policy. This belief ignores the fact that educational institutions – meaning mostly primary and secondary schools – would not be so successful if they could not count on the motivation of the young generation to learn English. The precarious state of other languages as school subjects is not the result of a mistaken approach to language pedagogy, but of a widespread (though by no means total) lack of motivation to learn them to the same degree as English.

History of Denmark and Danish Universities from a View of Language Choice

Denmark has always been multilingual to a certain extent, which is quite different from being a stable multilingual community, since the knowledge of a number of languages other than Danish has always been a particular attribute of certain groups within society. Multilingual individuals were found in elites and professional groups (such as actors and artisans), as well as autochthonous and migrant minorities (for a brief historical overview, see Haberland [2008a] and for the city of Copenhagen in particular, see Maegaard & Jørgensen [2015]). One of the elites in question is the academic community, and the locus of their language practices was, to a large extent, the university. While the first university-level teaching in Denmark took place at the short-lived *studium generale* in Lund from 1425 to 1536, the first university teaching within the geographical area of the present Danish state took place in Copenhagen after the foundation of a university there in 1479. In the beginning, Latin was the language of instruction, administration and (as far as it occurred) research. But Danish and other modern languages (especially German) gradually replaced Latin, until by the turn of the 19th century, most teaching was in Danish. By the second half of the 19th century, a Danish nation state had been established, and the university had been turned into a national institution, where Danish was used everywhere except for certain ceremonial functions, where Latin was still used. While the university was rather conservative in its language use, the Royal Academy of Sciences, a research institution founded in 1742, published its proceedings in Danish from the beginning. Other institutions of higher learning that had a more practical outlook used Danish in the area of teaching as well, like Sorø Academy (training diplomats) since 1747 and later the Royal Veterinary and Agricultural School from its start in 1858.

The period from about 1840 to 1990 was characterised by two complementary movements. On the one hand, in the area of teaching, Danish was established as the default language. In research publications, where Danish had been established much earlier, a number of modern languages were used (at first mostly German and French). During the 20th century, English played an increasingly prominent role and began to dominate research dissemination in some subjects after 1945.

While Danish had been the exclusive language of teaching until about 1990, this suddenly changed within a period of five to ten years. If we attribute this shift to English to *market* pressure, we need to be specific: On the one hand, we are talking about some administrators' (bureaucrats') understanding of the market. The following is a typical statement from the language policy of Denmark's Technical University (DTU):

> For an internationally known and recognized university, it is important to be able to function and develop in constant interaction with notable foreign universities. International exchange of students and teachers is important, and this can only be carried out consistently if the language of instruction is English.
>
> To ensure that universities have a strong international role and position, and to maintain a high number of MA students, it is important to be able to attract a large number of foreign BA students who will take their MA degree at Denmark's Technical University. From an economic point of view, this is only feasible if all teaching at the MA level is in English.
>
> The DTU produces graduates who can function in an international context, regardless of whether they find employment in Denmark

or abroad. By way of preparing them for this, it is essential to train the students in the use of the language of internationalization, i.e. English, for professional as well as everyday contexts. This is done most consistently by using English as the language of instruction. (*Universiteternes sprogstrategier*, 2009: 8, our translation)

But such a strategy can only be formulated seriously in a country where fluency in English is widespread among both average university students and a sufficiently large proportion of university teachers: there is a clear supply side to the issue, although it is often exclusively seen as a question of demand for English. The statement that 'from an economic point of view, this is only feasible if all teaching at the MA level is in English' only makes sense if it is not necessary to invest in the language proficiency of students and staff, since they have already acquired, or are considered to have acquired, the English language when the policy is to be implemented. The market aspect was articulated even more clearly by Børge Obel, dean of the Aarhus School of Business (part of Aarhus University), in an interview conducted in 2007:

English-language study programmes attract the best foreign teaching staff and students and create a unique international research and study environment which will help kickstart an international career for our students. (Bak, 2007)

This argument was repeated in a government paper published in 2009:

The universities ought to define relevant aims for programmes offered in English in order to be able to attract the best students and researchers nationally and internationally. (*Universiteternes sprogstrategier*, 2009: 5)

However, it is not clear why English-language study programmes would 'attract the best foreign teaching staff and students' unless one takes for granted that they are all English speakers, which is of course an unwarranted assumption.

The rationale behind this market orientation that university administrators developed after the turn of the millennium is probably to be found in a reorientation of the attitude of the state to university funding. Universities have become economically independent 'self-owned' institutions, which means that universities manage and are largely responsible for their own finances. The state is still their main source of funding, but funding is now strongly result oriented. There are

Table 2.1 Danish universities: Languages used and organizing principles

University type	Period	Legitimizing principle	Language
Medieval and early modern university	15th and 16th century	*Auctoritas* (authority)	Latin
Enlightenment university	17th and 18th century	*Ratio* (reason)	Latin, other European languages and Danish
National university	19th and 20th century	Nation	Danish
Post-national university	End of the 20th century and the 21st century	Market	Danish and English

strong expectations and even demands from the state that universities should attract a considerable amount of external funding. This is intended to create an atmosphere of competition, both nationally and internationally. One of the possible sources of external funding is fee-paying transnationally mobile students (from countries outside the EU). There is serious debate on the question of whether competing for international students really pays off for Danish universities (cf. Heltoft & Preisler, 2007), although the argument is often used as a rationale for creating more programmes taught in English. Most short-term exchange students and long-term foreign degree students are from other EU or European Economic Area (EEA) countries and do not pay fees. For a while, Chinese degree students were considered a lucrative market to tap, but as it turned out, they did not arrive in large enough numbers to make it worthwhile to set up special programmes for them.

To sum up, the use of languages at Danish universities has moved through history from a Latin-only scenario through a brief period with a multilingual scenario and a national language-based scenario to a scenario where Danish and English coexist. This can be set up in a model as in Table 2.1, a model inspired by Schiewe (2000) and Bull (2004) and first presented in Mortensen and Haberland (2012: 192).

Language Policy and Practices of Language Choice in Danish Universities

There is no nationwide university language policy in Denmark, except in the sense of 'general aims', either formulated by the ministry or arrived at by consensus. Danish universities were never expected to institute a common set of particular objectives and strategies, the mandate of an *ad hoc* language policy committee established in 2002 by the Association of Danish Universities was to provide inspiration for the universities to develop their own solutions (Lauridsen *et al.*, 2003). When the Danish Ministry of Science and Technology published a report on the language policies of individual universities in 2009, it stated that:

> While respecting the scientific autonomy of universities, the Government wishes to monitor closely the language strategies of the universities and development in their use of English, in order to ensure that the universities fulfil their double role as Danish cultural/educational institutions as well as institutions of the global community. [...] [The report also contains a section about the universities' work] on ensuring and developing the quality of teaching in English, this being an important aspect of university language policies. (*Universiteternes sprogstrategier*, 2009: 5)

One thing emerges from this statement: the government does not aim at defining a language policy for the universities, but there is one area in particular that it considers important to monitor in the policies of individual universities, namely, the teaching in English.

Rainer Enrique Hamel (2008: 196) has pointed out that in the sociolinguistic description of language use and language choice in the field of academia and research, one has to distinguish three areas, namely production of knowledge (*recherche scientifique*), dissemination (*diffusion*) and education (*formation*). Both explicit language policies and the practice of language choice can differ significantly between these areas. It is interesting that the Danish government report focuses on the monitoring of the language of teaching, and is mostly concerned with two things, namely whether there is teaching in English such that the universities can fulfil their role of institutions of the global community, and whether the quality of this teaching through the medium of English is the highest possible.

Teaching

Degrees in 'major' foreign languages and literatures (like French and German) have traditionally been taught in Denmark either exclusively or to a very large extent in the language being studied. But since the 1990s, an increasing number of university programmes are offered in English either instead of, or in parallel with, corresponding programmes taught in Danish.

It is difficult to give precise figures, though. Those given in Table 2.2 are from the Copenhagen Business School (2009), which is probably one of the Danish universities with the highest number of courses in English.

The perceived pressure on institutions of higher education to create whole degree programmes taught in English is tremendous. It is taken for granted that no university can participate in the international exchange of students and teachers without offering at least some of its educational components in a language that foreign students and professors can be expected to know (the demand side), but also which local staff is able to teach in and local students are able to work in (the supply side). In Denmark, it is usually argued that the choice of English is determined by the demand side, but it is an open question whether it is not equally or even primarily determined by the supply side. On top of everything else, the university is keenly aware that the use of English or other foreign languages must not lead to a lowering of academic standards. Thus, the main question is: how can the individual university define a language policy as an integrated part of its internationalization policy?

A general feature of the recommendations of the 2009 report referred to above is the call for a general strengthening of the language competences of Danish university students as regards Danish, English and other foreign languages, i.e. the strengthening of one language is not to be undertaken at the expense of another. But there are several possible strategies available, and any university can pick the strategies best suited for the particular institution. Already in 2006, Roskilde University had defined the relationship between Danish and English at the university as follows:

> RUC offers all of its approved educational programmes with Danish as the teaching language. *Wherever possible*, Roskilde University programmes

Table 2.2 Students at Copenhagen Business School enrolled in English-medium and Danish-medium programmes

	Bachelor programmes	Master programmes	Total
Number of students	6550	6162	12,712
Students in English-medium programmes	1570 (24.0%)	3475 (56.4%)	5,045 (39.7%)
Students in Danish-medium programmes	4980 (76.0%)	2687 (43.6%)	7,667 (60.3%)

Source: *CBS Observer* February 2009, p. 12.

are also offered in English. (*Sprogpolitik for RUC*, 2006; our translation and emphasis)

One recommendation in the ministry's 2009 report particularly deserving of mention was the institution of language competence centres, given this name (as distinct from 'language centres') because they were to service the university at all functional levels according to the needs of students, professors and administrators, running tailor-made courses in English or Danish (as a second language), coaching, translating research articles – anything to promote and improve language communication.

Such centres have subsequently been established in at least two universities: Roskilde University (Language and Intercultural Communication Services – LICS) and the University of Copenhagen (Centre for Internationalization and Parallel Language Use – CIP).

In 2011, the centre at Roskilde University (LICS) lost one of its two pillars of internationalisation when courses in Danish as a second language were abandoned due to funding problems. The other pillar, Academic English Services, remains in place. Along with a number of other services that are not specifically language-related, LICS continues to offer a two-week 'foundation course' before the start of the semester. The course introduces students at Roskilde University to the essentials of Danish culture and the bare essentials of the Danish language.

The centre at the University of Copenhagen, CIP is looking to become a permanent fixture at this university. On the basis of research in the field of parallel language use in an academic context, CIP offers diagnostic tests for staff teaching in English, language courses in Danish, English and recently other languages tailored to the various needs across the university, as well as facilitating language revision and translation of academic manuscripts.

In Denmark, an interesting debate has focused on whether, in language policies, Danish and English should be conceived of as 'parallel' or 'complementary' languages. Following recommendations by the Danish Language Council, the University of Copenhagen formulated a policy that contemplated Danish and English becoming 'parallel languages' in higher education in order to prevent diglossic development (Harder 2009). In this debate, diglossia is generally seen as undesirable because it entails a *hierarchy* of languages on the basis of *social conventions* of language use, the fear being that English would develop into the more prestigious language while Danish would become the language with lower status.

It seems that the term 'parallel' in this connection was used as early as 1998 in a paper by the Swedish Language Council (Kuteeva, 2011: 6). The

Swedish Language Council states that the aim is to give students the option to work in Swedish and English 'in parallel', i.e. as a measure to strengthen the role of Swedish at Swedish universities. Foreign staff should *not* expect to be able to avoid teaching in Swedish in the long run:

> It may prove necessary to take action to ensure that teaching staff have a sufficient knowledge of Swedish. New lecturers with a first language other than Swedish should be employed on a probationary basis and be required to pass a language test within two years in order to be eligible for a permanent post. Encouragement should be given to educational development work aimed at enhancing students' ability to use Swedish and English in parallel in their subjects. It is unfortunate if separate domains develop, with foundation courses predominantly in Swedish and more advanced courses only in English. (Swedish Language Council, 1998: 16)

What the Swedish Language Council saw as a potential problem and tried to avoid was a situation like the one Dean Børge Obel of the Aarhus Business School described in 2007 with approval:

> On all nine international MSc programmes, all subjects are taught in English, but students are free to do their exams and write their theses in Danish *if their teachers have a command of Danish*. (Bak, 2007)

The way that 'parallel teaching' is understood in Denmark today, parallelism is an offer made to students, not a requirement on the teacher.

It is interesting to note that 'parallelism' in the Swedish document refers explicitly to two languages only, English and Swedish, while the aims stated elsewhere in the document are much more ambitious:

> A possible objective would be for all Swedish speakers to be able to express themselves in and understand two foreign languages tolerably well, in addition to their mother tongue. To achieve this aim, more resources will primarily have to be devoted to the teaching of second and third foreign languages, perhaps at the expense of instruction in English. The objective suggested is in line with the EU's language policy goal, that every EU citizen should have a command of two Community languages apart from his or her native language. This would probably strengthen Swedish in relation to English, but above all it would result in Swedes being better equipped to function in a multilingual Europe. (Swedish Language Council, 1998: 19)

Similar observations can be made about a number of Danish language policy documents, where reference is made initially to 'English and other languages', while the discussion of concrete initiatives restricts itself mostly to the relationship between Danish and English.

It has never been quite clear if 'parallel language use' is a programme or a descriptive term. In Preisler (2009), it was proposed to describe the relationship between Danish and English as one of 'complementary languages' rather than 'parallel languages', as their relative distribution is determined not by social convention, such as in the hierarchical relationship between languages in a diglossic situation, but rather by the communicative needs of concrete social networks involving speakers with particular linguistic backgrounds: English is used when *not all* members of a transnational communicative network know Danish (well enough), and Danish is used when *all* members of a network can be expected to know Danish.[4] The argument is that if the particular language choice is a matter of communicative necessity (i.e. necessary if the interactants are to understand each other), issues of hierarchy and prestige cease to be relevant. It is obvious, though, that over the last 20 or 30 years, English has become the default language in situations where Danish cannot be used, while earlier it shared this function at least with German and French.

The problem with teaching in English is not so much a question of the English proficiency of transnationally mobile staff (whose mobility is assumed to imply that they are adequately proficient in English), but of the English proficiency of local staff (see also Hauge, 2011). There is no generally required level for teachers, such as C1 in the Common European Framework of Reference for Languages (CEFRL), but some universities are developing certification of language skills for English (though so far not for other languages, including Danish). The Centre for Internationalisering og Parallelsproglighed (CIP) at the University of Copenhagen has developed a procedure for the certification of university teachers' English proficiency known as TOEPAS (Test of Oral English Proficiency for Academic Staff, http://cip.ku.dk/certificering/; see Kling and Stæhr [2011]).

The first faculty of the University of Copenhagen that introduced certification as a requirement for all staff teaching in English was the Faculty of Life Sciences. According to the CIP website, it was expected that between 2010 and 2012 well over 250 staff members would have obtained a certificate of proficiency in English.

As for the expected language skills of students, demands vary, of course, depending on the programme that they follow. These demands also depend on what one can reasonably expect from students having gone through the Danish school system. The only compulsory languages in the Danish primary and secondary educational system are Danish (as first or second language) and English (as a foreign language). At the university level, Danish competence is required of foreign students except for programmes taught in English. In a number of subjects (especially in the humanities), students are still required to know two foreign languages, but it is increasingly difficult to use the second language in teaching, since the language competences of students have become so diverse (not least due to the intake of transnationally mobile students) that English is often left as the only language shared by all – a phenomenon that could be called 'the paradox of internationalization': the more international the programmes become, the fewer languages are used in them (probably first pointed out by Saarinen *et al.*, 2008). This is, although the students between them speak more languages, they share fewer languages than before, often only English.

There is no formal requirement for teaching staff members to know any languages other than Danish, except for a strong (and not always fully realistic) expectation in certain departments that all teachers are able to teach in English. Staff members who are to teach a foreign language are, of course, expected to teach *in* that language. International staff members are now implicitly expected to master English as a lingua franca if they do not speak it as their first language. This is different from the situation about 50 years ago, when language accommodation was often mutual and direct, and not necessarily via a lingua franca.

Publication

Another area where languages may compete is the publication of research (Hamel's *diffusion*). Danish is no doubt still used in academic publications, but – as the figures in Table 2.3, published by the Danish Ministry of Science and Technology for 2009, show – English dominates the output of academic publications even in the humanities.

For a single university (Roskilde), Figure 2.1 shows not only that the gap between English and Danish publications is increasing, but also that the number of publications in languages other than those two is small, though not totally insignificant. It is also rather stable.

According to a Danish Language Council report (Jarvad, 2001), English is particularly dominant in publications in the natural sciences, which can also be seen in Table 2.3. In the social sciences, Danish is used more frequently, though between a third and half of publications are in English. The situation is even more favourable for Danish in the humanities and

Table 2.3 Academic publications in Denmark, 2009, by field of research

	Humanities (%)	Social Sciences (%)	Natural Sciences (%)	Health Sciences (%)	Total (%)
Danish	42.2	38.9	2.1	16.5	15.9
English	49.6	58.4	97.3	83.2	82.5
Other	8.2	2.7	0.6	0.3	1.6

theology, where the objects of research are to a great extent Danish language and culture. The number of publications in languages other than Danish and English is still significant.

Research

One has to distinguish, however, between output in various languages (Hamel's *diffusion*) and the use of different languages in academic institutions, i.e. what academics speak when they do research (*production*). Madsen (2008) studied a natural science department at a Danish university and found that in their daily work the researchers *did* use Danish, unless it was not possible to do so, as, for example, in the case of colleagues who either were only in Denmark for a short period of time or had not been there for very long (though the latter might

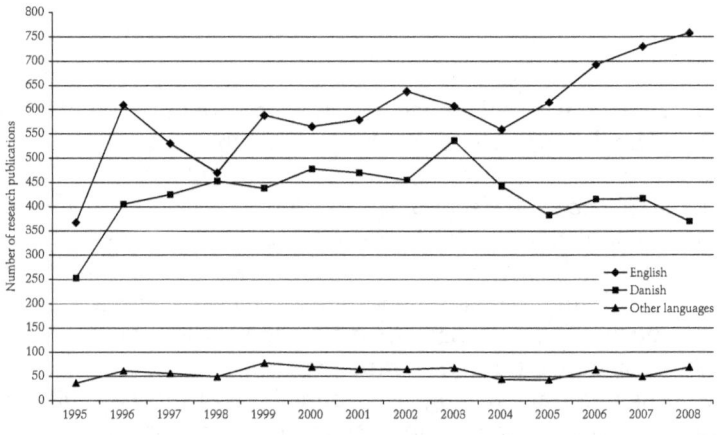

Figure 2.1 Research publications, Roskilde University, 1995–2008
Source: Mortensen and Haberland (2012: 189)

be expected to acquire Danish if they were to stay in the country, as mentioned above).[5]

The choice of language in these cases is again determined by the principle of complementary language use. What triggers language choice is the expected or experienced language repertoires of participants in social networks that exist within a given environment. If all the members of a network have Danish as their mother tongue or are expected to know Danish, then – everything else being equal – they will speak with or write to each other in Danish. If one or more of the actual or potential participants in the communication cannot be expected to know Danish – including the readership of an international scientific or scholarly journal – the language chosen will be one that the majority of participants would be familiar with, often English. If the participants have different mother tongues and are proficient in each other's languages, the factor determining which language will be chosen could, for example, be the topic, the situational context and/or the relationship between the participants.

Administrative staff

A fourth area within the university not even mentioned by Hamel is the administration of the universities. The secretarial staff (in the broadest sense) is an important interface between the university and the students. Members of the administrative staff are now generally expected to know enough English to be able to communicate with transnationally mobile students. Exam administrators routinely send their messages in Danish and English, but there is some resistance to the expectations that they should be able to use other languages as well. Due to Scandinavian receptive multilingualism (Zeevaert, 2007), Norwegian and Swedish students can still communicate with administrative staff in their first languages, and do not normally switch to English unless there is some special reason to do so, such as when a Norwegian student speaks a marked dialect of Norwegian that is not easily understood by his/her Danish interlocutor.

A Final Consideration

While many sociolinguists in Denmark have agreed to dismiss the domain concept as analytically blunt (see above), there is still a widespread public fear that Danish is 'losing domains' to English. 'Domain' in this case is a popular notion based on an interpretation of Fishman's (1967) concept, which applies to stable multilingual communities (Simonsen, 2008; Thelander, 1974: 51) and is conceived of as an area of social practice, e.g. education, advertising, the military and the courts. 'Domain loss' refers to a 'Danish' domain (e.g. higher education) becoming 'internationalized' through (predominant) use of the English language. The feared (by many) worst-case scenario is that English will take over the 'important' (public, official) domains, whereas Danish will get to keep the 'unimportant' (private, unofficial) domains, a situation known as diglossia.

This chapter has attempted to show that what seems to happen is not that English takes over domains from Danish, but that in some areas, particularly academic publications, English has taken over where French, German and to some extent Spanish used to play a bigger role than today (Haberland, 2008b; Preisler, 2008, 2010). This has been confirmed not just for higher education but also for science and business by Danish sociolinguist Normann Jørgensen:

> Scarce as it is, the research on the matter nevertheless suggests that Danish is not in danger of being pushed aside by English in these domains, but draws attention to another danger – that of depending exclusively on English-speaking sources to understand the rest of the world, due to the decreasing familiarity with other major languages. (Jørgensen, 2009: abstract; see also Jørgensen, 2013: 54–55)

In the complex interplay between many languages – as is unavoidable in research and higher education – a frequent question is how many languages we actually need for our communities of practice to work. One recurring answer is that two languages are enough. Lluís V. Aracil, the father of Catalan sociolinguistics, wrote:

> Perquè tothom pugui comunicar-se amb tothom, n'hi ha prou que cadascú sàpiga només *dos* idiomes: el seu propi i una *interlingua* comuna a tots. [...] I la lògica ens diu que la *interlingua* europea farà automàticament inútils les *interlinguas* dels imperis parroquials.[...] En primer lloc, en contrast amb el llatí, [la nova interlingua] no serà pas el privilegi esotèric d'una *élite*. (Aracil, 1982: 37)[6]

The idea is that successful communication is not dependent on the languages of semi-wide communication, the 'interlanguages of parochial empires'; we can make do with two languages for everybody: a common language for all and the individual language user's own language. A similar idea is expressed by David Crystal, although he does not argue from the point of view of communicative efficiency alone, but rather associates the need for a local language (*l'idioma propi*) with issues of identity:

> Arguments about the need for national or cultural identity are often seen as being opposed to those about the need for mutual intelligibility. But this is misleading. It is perfectly possible to develop a situation in which intelligibility and identity happily coexist. The situation is the familiar one of bilingualism – but a bilingualism where one of the languages within a speaker is the global language, providing access to the world community, and the other is a well-resourced regional language, providing access to a local community. The two functions can be seen as complementary, responding to different needs. And it is because the functions are so different that a world of linguistic diversity can in principle continue to exist in a world united by a common language. (Crystal, 2003: 22)

Similar ideas have occasionally been expressed in Denmark: if all Danes were bilingual in Danish and English, all communication problems would be solved (as long as everybody else was bilingual in English and their own language). It is no accident that in this argumentation, the second language that comes into the picture here apart from Danish is English, and not any other language. This is in the first place a consequence of the role that English plays in Danish society (and academia as a part of it), a role that is by no means unique but certainly not universal either. In few other countries is English spoken and understood by as large a section of the population (academic or otherwise) as in Denmark. In Denmark, it has been rather easy to accept the idea that English is 'the' lingua franca of the world, simply because it puts Danes into the comfortable position that access to this lingua franca is widespread and not restricted to an elite, a comfortable position that Denmark shares with a number of, but certainly not all, other countries. But the step from comfort to complacency is often small. Not everybody in the world outside Denmark speaks English; and French, Spanish and German still have a strong position in Europe, Spanish also in Latin America, French in West Africa, Swahili in East Africa, Chinese in South East Asia and Japanese in East Asia. Even in the academic world there is not just *one* world language.

Acknowledgment

Based on a paper given in Barcelona, 27 October 2011. Thanks to many people for help with references and information: Kimberly Chopin, Josep M. Cots, Petra Daryai-Hansen, Anne H. Fabricius, François Grin, Therese Hauge, Ebbe Klitgård, Linus Salö and especially Janus Mortensen as well as to an anonymous referee for helpful comments.

Notes

(1) 'If we concentrate exclusively on repertoire-related criteria, we could say that small languages are dominated more often than they dominate, and that they are rarely used as a lingua franca'.
(2) Foreign TV programmes and films even for school children are increasingly dubbed into Danish, which means that children in the age bracket where they are most impressionable (linguistically and otherwise) are no longer exposed to other languages when they watch these media. From the standpoint of foreign language acquisition, this is obviously an unfortunate development, which does not appear to be based on an explicit language policy.
(3) The youth cultural context of this example has been described in Preisler (1999a: 156f.) in connection with the discussion of a similar extract from the same material.
(4) This is not an exhaustive definition of *the principle of complementary languages* – only of its most general manifestation. Preisler (2008: 245) mentions other potentially relevant parameters. The defining criterion of a complementary, non-diglossic relationship between languages x and y is that, in the contexts where language x is chosen, this happens for the sake of communicative necessity or convenience, thus precluding language y for the same reasons – and vice versa.
(5) Similarly, Lønsmann's (2011) case study of an industrial research department showed that language choice was a complex process that followed basically the same principle: Danish where possible, English where necessary, other languages occasionally.
(6) 'To make it possible that everyone can communicate with each other, it is sufficient that everybody can use just two languages: his or her own and a lingua franca which is common to all... Logic tells us that the European lingua franca will automatically turn useless the linguae francae of parochial empires... First of all, in contrast with Latin, [this new lingua franca] will not be the esoteric privilege of an élite'.

References

Ammon, U. (1991) *Die internationale Stellung der deutschen Sprache*. Berlin: de Gruyter.
Ammon, U. (2003) The international standing of the German language. In J. Maurais and M.A. Morris (eds) *Languages in a Globalising World* (pp. 231–249). Cambridge: Cambridge University Press.
Ammon, U. (2010) World languages: Trends and futures. In N. Coupland (ed.) *The Handbook of Language and Globalisation* (pp. 101–122). Oxford: Oxford University Press.
Aracil, L.V. (1982) Conflicte lingüístic i normalització a l'Europa nova. In L.V. Aracil (ed.) *Papers de Sociolingüística* (pp. 23–38). Barcelona: Edicions de la Magrana (Els Orígens, 9).

Bacher, P., Clemmensen, N., Jacobsen, K.M. and Wandall, J. (1992) *Danskerne og fremmedsprog: en undersøgelse af den voksne befolknings sprogfærdigheder*. København: Udviklingscentreet for folkeoplysning og voksenundervisning.

Bak, H.F. (2007) Kickstart your English, interview with Dean Børge Obel, Aarhus School of Business. See http://www.asb.dk/omos/institutter/erhvervsoekonomiskinstitut/nyheder/nyhed/artikel/kickstart_your_english/ (accessed 10 February 2012).

Blommaert, J. (2009) A sociolinguistics of globalisation. In N. Coupland and A. Jaworski (eds) *The New Sociolinguistics Reader* (pp. 560–573). Basingstoke: Palgrave Macmillan.

Bull, T. (2004) Dagens og gårdagens akademiske lingua franca. Eit historisk tilbakeblikk og eit globalt utsyn. In D.F. Simonsen (ed.) *Språk i kunnskapssamfunnet. Engelsk – elitenes nye latin?* (pp. 35–45). Oslo: Gyldendal Akademisk.

Crystal, D. (2003) *English as a Global Language* (2nd edn). Cambridge: Cambridge University Press.

Daryai-Hansen, P.G. (2010a) Begegnungen mit fremden Sprachen: Sprachliche Hierarchien im sprachenpolitischen Diskurs im Dänemark und Deutschland der Gegenwart. PhD thesis, Roskilde University.

Daryai-Hansen, P.G. (2010b) Repræsentationernes magt – sproglige hierarkiseringer i Danmark. In J.N. Jørgensen and A. Holmen (eds) *Sprogs status i Danmark 2021* (pp. 87–105). Copenhagen: Københavns Universitet, Humanistisk Fakultet.

de Swaan, A. (2001) *Words of the World: The Global Language System*. Cambridge: Polity Press.

de Swaan, A. (2007) The language predicament of the EU since the enlargements. *Sociolinguistica* 21, 1–21.

EBLUL (2010) Ireland. See http://eblul.eurolang.net (accessed 4 December 2013).

Ethnologue (2013) Denmark. See http://www.ethnologue.com (accessed 18 February 2014).

Eurobarometer (2006) *Europeans and Their Languages*. European Commission. See http://ec.europa.eu/public_opinion/archives/ebs/ebs_243_en.pdf (accessed 10 February 2013).

Eurobarometer (2012) *Europeans and Their Languages*. European Commission. See http://ec.europa.eu/public_opinion/archives/ebs/ebs_386_en.pdf (accessed 21 February 2013).

Fishman, J. (1967) Bilingualism with and without diglossia; diglossia with and without bilingualism. *Journal of Social Issues* 23, 29–38.

Haarmann, H. (1973) *Soziologie der kleinen Sprachen Europas, Band 1. Dokumentation*. Hamburg: Buske.

Haberland, H. (1993) Probleme der kleinen Sprachen in der EG: Beispiel Dänisch. *Heteroglossia, quaderni dell'Istituto di Lingue Straniere* 5, 79–128.

Haberland, H. (2008a) Dänisch. In U. Ammon and H. Haarmann (eds) *Wieser Enzyklopädie der Sprachen des europäischen Westens, Band 1* (pp. 131–153). Klagenfurt/Celovec: Wieser Verlag.

Haberland, H. (2008b) Domains and domain loss. In B. Preisler, A. Fabricius, H. Haberland, S. Kjærbeck and K. Risager (eds) *The Consequences of Mobility: Linguistic and Sociocultural Contact Zones* (pp. 227–237). Roskilde: Roskilde University.

Haberland, H. and Mortensen, J. (2009) Engelsk – et nøgleord fra RUC til Tokyo. In K. Farø, A. Holsting, N.-E. Larsen, J.E. Mogensen and Th. Vinther (eds) *Sprogvidenskab i glimt. 70 tekster om sprog i teori og praksis* (pp. 385–388). Odense: Syddansk Universitetsforlag.

Hamel, R.E. (2008) Les langues des sciences et de l'enseignement supérieur: état actuel et perspectives d'avenir. *Séminaire international sur la méthodologie d'observation de la langue française dans le monde, Paris, du 12 au 14 juin 2008. Synthèse des ateliers et contributions écrites* (pp. 193–204). Paris: Agence Universitaire de la Francophonie et Organisation Internationale de la Francophonie.

Hauge, T. (2011) Language excellence – a necessary skill? University lecturers' dilemmas in teaching content courses in English as an international language. In R. Cancino, L. Dam and K. Jæger (eds) *Policies, Principles, Practices: New Directions in Foreign Language Education in the Era of Educational Globalisation* (pp. 161–187). Newcastle upon Tyne: Cambridge Scholars Publishing.

Harder, P. (2009) Parallel language use: A case for active social construction. In P. Harder (ed.) *English in Denmark: Language Policy, Internationalization and University Teaching*. Special edition of *Angles on the English-Speaking World*, Vol. 9 (pp. 109–128). Copenhagen: Museum Tusculanum Press.

Heltoft, L. and Preisler, B. (2007) Sigtet med en sproglov [The aims of a language law]. *Sprogforum* 39, 4–7.

Hilmarsson-Dunn, A.M. (2006) Protectionist language policies in the face of the forces of English. The case of Iceland. *Language Policy* 5, 293–312.

Jarvad, P. (2001) *Det danske sprogs status i 1990'erne med særligt henblik på domænetab*. Copenhagen: The Danish Language Council.

Jørgensen, J.N. (2009) Challenges facing Danish as a medium-sized language. Lecture for the project Comunitats Lingüístiques Mitjanes, Linguamón/CUSC, Barcelona. See http://www.ub.edu/cusc/llenguesmitjanes/?conferencies=%E2%80%9Cchallenges-facing-danish-as-a-medium-sized-language%E2%80%9D (accessed 27 July 2014).

Jørgensen, J.N. (2013) Challenges facing Danish as a medium-sized language. In F.X. Vila (ed.) *Survival and Development of Language Communities: Prospects and Challenges* (pp. 38–57). Bristol: Multilingual Matters.

Kling, J. and Stæhr, L.S. (2011) Assessment and assistance: Developing university lecturers' skills through certification feedback. In R. Cancino, L. Dam and K. Jæger (eds) *Policies, Principles, Practices: New Directions in Foreign Language Education in the Era of Educational Globalisation* (pp. 213–245). Newcastle upon Tyne: Cambridge Scholars Publishing.

Kloss, H. (1974) Die den internationalen Rang einer Sprache bestimmenden Faktoren. Ein Versuch. In H. Kloss (ed.) *Deutsch in der Begegnung mit anderen Sprachen* (pp. 7–77). Tübingen: Narr.

Kuteeva, M. (2011) Editorial: Teaching and learning in English in parallel-language and ELF settings: debates, concerns and realities in higher education. *Ibérica* 22, 5–12.

Lauridsen, K.M., Götzsche, H., Helmersen, O., Iversen, N., Jakobsen, K.S., Just, F., Kuhlmann Madsen, J. and Preisler, B. (2003) Sprogpolitik på de danske universiteter. Rapport med anbefalinger. Copenhagen: The Danish Rectors' Conference. See http://www.rektorkollegiet.dk/fileadmin/user_upload/downloads/Sprogpol.pdf (accessed 27 July 2014).

Li, D.C.-S. (2012) Review of [Harder 2009]. *International Journal of the Sociology of Language* 216, 199–204.

Lønsmann, D. (2009) From subculture to mainstream: The spread of English in Denmark. *Journal of Pragmatics* 41, 1139–1151.

Lønsmann, D. (2011) English as a corporate language. Language choice and language ideologies in an international company in Denmark. PhD thesis, Roskilde University.

Mac Mathúna, L., French, N., Murphy E. and Singleton D. (eds) (1988) *The Less Widely Taught Languages of Europe*. Dublin: IRAAL/Cumann na Teangeolaíochta Feidhmí.
Madsen, M. (2008) 'Der vil altid være brug for dansk'. En undersøgelse af 11 naturvidenskabelige forskeres grunde til at vælge henholdsvis dansk og engelsk i deres arbejde. Copenhagen: Københavns universitet, Humanistisk Fakultet. Københavnerstudier i tosprogethed, 48.
Maegaard, M. and Jørgensen, J.N. (2015, in press) Language in Copenhagen: Changing social structures, changing ideologies, changing linguistic practices. In E. Boix-Fuster (ed.) *Multilingual Cities and Medium-Sized Language Communities*. Bristol: Multilingual Matters.
Mahncke, H. and Nymark, J. (2010) *The Expat Study 2010*. Copenhagen: Oxford Research A/S and Copenhagen Post. See http://www.oxfordresearch.dk/publikationer/expat-2010.aspx (accessed 27 July 2014).
Ministry of Children and Education (2005) Vejledning om undervisningstimetal i folkeskolen. See http://www.carolineskolen.dk/filer/undervisningministeriets vejledendetimefordelingsplan.pdf (accessed 6 May 2012).
Ministry of Children and Education (March, 2006) Evaluering af tidligere start på fremmedsprogsundervisning – en spørgeskemaundersøgelse om engelsk i 3. klasse. http://www.uvm.dk/aktuelt/~/UVM-DK/Content/News/Udd/Folke/2002/Nov/~/media/UVM/Filer/Udd/Folke/PDF08/ESIB/060301_tidligere_fremmedsprogsstart_engelsk.ashx (accessed 6 May 2012).
Ministry of Children and Education (updated 2012) See http://www.uvm.dk/Uddannelser-og-dagtilbud/Gymnasiale-uddannelser/Internationale-aktiviteter-paa-det-gymnasiale-omraade/Undervisning-paa-andre-sprog (accessed 6 May 2012).
Mortensen, J. and Haberland, H. (2012) English – the new Latin of academia? Danish universities as a case. *International Journal of the Sociology of Language* 216, 175–197.
Peeters, Y.J.D. (1988) State and non-state supported less widely taught languages: Statutes beat numbers. In L. Mac Mathúna, N. French, E. Murphy and D. Singleton (eds) *The Less Widely Taught Languages of Europe* (pp. 101–110). Dublin: IRAAL/Cumann na Teangeolaíochta Feidhmí.
Preisler, B. (1999a) *Danskerne og det engelske sprog* [*The Danes and the English Language*]. Frederiksberg: Roskilde Universitetsforlag/Samfundslitteratur.
Preisler, B. (1999b) Functions and forms of English in a European EFL country. In T. Bex and R. Watts (eds) *Standard English: The Widening Debate* (pp. 239–267). London: Routledge.
Preisler, B. (2008) Deconstructing 'the domain of science' as a sociolinguistic entity in EFL societies: The relationship between English and Danish in higher education and research. In B. Preisler, A. Fabricius, H. Haberland, S. Kjærbeck and K. Risager (eds) *The Consequences of Mobility: Linguistic and Sociocultural Contact Zones* (pp. 238–248). Roskilde: Roskilde University.
Preisler, B. (2009) Complementary languages: The national language and English as working languages in European universities. In P. Harder (ed.) *English in Denmark: Language Policy, Internationalization and University Teaching*. Special edition of *Angles on the English-Speaking World*, Vol. 9 (pp. 10–28). Copenhagen: Museum Tusculanum Press.
Preisler, B. (2010) The influence of English in Scandinavia: Three studies of language attitudes and change. *International Journal of the Sociology of Language* 204, 161–169.
Risager, K. (2012) Language hierarchies in the international university. *International Journal of the Sociology of Language* 216, 111–130.

Saarinen, T., Pöyhönen, S. and Nikula, T. (2008) The language situation in Finnish higher education – from a nationalist project towards answering multilingual demands. Paper given at the CALPIU'08 conference on Transnational student mobility, Roskilde, December 2008.

Schiewe, J. (2000) Von Latein zu Deutsch, von Deutsch zu Englisch. Gründe und Folgen des Wechsels von Wissenschaftssprachen. In F. Debus, F.G. Kollmann and U. Pörksen (eds) *Deutsch als Wissenschaftssprache im 20. Jahrhundert* (pp. 81–104). Mainz: Akademie der Wissenschaften und der Literatur and Stuttgart: Franz Steiner.

Sevaldsen, J. (1992) Culture and diplomacy: Anglo-Danish relations 1945–49. In J.E. Nielsen (ed.) *The Twain Shall Meet. Danish Approaches to English Studies* (pp. 9–46). Copenhagen: University of Copenhagen. (POET, 18)

Simonsen, D.F. (2008) Over the fence–and into English? Reflections on adolescents, academics, linguistic development and language policy in Norway in the early 2000s. In B. Preisler, A. Fabricius, H. Haberland, S. Kjærbeck and K. Risager (eds) *The Consequences of Mobility: Linguistic and Sociocultural Contact Zones* (pp. 269–271). Roskilde: Roskilde University.

Sprogpolitik for RUC (2006) Roskilde: Roskilde University. See http://rudar.ruc.dk/bitstream/1800/5227/1/sprogpolitik_endelig_version_2006.pdf (accessed 24 October 2011).

Swedish Language Council (1998) Draft Action Programme for the Promotion of the Swedish Language. See http://www.sprakochfolkminnen.se/om-oss/kontakt/sprakradet/om-sprakradet/in-english.html (accessed 27 July 2014).

Thelander, M. (1974) *Grepp och begrepp i språksociologin*. Lund: Studentlitteratur.

Universiteternes sprogstrategier [The Language Strategies of the Universities] (2009) Copenhagen: The Ministry of Science, Technology and Development. See http://www.ubst.dk/publikationer/universiteternes-sprogstrategier/Universiteternes%20sprogstrategier.pdf. (accessed 14 November 2011).

Wee, L. (2011) The ranked list as panopticon in enterprise culture. *Pragmatics and Society* 2, 37–56.

Zeevaert, L. (2007) Receptive multilingualism and inter-Scandinavian semicommunication. In J.D. van Thije and L. Zeevaert (eds) *Receptive Multilingualism* (pp. 103–135). Amsterdam: Benjamins.

3 The Position of Czech and Other Languages at Universities in the Czech Republic: Some Initial Observations[1]

Tamah Sherman

Introductory Remarks

This chapter outlines some emerging issues concerning language policy in higher education in the Czech Republic. It contains two points of departure. The first is the issue of Czech as a medium-sized language in Europe. Czech is the language spoken as a first language by the majority of the population (over 90%)[1] and, in this respect, it shares characteristics with other European nation states of similar size.[2] The second point of departure is the commonly discussed issue of English in the higher education sphere – as an additional language of instruction, as a language of universities' outward presentation, as a language of international collaboration and research publications, and the like. Although I will offer a rough characterization of the issues involved in these two points of departure, I will argue that the issue of multilingualism in the Czech higher education context should be viewed in a more complex manner than as a question of the national language vs. English in conjunction with Czech's size as defined by the number of speakers.

The text will not present an exhaustive overview of language policy in higher education in the Czech Republic. Rather, I will attempt to identify a number of areas of the higher education domain[3] in which observable *language management* occurs, with a focus on the specific situation of the humanities and social sciences. The ideas contained in the text will, thus, hopefully be able to serve as a bridge to further research projects. I will begin by presenting a brief overview of some of the relevant characteristics of the higher education system in the Czech Republic. Then, I will introduce the theoretical perspective utilized in this chapter. This will be followed by an analysis of the specific languages and areas that are managed in the Czech higher education context, which reflect the main sociolinguistic issues involved in the Czech higher education sphere and which are worthy of more in-depth attention.

The Czech Republic and its Higher Education

The Czech Republic has existed as an independent nation state only since 1993, following the split of Czechoslovakia, but the Czech lands (in rough terms, the territory of the contemporary Czech Republic) have undergone a series of sociopolitical changes over the centuries which have been reflected in language policy and use in all areas of life, including the university sphere. Following the shift from Latin to German as the primary language of instruction in the 18th century and the increasing demand for Czech instruction in the late 18th century and throughout the 19th century, the most recent history includes separate Czech and German universities from 1882 up until World War II, and Czech–Slovak bilingualism during the periods of the Czechoslovak state (1918–1938, 1945–1993). Since 1993, Czech has been understood as the *de facto* official university language with the increase in the use of English over the past two decades.[4] In addition to the direct relationship between historical and political events and language policy, there are also several relevant facts which characterize the current state of higher education in the Czech Republic and may influence the language policy and practices of multilingualism *indirectly*. These include the following:

(1) As of 2013, basic public and state university programs are free of charge, though a transition to a tuition system has been the subject of public discourse since the 1990s. In practice, this means that anyone, regardless of his or her country of origin, may study tuition-free on the condition that he or she passes the entrance exams, which, for most programs, are held in the Czech language.[5]
(2) There has been a recent increase each year in the percentage of Czech secondary school graduates who go on to attend university. This is partially due to a population curve, as birth rates in the 1990s were significantly lower than in the 1970s and 1980s, leading to a decrease

in competition for places in study programs. It is also connected to a sharp increase in the number of accredited universities and study programs, particularly at private institutions. To illustrate – in 2000, there were 23 public universities, 8 private universities and 2 state universities[6] in the Czech Republic, while in 2012, there were 26 public universities, 46 private universities and 2 state universities. To use economic metaphors, this development has led to a shift in the Czech university sphere from a 'seller's market' to a 'buyer's market'.

(3) The Czech university system is in the final phases of its implementation of the Bologna Process. In 2012, the final subjects of study, in the humanities in particular, were transitioning from longer (5-year) master's programs to separate bachelor's and master's degree programs (3-year and 2-year, respectively).

(4) In 2012, there were 74 accredited higher education institutions in the Czech Republic and 7992 accredited study programs (2678 bachelor's programs, 745 5-year master's programs, 2631 2-year master's programs and 1938 PhD programs,).[7] Of these, 1692[8] study programs are accredited in English (340 bachelor's programs, 68 5-year master's programs, 555 2-year master's programs, 729 PhD programs), 86 in German (29 bachelor's programs, 33 2-year master's programs, 24 PhD programs), 7 in Russian (6 bachelor's programs, 1 2-year master's program), 4 in French (2 2-year master's programs, 2 PhD programs), 1 in Italian (bachelor's program), 1 in Dutch (2-year master's program) and 1 in Polish (PhD program).[9] At first glance, the numbers of programs accredited in foreign language reflect the range of languages prevalent in the Czech context. However, there are no available data on whether the foreign language programs are actually opened (i.e. it is entirely possible that some programs exist in name only) or the number of students currently studying in these programs. There is also no information publicly available on what linguistic backgrounds the students and teachers in these programs have, e.g. it can be observed that programs in English are often attended by students whose first language is Russian.

Language Problems and their Management

Facts and figures specifically related to explicit language policy are generally unavailable in the Czech context. This reflects the fact that the policy itself in the Czech higher education context (and in general in the Czech Republic, which does not have an all-encompassing language law) is rarely explicit. For this reason, I take an ethnographic approach to the way in which practices of multilingualism are managed. I understand language management as metalinguistic behavior, including all forms of language policy, which is oriented towards language problems (see Nekvapil & Sherman, 2009; Neustupný & Nekvapil, 2003). Language management can be analysed as a process of several phases: noting and evaluation of deviations from norms or expectations, and the design and implementation of adjustments (or the lack of it). In other words, this text poses the questions of when and where individual or organizational actors in the university sphere find problems, even those at the most micro level of communication, and how they deal with them. This complex approach which attempts to identify the multiple instances of language management occurring in single institutions or groups of institutions, with all of their associated ideologies, is inspired in part by previous research on multinational companies in the Czech Republic (see, e.g. Nekvapil & Sherman, 2009, 2013).

Methodology

The research for this chapter was conducted over a four-year period, consisting primarily of the systematic observation of instances of language management. These instances typically occurred in situations which are typical for the everyday existence of the academic sphere – teaching, research and administrative activities. There is a specific focus on the Faculty of Arts at Charles University in Prague. There are, thus, certain limitations related to this faculty's highly specific character. In particular, the range of languages used at this faculty is most likely broader than that of any other similar-sized institution in the country.[10] Examples are taken from participant observation—the author has been an employee at this faculty since 2003 (having taught classes and conducted research in both Czech and English) and was a student there from 1998 to 2007. It should, however, be noted that the author's interpretations may be influenced by her experiences as a native speaker of English and as a non-native speaker of Czech. The observed examples are supplemented with data from official and unofficial documents produced by the faculty, university and Ministry of Education, many available on the web. As language problems are managed on a daily basis, examples have been taken from as late as March 2012, when the first version of this chapter was submitted.

The Languages

There are four languages which are observed to be most typically the subject of language management in the Czech higher education setting.

The first of these is Czech. It is the primary language of instruction in higher education and is spoken by approximately 10 million people. In the 2001 census, it was the declared mother tongue of 95% of the population of the Czech Republic, in the 2011 census approximately 91%.[11] These basic facts are reflected in the commonly expressed ideologies 'Czech is a small language spoken only by the Czechs' (see Nekvapil & Sherman, 2013) and 'In the Czech Republic, only Czech is (and should be) spoken' (cf. Sloboda, 2010). It is important to note that the status of Czech as the language of instruction in universities is not commonly questioned, for example in media discourse, yet at the same time there are several important issues regarding this status which are not typically considered. The first is that Czech's position as the *de facto* official language enables the protection of national networks, the national economy and Czech-speaking individuals within it, as non-Czech-speaking potential students and employees are less likely to compete for positions. However, the perceived economic value of Czech by individuals from 'older' European Union (EU) states, given the average salaries for academic employees, which are considerably lower,[12] in combination with the fact that it is spoken by 'only' 10 million people and may be perceived as not contributing to international mobility, may limit the influx of talented students and employees from abroad and thus threaten the Czech university's ability to internationalize.

A second language used in the Czech university sphere is Slovak, which is spoken by approximately 5 million people. Slovak and Czech speakers lived for many years in the single, officially multilingual republic, Czechoslovakia, the two languages being mutually intelligible, enabling semi-communication, i.e. communication in which speakers of such mutually intelligible languages use their own native languages.[13] Slovaks continued to live in the Czech Republic and to migrate there even after the split of Czechoslovakia in 1993. They are active in all domains of Czech life, which includes students attending Czech universities. The relevant question, then, is: in which situations is Slovak actually a foreign language in the Czech context? In other words, when is the use of Slovak permitted? As the following example, taken from a list of 'frequently asked questions' at the Faculty of Arts, shows, this issue is not one that is taken for granted and is universal for all fields of study.

> Question: (In Slovak) Hello, I'd like to ask for information, whether it's possible to study translation and interpretation in the combination of two languages (English and French and English and Swedish) Do I have to take entrance exams from both languages? As a Slovak, do I have to know Czech perfectly? Thank you for your answer.

Answer: ((In Czech)) Hello, the combinations mentioned are possible, if the majors listed are opened in the given year. It is necessary to take the entrance exams from both languages and because it is the field of translation and interpretation, very high proficiency in Czech is necessary.[14]

Initial observation of everyday practices at the university reveals that this example is highly field specific – the Czech language is only explicitly required for fields in which it is the object of study (Czech language and literature, translation studies). Observation at the university suggests that Slovak is in fact permitted for a range of academic purposes, including oral participation in seminars and readings and written assignments. But there are situations in which Slovak is viewed as a foreign language. For example, it is possible to find Slovak students in the 'Czech for Foreigners' program, a bachelor's and master's program for students for whom Czech is not their native language. Slovak is also the subject of extensive debate as a language used by teachers – in language management terms, it is noted by students (they are aware that the teacher is speaking Slovak), occasionally evaluated negatively, and in such cases, one proposed adjustment is that these teachers use Czech instead.

In addition to these two languages which have traditionally been spoken on Czech territory is a third, German. A language once used heavily (and, in fact, officially) in universities on the territory of the contemporary Czech Republic, German currently holds the status of a foreign language and is the official language of two neighbouring states, Austria and Germany. Interest in learning German has dropped overall at the Czech primary and secondary school levels, mostly in connection with increased interest in English.[15] In the higher education sphere, this drop is subsequently reflected in students' willingness to read texts and work with written material in German and travel abroad for German courses and exchange programs, which can be demonstrated through data revealing the management of this problem, as in the following example observed on the web page of the Department of Czech Literature in March 2012:

In consideration of repeated questions and unclear issues and the fact that that there has thus far been no interest in the exchange programs to Germany, the Department of Czech Literature announces that the nomination process for the Erasmus program will take place on Friday, March 30 (in room 413) at 1pm.

We ask all those interested to attend. We ask students consider whether they insist on going only to English-speaking countries, whether it is not more advantageous to go to a country whose language they do not know so well and in which they should, rather, improve their skills. German universities are outstanding universities and they work in a different way. In addition, Czech language and literature scholars should know German. And studying German literature and literary science is important for Czech language and literature scholars in general.[16]

In the higher education sphere, then, expectations that students will read in German has gone from general to field and region specific, i.e. German is still expected in fields such as history or philosophy and in regional universities near the German and Austrian borders, though in some cases, the students are openly reminded of this expectation by their teachers (as the example above shows). Efforts to promote German are also put forth at more organized levels, such as by the Czech Union of German Scholars or the Goethe Institute. German native-speaking teachers at German departments are also typically financed from external sources – the German and Austrian governments and private foundations.

Finally, there is English, which is common to all medium-sized languages in Europe in terms of its role as a language which is increasingly in demand. The specific nature of the relationship between Czech and English is connected, on the one hand, to the fact that knowledge of it is highly generationally tied to perceptions of the Czechs as a nation whose English skills are poor overall, particularly in comparison with countries such as Germany, the Netherlands and the various Scandinavian countries (Sherman & Sieglová, 2011). On the other hand, English as a foreign language is viewed as a neutral alternative to languages such as German or Russian, which are ridden with symbolic ties to historical and political relationships, in which case they may be evaluated negatively. The more general character of English in the Czech Republic is, of course, that it is the language of many top-tier academic journals, in which there is growing pressure for Czech academics to publish.

English, thus, frequently serves as a lingua franca in contexts in Czech higher education, including private universities which cater to both Czech and international students,[17] English-medium programs in public universities (some of which involve tuition fees), programs for foreign students, e.g. Erasmus, scientific contexts such as research, lectures, conferences and publishing, and administrative contexts, e.g. communication with other universities. This use of English is one which is becoming ever more relevant in the countries of the 'expanding circle', where it is a foreign language rather than a native or official one (as defined by Kachru, 1985). Moreover, in the Czech Republic, foreign language competence, in particular that of English, serves as an important fuel for individuals in the knowledge economy (cf. Piech & Radosevic, 2006; Prendergast, 2008).

Given this combination of languages present in the Czech higher education context, we can pose the question of the specific position of Czech, and in doing so, we can point to some language ideologies which are represented by two statements regarding Czech. The first can be paraphrased as 'Czech is enough', accompanied by the argumentation that the power of the Czech language helps protect national interests and national research topics, that Czech is fully functional in all domains and should be cultivated further. The second can be paraphrased as the opposite, i.e. 'Czech is not enough', with the arguments being that the dominance of Czech impedes internationalization, scientific growth and the influx of foreign students and employees. Both of these statements can be observed in a constant state of tension in public universities. This corresponds with an observation made by Czech researchers Melichar and Pabian (2007), who use the concept of centre and periphery as a metaphor for the professional situation of Czech academics, who they claim are at the centre of the international periphery, enjoying a significant degree of local success, which in many cases is a sufficient (and even highly desirable) career base, but are virtually unknown abroad. This metaphor is reflected in various ways in the higher education domain, as we will see below.

Areas of Language Problems

This section will provide a brief overview of the areas of the higher education domain in which language problems are experienced. The first relevant area is that of study programs. At the faculty under study, for years the predominant language problem in this area has been that of integrating students from abroad, non-native speakers of Czech. Since the 1990s, the most common management act has been the creation of programs specifically for non-native Czech speakers, the students of which are, for the most part, isolated from the Czech-speaking students in other programs.

There are two types of such programs which are typically created. The first type includes programs in Czech which are part of the regular offer of university study programs and are, thus, free of charge. The most well-known major study program in the humanities context of this type is called

'Čeština pro cizince' or 'Czech for Foreigners', and offers a BA and MA course of study parallel to that of Czech Language and Literature programs. Another is in the field of Translation Studies. During the past decade, for example, it was noted that many students from abroad were applying to the Translation Studies programs with excellent knowledge of the second translation language (English, German, Russian, French, Spanish), but with poor knowledge of Czech. For this reason, new Translation Studies programs were accredited specifically for non-native speakers of Czech. The second type of program is one which is designated primarily for students from abroad and is conducted entirely in a foreign language, most commonly English, with minimal to no exposure to Czech. Fees are typically charged for these programs.

In between these two types of programs, however, there is the problem of classes for Erasmus students, who do not pay fees and many of whom do not speak Czech. This means that on the one hand, they may not be given places in the classes for fee-paying students in foreign languages, and on the other hand, they are not able to attend the courses in Czech. The result of this is extensive management on an *ad hoc* basis. An example of this is taken from an email sent to all departments at the beginning of the semester, which, in addition to requesting a list of courses offered by the department in foreign languages, stated the following:

> If you know that a teacher in your department provides individual instruction/consultation/block seminars for foreign students, it is appropriate to pass this information on... if you do not offer any foreign language courses in your department, send me this information and also information on who in your department short-term Czech-speaking students should address if they would like to attend courses in your department... (Originally in Czech, translation by the author)

This indicates both that there is a shortage of courses for Erasmus in general and that the general information about these courses is dynamic and typically not available centrally.

Language of Departmental Websites

The question of choosing languages in which to convey information which is made publicly and centrally available, i.e. on university websites, is a further area of problems. As the websites of Czech universities generally appear in Czech and/or English (with the exception of the web pages of selected language departments), there are two relevant issues in terms of regulation: (1) which information should appear in which languages on the website and (2) the question of the default language – which language should appear first on the website. One example of this is the case of departmental websites at the Faculty of Arts, Charles University. In terms of (1), the faculty administration requires information about the department, studies, research, information for potential students and study abroad to be in Czech. The required Czech information appears in an extensive list with five to six points for each area. The required English information is considerably briefer, consisting of the following: What we teach, Graduate/Post-graduate profile; Science & Research (Major research themes, Profile subjects, Publishing activities, Cooperation, Conferences/Events); Links to International Office a (sic) Registrar of the Faculty of Arts of Charles University; Contact (Address; Telephone/Fax; Email; Webmaster; Management: Director, Assistant Director, Secretary, Administrative support and English-speaking contact).[18]

The faculty administration thus designates which minimum of information should be on a department website in Czech and English, but it does not designate the order in which this information should appear. In terms of (2), the default web page language (the language which appears first when the link to the department is clicked upon) of all departments (46) but five was Czech at the time this chapter was being written.[19] The exceptions to this are two departments (English Literature, Theoretical and Computational Linguistics) with English as the default language, one department with two languages equally represented as the default language (Classical Archaeology), one department with three languages in this function (German Studies – Czech, German and English) and one department with a mix of Czech and English (Sociology).

Language Competence of Teaching Staff

The language competence of teaching staff is not regulated at the national or university levels, and typically not at the faculty level, either. Rather, it is regulated at the departmental level. This means that departments can determine the linguistic requirements for their staff upon hiring.[20] A selection of language requirements from job advertisements from the Faculty of Arts[21] from 2010 and 2011 provides a small sample.

In the context of this sample, we can observe several tendencies. One is the use of the concept of the 'world language', which is sometimes defined and sometimes not. This concept appears in formulations such as 'Active knowledge of at least two world languages' (Comparative Literature),

'Active knowledge of at least two world languages (English, German, French), ability to teach and publish in at least one of them' (Philosophy), 'Active knowledge of another world language and ability to teach in it' (Far East, for a Chinese-teaching job), 'Active knowledge of at least one world language, ability to teach and publish in a world language' (Theatre Studies), 'Active knowledge of another world language and ability to teach and publish in it' (Far East, Japanese teaching job), 'Active knowledge of at least one world language' (Art History), 'Active knowledge of English and partial knowledge of another world language' (German), 'Advanced knowledge of at least two world languages (English, French, German, Spanish, Russian) and ability to teach and publish in at least one of them' (Far East, Chinese teaching job).

There are many job advertisements which only mention English. They include: 'Ability to teach in English' (Art History), 'Active knowledge of English' (Physical Education), 'Very good knowledge of specialized English' (Phonetics), 'Active knowledge of English considered automatic' (Ethnology, for job in Indonesian program), 'Experience with teaching in English' (Linguistics), 'Knowledge of English for the purposes of teaching in it' (Central European Studies), 'Ability to teach in English' (Social Work).

There are also advertisements which offer some combination of the requirements above, or which speak more generally of 'language knowledge' or 'language skills' and often further specify the relevant languages. They include 'Relevant language knowledge' (Central European History), 'Active knowledge of English and German (at a high level), ability to teach in these languages' (Economic and Social History), 'Language skills (English, Spanish, potentially other languages)' (World History), 'Good knowledge of another Slavic language' (Czech Language), 'Excellent knowledge of English, knowledge of another language welcome' (Czech as a Foreign Language), or 'Language skills' (Latin, German, English) or (English, German, French), depending on position (World History).

A significant number of departments advertised jobs with no explicit extra language requirements, though in cases of language-teaching or areal studies positions, requirements relating to the specific language may have applied.[22] These departments were: Aesthetics, Cultural Studies, Adult Education and Personnel Management, Comparative Linguistics, Musicology, South Slavic and Balkan Studies, Czech Language, Education, Central European Studies, Psychology, Eastern European Studies, Logic, Romance Languages, Greek and Latin Studies, Information and Library Studies, Linguistics, Czech History, South and Central Asian Studies (Mongolian, Hindi, Tibetan and Romany language teaching jobs), Political Science, Prehistoric Archaeology, Czech National Corpus, Classical

Archaeology, Translation Studies, Ethnology, Middle East and African Studies, Czech Literature, and the Language Centre.

Some departments advertised more than one job during this period, but their tendencies towards language requirements did not change (including the specific formulations in the job advertisements). The behaviour of the departments which did not make explicit language requirements can be interpreted in a number of ways, including:

(1) Languages other than Czech (and potentially also language-teaching or area studies requirements) are truly not assumed to be necessary for the job.
(2) It is assumed that anyone thinking of applying for the job would automatically be a native speaker or a highly competent user of Czech (the advertisements are published in Czech) and has knowledge of languages other than Czech, particularly English.

It is also worth mentioning that there were some departments which advertised jobs for which it was expected that the applicants would be non-native speakers of Czech, and the following requirements could be observed: 'Knowledge of Czech' (English), and 'Basic knowledge of Czech' (Eastern European Studies, Ukrainian teaching job). These jobs were language-teaching jobs for which it was deemed desirable that the language in question be taught by a native speaker or that the only available job candidates (or the majority of them) would be native speakers. This indicates another language-related issue at the faculty: the demand for speakers of specific languages in combination with the low likelihood of those speakers having competence in Czech. While it is true that Czech may not be required to teach classes, there are other job tasks for which not having knowledge of Czech is a serious limitation.

Potential conflicts in this area lie not in the fact that the other employees at the faculty do not speak other languages, e.g. English, but rather, that the majority of the employees at the faculty are native speakers of Czech, and Czech is the language used in most communication situations. Therefore, whereas communication in other languages may not be a problem for individual face-to-face dialogical communication with colleagues and students, lack of Czech knowledge limits access to social networks and to the important information shared within those networks and also creates extra work for other employees, who must serve as interpreters at official events or department meetings or meetings of faculty organs.

Language of Written Work

The language in which students submit papers and write qualifying theses is also the object of management, and this is one area where it is possible to find explicit documented policy on a variety of levels. These are: (1) ministry level, (2) faculty level, (3) department level and (4) instructor/course level. At the faculty level, the management is a question of explicit written regulations, limited to written texts such as final theses. For example, Article 18a of the faculty's study regulations regarding publication of final theses states:

> 9. Except in the case of bachelor's theses, the final thesis must contain an abstract. In this case the student by the date and in the manner according to paragraph 8 must also submit an extra abstract of the thesis in Czech and in English, or in the language of the study program in which the student is registered;[23]

As can be observed, the explicit policy is characterized by a certain vagueness which is particularly apparent when the policy is applied in practice. Part of this vagueness is also connected to the concept of 'language of accreditation', which is defined in official documents from the Ministry of Education as follows:

> Note: By 'instruction in a foreign language' we mean instruction in the full range of the study program/major, not the instruction of selected individual subjects or parts of them in a language foreign to the accredited program/major.[24]

The combination of these official policies at the national level, and, subsequently, at the level of the faculty, often translates to the shifting of decisions about language use in written genres to the level of the department as well as the individual instructors. For example, in the study program in General Linguistics, which officially has Czech as its language of accreditation, theses are submitted in languages other than Czech, e.g. English, with the language of the individual thesis being a matter of agreement between the student, the student's advisor and other evaluators of the work (committee members).

At the department level, the language of written work is managed above all in departments that accept a large number of student papers, e.g. departments that offer courses that fulfil general education requirements for students from the entire faculty. For example, all doctoral students at the Faculty of Arts are required to write a paper in Philosophy, the grading of which is organized by the philosophy department. On the philosophy department web page, teachers declare which languages in which written work may be submitted.

> The paper can be written in Czech, Slovak, English, German, or French. Exceptionally, upon the agreement of the contact person, in another world language. If the doctoral student intends to submit the paper in a language that is not his native language, it should be checked by a native speaker or a person who knows the language well.[25]

Finally, within individual courses, instructors are free to determine the language in which papers can be submitted. Like the department-level management of written work, this management typically occurs in the form of semiformal announcements or personal arrangements between instructors and students, particularly in fields where classes are small. The following example, from the web page of a teacher in one of the linguistics departments, exemplifies this:

> The language of the paper can be Czech (Standard Czech, or for those who dare, Common Czech) or English, and for non-native speakers of Czech – by agreement – even their native language.[26]

Here, it should be noted that in the course of instruction, language issues also come up when syllabi are created, particularly in the question of which languages students should be able to read. Though the above mentioned 'world language' is a mandatory part of all humanities programs, frequently noted issues on the part of teachers are that (1) students are reluctant to read texts that are not in Czech or Slovak and (2) students are reluctant to read texts in foreign languages other than English – this is marked in general by the decline in students' ability to read texts in German and Russian. The most common management act in this area is the extensive translation of canonical texts into Czech and Slovak, and, in fact, the establishment of entire book series devoted to translations of texts in certain specialized areas of study (e.g. Linguistics).

Language of Research

The selection of languages for publishing research results and applying for national research funding is, as in any country, highly field dependent, and, as has been pointed out by a number of scholars (e.g. Ferguson *et al.*,

2011; Gazzola, 2012), non-native English-speaking scholars are typically at a disadvantage in general when publication in impacted journals, most often in English, is increasingly required due to the quantification of the evaluation of research results. For this reason, in this section, I will merely point to three interesting acts of language management that have been observed over the past decade. In combination, they appear to place emphasis on a general orientation towards internationalization (which occasionally defeats its own purpose, as we will see), combined with the acknowledgement that languages other than English are essential to the research in certain fields, as well as the ongoing need to cultivate the Czech language.

The first of these is the universal requirement of the Czech Science Foundation that the major text section of all grant applications be written in English. There is one exception to this – grants that are 'bound exclusively toward the Czech language domain'.[27] This requirement, however, merely allows for the possibility of sending the grant applications abroad for evaluation – it does not ensure that the applications will be reviewed abroad, and in fact, many evaluations, particularly in the humanities and social sciences, continue to be evaluated by Czech reviewers. The remaining portion of the grant application, e.g. budget information and explanation of costs, is to be written in Czech. Interestingly, this constitutes an instance in which Slovak, which, as mentioned above, is mutually intelligible with Czech, is not permitted. Both of these acts of language management (preference for English, penalization for Slovak) were revealed in an email from the faculty grant coordinator to potential grant applicants in early 2010:

> GOOD ADVICE considering the results of last year's competition: do not fill in any part of the project, not even the slightest bit, in Slovak – it is grounds for disqualification. If you do not have a very well-argued reason, do not submit the project in Czech – last year this led to disqualification in 100% of cases.[28]

The second is the issue of Czech journals. Czech language journals dominate humanities and social sciences, and some are listed in the Thomson Reuters Web of Science and other databases such as Scopus. There are an increasing number of Czech journals which publish some or all of their articles in English. However, it is necessary to pose the question of whether local publications in English are actually read by an international audience, a question motivated by the observance of what can be called 'English overkill', or excessive publication in English, but not in top-tier journals, and often not suitable in terms of either content or style (or both) for an English-speaking readership. In the humanities and social sciences, another act of language management has been implemented, which can be called 'building parallel discourses'. This consists of publishing articles and books in dual versions, typically Czech and English. The two versions are either direct translations of each other or (more typically) different versions of the same publication, with various adaptations in the content and style made to suit different groups of readers, e.g. with special consideration given to those readers' assumed backgrounds.

Thirdly and most importantly, at present, there is the relationship between language choice and research-based institutional financing. The Czech system for such financing is currently partially based on point system for research results. What is interesting in this system is the establishment of the so-called National Reference Framework of Excellence fields,[29] created in early 2008 in order to balance out what was viewed as discrimination against the humanities in particular. These fields are: Philosophy, Religion, History, Archaeology, Anthropology, Ethnology, Political Science, Management and Administration, Legal Studies, Linguistics, Literature, Media Studies, Art and Architecture and Education. An example of the way in which this system functions is as follows: In 2011, for a monograph in the areas of Philosophy, Religion, History, Archaeology, Anthropology, Ethnology, Political Science, Management and Administration, Legal Studies, Linguistics, Literature, Media Studies, Art and Architecture and Education, there were 40 points, regardless of the language. For a monograph in all other areas, there were 40 points for a monograph in a 'world language' (English, Chinese, French, German, Russian, Spanish) and 20 points for a monograph in any other language, including Czech.[30]

Concluding Remarks

In this chapter, I have provided an overview of some of the most current problems regarding the position of Czech and other languages in higher education institutions in the Czech Republic. In attempting to characterize this highly complex situation overall on the basis of observed multiple acts of language management, it is possible to articulate several overarching themes. First of all, returning to the original vantage point of Czech as a medium-sized language,[31] it can be stated that Czech's 'size' is not only a question of numbers of speakers, but also one of political and economic power, which is frequently made relevant in the higher education sphere. Unlike in some other countries discussed in this volume, foreign students coming to study at Czech universities and foreign lecturers coming to teach there are not universally expected to learn and use Czech, and instructors teaching in English as part of special programs for foreign students are paid at a higher hourly rate than instructors teaching in Czech. Higher education is an exceptionally multilingual domain in the Czech Republic, which is, from a contemporary demographic perspective based on census results, a highly ethnolinguistically homogeneous state. Yet in this multilingual domain, the individual languages may not be valued in the same way.

In general, it can be stated that at present, there does not appear to be a fear of domain loss for Czech in favour of English in the higher education sphere, particularly in the social sciences and humanities. In terms of Language Management Theory, it is not the absence of Czech in certain domains, but rather, the lack of proficiency in foreign languages, above all English, which is more typically noted as a deviation from the norm. Such noted deviations lead to hyper-corrective measures, such as making English the default language of a Czech university website, or the publication of local journal articles in English despite the lack of an appropriate readership.

Many issues concerning language use in the Czech university system are not managed at all, or the management is not top-down. As we have seen in the examples above, much of the management that occurs specifically at the Faculty of Arts is done at the levels of the faculty, department and individual courses. This can be observed along with ideological assumptions about English as an international language, about German as a language which is undesirable in various ways, and above all, about Czech as a language which can, at present, stand to be 'left alone' in terms of its official status. The cultivation of Czech as an academic and non-native language for both employees and students, currently most observable in less prominent contexts and not the subject of extensive discourse, can be anticipated as a challenge which will continue to grow.

Acknowledgements

Work on this publication was supported by Charles University Research Development Program no. 10 - Linguistics, subprogram Language Management in Language Situations. I am grateful to Jiří Nekvapil, Vít Dovalil, Karla Tvrdá and the participants in the workshop 'Language in Higher Education. Challenges for Medium-Sized Language Communities' at the University of Barcelona on 28 October 2011 for their kind assistance in directing me to various data sources that were used.

Notes

(1) Source: Czech Statistical Office, http://www.scitani.cz, tab. 614b.
(2) For an analysis of Czech as a medium-sized language, see Nekvapil (2013).
(3) In this text, I will use the term 'domain' while at the same time acknowledge the problematic character of this term as elaborated by Haberland (2008). In the Czech context, unlike, for example, the German and Danish contexts, there is little or no public discourse articulating the concept of 'domain loss' (see Haberland & Preisler, this volume).
(4) Although we can assume that on Czech territory, it was the predominant language even during the periods of the Czechoslovak state.
(5) There are, of course, some exceptions to this, as fees are charged for students who study longer than the standard period of time and for students who take on additional study programs.
(6) The Police Academy and the Military Academy.
(7) Source: Czech Ministry of Education, http://www.msmt.cz/file/15150/, overview from 30 January 2012.
(8) One study program was accredited in both English and German, and two in both English and Russian.
(9) This means that the language of instruction is entirely in the given language; see the explanation of the 'language of instruction' below.
(10) This evaluation is based on several factors: (1) it is the largest faculty of the largest university in the country and (2) it is the nation's centre for the teaching of national languages and literatures (usually based on the concept of philology, but with a more recent tendency towards area studies). This latter fact is reflected in a statement on the (Czech language version of the) faculty's web page that 'The Faculty of Arts offers instruction in the greatest number of humanities fields in the Czech Republic and *is the only faculty in Europe at which it is possible to study (in various forms) all languages spoken in the member states of the European Union*. (http://www.ff.cuni.cz/FF-17.html, translation from Czech and italics by the author).
(11) In the 2001 census, of 10,230,060 respondents, 9,707,397 declared their mother tongue to be Czech (as reported in Nekvapil et al., 2009:15). In the 2011 census, of 10,436,560 respondents, 9,467,610 declared Czech to be at least one of their mother tongues (source: Czech Statistical Office, http://www.scitani.cz, tab. 614b).
(12) According to the official university salary tables defined in 2007, the monthly salary for an assistant professor was the CZK equivalent of 747–1062 EUR, for an associate professor 905–1259 EUR, and for a full professor 1101–1495 EUR. (http://www.cuni.cz/UK-2547-version1-UZVMzdyUK.pdf, conversions from 11 December 11 2011)
(13) For an extensive exploration of Slovak-Czech semi-communication, see Nábělková (2008).
(14) This example was taken from an individual question (which also included the inquirer's name) on the website of the Faculty of Arts in July 2010, but was later removed when the web page was upgraded. Instead of answering individual

questions, the faculty adopted a policy of listing the most general ones. The issue of using Slovak was not included among these.
(15) See Dovalil (2010) for more on the decline of German.
(16) See http://cl.ff.cuni.cz/cs/uvodni-stranka (accessed 29 March 2012), originally in Czech, translation by the author.
(17) According to the Ministry of Education, there are only three private higher education institutions which have accredited programs exclusively in English. However, there are numerous other institutions teaching in English which are located physically in the Czech Republic, but are accredited elsewhere.
(18) This information is taken from a provision made by the dean of the faculty, numbered 7/2011. See http://www.ff.cuni.cz/FF-8746.html, translation from Czech by the author.
(19) This list represents the state of the respective web pages in November 2011.
(20) In other words, the departments are in a position to actually hire people without any Czech language knowledge if they so desire.
(21) All available in Czech. See http://www.ff.cuni.cz/FF-8157.html (accessed 18 December 2011).
(22) Some departments advertised more than one position over the observed period and explicitly required extra language knowledge for some positions, but not for others.
(23) See http://www.cuni.cz/UK-2535-version1-02UKuzVISZRUK.pdf, p. 17, translation from Czech by the author.
(24) See http://www.msmt.cz/vzdelavani/pozadavky-pro-akreditaci-studijniho-programu-studijniho-oboru-s-vyukou-v-cizim-jazyce, translation from Czech by the author.
(25) See http://ufar.ff.cuni.cz/6/zkouska-z-filosofie-v-doktorskem-studiu, translation from Czech by the author.
(26) See http://ulug.ff.cuni.cz/lingvistika/elsik/Elsik_PP.pdf, translation from Czech by the author. It should be noted that this comment on the web page serves multiple purposes – one is to let students know that they are welcome to submit papers in languages other than Czech, while the other is to add a humorous element to the guidelines for written work, as Common Czech is a variety typically associated with informal spoken genres as opposed to written ones.
(27) Originally in Czech. See http://www.gacr.cz/wp-content/uploads/2012/03/ZD_ST_2013_Final-.pdf, translation by the author.
(28) Originally in Czech, translation by the author.
(29) In Czech, Národní referenční rámec excelence (NRRE).
(30) It should be noted, however, that the evaluation criteria for research results are adapted on a yearly basis. This information was valid for results in 2011. Evaluation criteria for the individual years are available in Czech. See http://www.vyzkum.cz/FrontClanek.aspx?idsekce=18748.
(31) The application of Czech to the concept of medium-sized languages (see Vila, 2013) has been discussed, among others, in Nekvapil (2010).

References

Dovalil, V. (2010) Sind zwei Fremdsprachen in der Tschechischen Republik realistisch? Zu den aktuellen Problemen der tschschischen Spracherwerbsplanung. *Sociolinguistica* 24, 43–60.

Ferguson, G., Pérez-Llantada, C. and Plo, R. (2011) English as an international language of scientific publication: A study of attitudes. *World Englishes* 30 (1), 41–59.

Gazzola, M. (2012) The linguistic implications of academic performance indicators: General trends and case study. *International Journal of the Sociology of Language* 216, 131–156.

Haberland, H. (2008) Domains and domain loss. In B. Preisler, A. Fabricius, H. Haberland, S. Kjaerbeck and K. Risager (eds) *The Consequences of Mobility: Linguistic and Sociocultural Contact Zones* (pp. 227–237). Roskilde: Roskilde University.

Kachru, B.B. (1985) Standards, codification and sociolinguistic realism: The English language in the outer circle. In R. Quirk and H.G. Widdowson (eds) *English in the World* (pp. 11–30). Cambridge: Cambridge University Press.

Melichar, M. and Pabian, P. (2007) Shifting peripheries: A state of the art report on the Czech academic profession. In W. Locke and U. Teichler (eds) *The Changing Conditions for Academic Work and Career in Select Countries* (pp. 37–56). Kassel: Incher University of Kassel.

Nábělková, M. (2008) *Slovenčina a čeština v kontakte: Pokračovanie príbehu* [*Slovak and Czech in Contact: Continuation of the Story*]. Bratislava, Praha: Veda, Univerzita Karlova v Praze, Filozofická fakulta.

Nekvapil, J. (2010) Hlavní výzvy pro češtinu jako středně velký jazyk na začátku 21. století. [The main challenges for Czech as a medium-sized language at the beginning of the 21st century]. *Přednášky z 53. běhu Letní školy slovanských studií* (pp. 19–35). Praha: Univerzita Karlova v Praze, Filozofická fakulta.

Nekvapil, J. (2013) The main challenges facing Czech as a medium-sized language: The state of affairs at the beginning of the 21st century. In F.X. Vila (ed.) *Survival and Development of Language Communities: Prospects and Challenges* (pp. 18–37). Bristol: Multilingual Matters.

Nekvapil, J. and Sherman, T. (2009) Pre-interaction management in multinational companies in Central Europe. *Current Issues in Language Planning* 10, 181–198.

Nekvapil, J. and Sherman, T. (2013) Language ideologies and linguistic practices: The case of multinational companies in Central Europe. In E. Barát, P. Studer and J. Nekvapil (eds) *Ideological Conceptualizations of Language: Discourses of Linguistic Diversity* (pp. 85–117). Frankfurt am Main: Peter Lang.

Nekvapil, J., Sloboda, M. and Wagner, P. (2009) *Mnohojazyčnost v České republice. Základní informace* [*Multilingualism in the Czech Republic. Basic Information*]. Praha: Nakladatelství Lidové noviny.

Neustupný, J.V. and Nekvapil, J. (2003) Language management in the Czech Republic. *Current Issues in Language Planning* 4, 181–366. Reprinted in R.B. Baldauf and R.B. Kaplan (eds) (2006) *Language Planning and Policy in Europe, Vol. 2: The Czech Republic, The European Union and Northern Ireland* (pp. 16–201). Clevedon: Multilingual Matters.

Piech, K. and Radosevic, S. (2006) *The Knowledge-Based Economy in Central and Eastern Europe. Countries and Industries in a Process of Change.* Basingstoke: Palgrave MacMillan.

Prendergast, C. (2008) *Buying into English: Language and Investment in the New Capitalist World.* Pittsburgh, PA: University of Pittsburgh Press.

Sherman, T. and Sieglová, D. (2011) Perceptions of ELF in Czech secondary schools: National identity and social differentiation. In A. Archibald, A. Cogo and J. Jenkins (eds) *Latest Trends in ELF Research* (pp. 229–249). Newcastle upon Tyne: Cambridge Scholars Publishing.

Sloboda, M. (2010) Menej používané jazyky v Česku: problémy rozvoja v jazykovo homogénnom' národnom state [Lesser-used languages in the Czech Republic: Development problems in a linguistically 'homogenous' state]. In A.M. Papp (ed.) *Kevésbé használt nyelvek helyzete a Visegrádi Négyek országaiban* [*The Situation of the Lesser Used Languages in Visegrád Four Countries*] (pp. 38–55). Budapest: Országos Idegennyelvű Könyvtár.

Vila, F.X. (ed.) (2013) *Survival and Development of Language Communities: Prospects and Challenges*. Bristol: Multilingual Matters.

4 The Position of Finnish and Swedish as well as Other Languages at Universities in Finland

Sabine Ylönen

Introduction

Finland has two national languages: Finnish and Swedish, and language policy is regulated by the Finnish Constitution (731/1999) and the Language Act (423/2003). About 90% of the population speaks Finnish and 5% Swedish as their mother tongue. The Swedish-speaking minority lives mainly in the areas around the south-west coast of Finland. Over 90% of native speakers of Swedish live in the autonomous province of Åland, a group of islands in the Baltic Sea between Finland and Sweden, where the only official language is Swedish. There are four other minority languages – Sami, Romani, Finnish sign language and the Karelian language – but Statistics Finland databases only give information on the number of speakers of Sami. At 0.04% of the population, their number is very low despite the relatively large size of the area in the north of Finland where Sami speakers live. In 2012, about 5% of the population had mother tongues other than the three mentioned above, and only 3.6% were foreign citizens (Statistics Finland, 2013: 5, 7).

Given the bilingual situation, there is a fairly explicit regulation of language policy in Finland. In addition to the Finnish Constitution (731/1999) and the Language Act (423/2003), several other acts and decrees regulate language practices in specific societal domains. These include the Government Decree on Demonstrating Proficiency in Finnish and Swedish in the Public Administration (481/2003), the Universities Act (558/2009) and the Government Decree for Universities (770/2009). These legislative regulations deal mainly with the position of the national languages, Finnish and Swedish. Moreover the new government strategy for the national languages of Finland (Prime Minister's Office, 2012: 9) does not address the position of foreign languages and their possible influence on language practices in Finland, particularly the influence of English in various societal domains such as science and education, except for an appeal to use Finnish and Swedish 'in all walks of life', including sciences, to maintain diverse vocabulary and expressions. Otherwise the use of English is characterised as 'a natural development' 'in view of the international dimension of science' (Prime Minister's Office, 2012: 9). This government strategy meets the aims of diversifying the national language resources and diversifying language programmes in basic education, postulated in the programme of Prime Minister Jyrki Katainen's government (Prime Minister's Office, 2011: 51, 53), only with respect to the national languages. The autonomy of Finnish universities guarantees them freedom to regulate language practices independently, and the Finnish Ministry of Education (2008: 44) expects universities to develop language strategies.

In the following sections, I will provide an overview of language policies and practices in Finnish universities. I will examine language policies at the governmental and university level, look at language practices in teaching and research and consider discourses about languages in the higher education context in Finland. The section on language policy at university level will explore six questions related to language policy in Finnish universities. The first focuses on regulations governing language practices and the second on those concerned with language competences. The third and fourth questions deal with autonomy and differences between the language policies of different universities. The fifth is related to the fourth question, and is concerned with the role of academic disciplines in defining university policies. Finally, the answers to these five questions will be summarised by considering the question of whether Finland has a nationwide university language policy. In the next section, the focus shifts to language practices in instruction and research. Specifically, I will consider which languages are used by staff and students at universities in Finland in general. I will then go on to look at the language of instruction at different degree levels (undergraduate, master, doctorate and lifelong learning) and what practical language requirements teaching staff, students and administrative staff have to meet. I will also indicate which national and foreign languages they are expected to know, and discuss whether language competence is officially verified in any way. In this section on language practices, I will finally focus on language use for research (first, in scientific publications and second, in PhD dissertations). Finally, discourses about language policy at university level will be discussed followed by a brief summary and conclusions.

This chapter is based on a thorough analysis of a number of different types of texts, including Finnish legislative documents, documents of the Finnish Ministry of Education (and Culture), university documents, statistical data provided by the Centre for International Mobility (CIMO) and the National Statistics Centre of Finland, research publications and surveys as well as media news archives. The data on language use stem from two large surveys among students (about 3500 answers) and staff (about 3600 answers) of universities in Finland conducted in 2008 and 2009 within the FinGer project (German as a vehicular language in academic and business contexts in Finland, cf. Ylönen & Kivelä, 2011; Ylönen & Vainio, 2010). In addition, two extensive analyses were conducted for the purpose of this chapter: First, survey and archival research designed to explore the state and contents of university language policies, and second, a search through existing bibliographic sources to document the languages used for writing PhD dissertations from the 17th century to 2009. The study of university language policies was conducted in 2011 by contacting the rectors of 14 universities and 2 heads of the respective language policy working groups (there were 16 universities in Finland in 2011). In addition to analysing the language policy documents forwarded to me, information was gathered via email correspondence and telephone interviews to explore the role of different academic areas in preparing language policies. The study of language choices for PhD dissertations was conducted in 2011 with the help of the register of all PhD dissertations in Finland purchased from the Finnish National Bibliography (FENNICA) database, which contained 45,592 titles. These data were analysed statistically using cross-tabulation frequencies. The analyses carried out in 2011 were complemented with some new information during the editing of this chapter in August 2013.

Language Policy at University Level

Are language practices regulated in an explicit way?

University language practices are regulated explicitly by law because of the bilingual situation in Finland. In 2010, Finnish universities underwent reform when the number of universities was reduced from 21 to 17. In 2013, three more universities (the Finnish Academy of Fine Arts, the Sibelius Academy and the Theatre Academy, all located in Helsinki) merged to jointly establish the Arts University; consequently, Finland has 15 universities since the beginning of 2013. Fourteen of these are regulated by Finnish legislation, and these regulations also affect language practices (Universities Act, 2009). The 15th university is the Finnish National Defence University in Helsinki, which is not under civil jurisdiction because its administrative organisation is military rather than civilian. Northern Finland is very sparsely populated and there is only one university in Rovaniemi: the University of Lapland. Most of the 14 civilian universities are located in Southern Finland, and four of them are in Helsinki. There are 10 multidisciplinary universities and four specialised universities (see Appendix 4.1).

The languages of instruction and examination in Finnish universities are regulated by Section 11 of the Universities Act 558/2009. Nine universities are Finnish-medium universities, two are Swedish-medium and three are bilingual Finnish–Swedish. In addition, two universities have separate units with special language regulations: the Swedish School of Social Science is attached to the University of Helsinki as a separate Swedish-language unit, and at the former Helsinki School of Economics (part of Aalto University since 2010), the language of instruction and examination is Finnish. The other two units that merged to form Aalto University – the University of Art and Design Helsinki and the Helsinki University of Technology – are Finnish–Swedish bilingual universities. This arrangement is based on the new Universities Act (558/2009, Section 11/1), under which the languages of instruction and examination at Aalto University are regulated by the provisions of its constituent schools, which are set out in Section 9 of the Universities Act of 1997 (645/1997).

Seven universities have the responsibility to educate 'a sufficient number of persons proficient in Swedish for the needs of the country': the Åbo Akademi University, the Hanken School of Economics, the University of Helsinki, the Finnish Academy of Fine Arts, the Sibelius Academy, the Theatre Academy and Aalto University (Universities Act 558/2009, Section 12/1).

The language of university administration is regulated by Section 35 of the Universities Act 558/2009. Generally, the administrative language at a university in Finland is Finnish. However, at two universities (Åbo Akademi University and the Hanken School of Economics) and at the Swedish School of Social Science of the University of Helsinki, the language of administration is Swedish. In addition, Section 35 regulates the right of everyone to use Finnish or Swedish and to receive documents in the language he or she uses: 'Everyone shall have the right to use Finnish or Swedish in matters concerning them and to obtain a document in the language he or she uses' (Universities Act 558/2009, Section 35/3).

Are language competences regulated in an explicit way?

The reform of Finnish universities has also affected the legislative position of languages at the university level. The new Universities Act (558/2009) and the Government Decree (770/2009) came into force in January 2010. The main outcome of the reform was that Finnish universities are now independent legal bodies, and staff are no longer employed by the government. Because staff at Finnish universities are no longer considered civil servants, their employment contracts had to be renewed. Section 35 of the Universities Act provides that Finnish and Swedish language proficiency requirements for teaching and research staff and other personnel are established in the government decree. However, this decree only contains regulations for teaching and research staff. In the first section (Government Decree 770/2009, Section 1), language competences are regulated as follows:

- University teaching and research staff are required to be proficient in the language – Finnish or Swedish – that they are supposed to use for instruction.
- Requirements with respect to proficiency in the language of instruction may be specified in university regulations.
- At universities where a degree may be taken in either Finnish or Swedish, teaching and research staff must have at least satisfactory oral and written proficiency in Finnish or Swedish.
- The university may grant exemptions from these language proficiency requirements as provided in university regulations.

Compared with the previous decree (463/1998), these regulations are less rigorous because teaching and research staff were formerly considered civil servants and competence in both Finnish and Swedish was required under the Act on the Language Skills of Civil Servants (149/1922; full proficiency in the majority language of the university as well as proficiency in understanding the second official language). This act was replaced in 2003 by the Act on the Knowledge of Languages Required of Personnel in Public Bodies (424/2003), under which employees were required to have the language proficiency needed to perform their duties.

One exception is Åbo Akademi University, where the university defines its own policy and no separate decree regulates the requirements for teaching and research staff. These regulations have not been radically changed compared to the previous Universities Act (645/1997). Section 78 of the new Universities Act (2009) contains the following provisions:

A requirement for a teaching position at Åbo Akademi shall be full proficiency in the Swedish language and an ability to understand the Finnish language. The decision on the proficiency in Swedish and Finnish required of a foreigner or a non-native Finnish citizen shall rest with Åbo Akademi. Åbo Akademi has a language board to which the proficiency in Swedish referred to in subsection 1 can be demonstrated. (Universities Act 558/2009, Section 78)

Because staff members are no longer civil servants, language competences for other university personnel are not as clearly regulated today as they were before the 2010 university reform. In this respect, the university reform was probably conducted too hastily, without considering the consequences in terms of the language requirements that apply to this group of 'other personnel'. It is now up to universities to define language requirements for recruitment purposes.

To what extent are universities autonomous in defining their language policy?

As discussed above, universities today are more autonomous in defining their language policy than before the 2010 reform. This applies especially to the language competence of other personnel. As regards instruction and examination, universities have been free to use languages other than Finnish and/or Swedish for instruction and examination since 2004 (Universities Act 645/1997, Amendment 715/2004), and the new Universities Act does not differ much in this respect: 'In addition, the university may decide to use a language other than that referred to in Article 1 as a language of instruction and examination' (Universities Act 558/2009, Section 11/2).

In relation to the previous Universities Act 645/1997 and its amendment (715/2004), the only new words introduced are 'in addition', which highlights the fact that the university has to ensure the role of the national languages, Finnish and Swedish, by emphasising that no foreign language may replace the language(s) of instruction and examination as regulated by the new Universities Act, Section 11 (see Appendix 4.1).

When recruiting new staff, universities regulate the language proficiency required for the performance of the duties associated with a position. Announcements of new vacancies generally contain case-specific requirements for teaching, research and other personnel. In most cases, English proficiency (speaking and understanding) is now specified as being either a requirement or an advantage to perform the duties associated with posts.

The Ministry of Education expected all universities to formulate their own language policies during 2009, and to include measures for demonstrating the language proficiency required to teach in a foreign language:

> Higher education institutions will draw up language strategies covering their entire operations during 2009. Higher education institutions will require that teachers teaching in a foreign language demonstrate their skills in the teaching language with a language proficiency certificate or in another recognisable manner. (Ministry of Education, 2008: 44)

The extent to which such university language policies have been developed will be discussed in the next section.

Do different universities have different language policies?

Information on university language policies was difficult to obtain, because policy documents are often for internal use only. Some language policies were found on the public web pages of the universities. They had usually been prepared by working groups appointed by the rector of the university in question. To obtain further information, emails were sent to the rectors of 14 universities in October 2011. At two universities, the heads of the respective working groups were contacted directly. Our aims were to explore whether the universities had developed or were developing their own language policies, and to find out which academic areas were relevant to the process of defining them (see next question).

We received answers from 13 universities. At the end of 2011, 7 of the 16 universities had developed language policies, and 1 had developed a 'language policy for support and administrative services'. One of the predecessors of the University of Eastern Finland (the University of Joensuu, which merged with the University of Kuopio in 2010) had already developed a language policy in 2006, and the new language policy for both units came into force in December 2011. At three more universities, language policies were being prepared to come into effect in 2012 at the earliest. The oldest language policy at any European university (adopted in 2004) – the one in place at the time of this study in 2011 at the University of Jyväskylä – was being updated at the time of the study. Table 4.1 shows the state of university language policies in Finland in January 2012 (upper part) supplemented with information gathered in August 2013 (lower part of the table).

Table 4.1 Language policies at Finnish universities (in January 2012 and August 2013)

	Year of approval	Name	Document language(s)	Length (pages)
Results of the first study (January 2012)				
University of Jyväskylä	2004	Language Policy	FI, EN	9
	2012	Kielipolitiikka (Language Policy)	FI (EN in preparation)	15
Hanken School of Economics	2005	Språkstrategi	SE	6
University of Helsinki	2007	Language Policy	FI, SE, EN	61 (about 20 per language)
Åbo Academy	2009	Language Policy Programme	SE, EN	3
University of Vaasa	2010	Kielilinjaukset (Language Guidelines)	FI	3
Aalto University	2010	Language Guidelines	FI, SE, EN	3
University of Eastern Finland (University of Joensuu)	2011	Kielipoliittinen ohjelma (Language Policy Programme)	FI (to be translated into EN)	20
	(2006)	Kielistrategia (Language Strategy)	FI	34
Theatre Academy (merged with Sibelius Academy and the Academy of Fine Arts to the Arts University in 2013)	2010	Tuki- ja hallintopalveluiden kieli- ja käännösperiaatteet (Language Policy for Support and Administrative Services)	FI	9
Results of the updated study (August 2013)				
University of Turku	2012	Kieliohjelma (Language Policy)	FI, EN	14
Tampere University of Technology	2012	Kielisuunnitelma (Language Plan)	FI, EN	9
University of Tampere	2013	Kieliperiaatteet (Language Strategy)	FI, EN	4

Two universities responded that they were not planning to develop a university language policy and did not consider this an important issue. Three universities did not respond. It is assumed that they have no language policies and are not currently developing any. One reason may be that smaller universities in particular do not have the resources to focus on developing language strategies, because a lot of their energy is still going into the implementation of the university reform. Also, another merger of three universities to establish the Arts University was planned at the time of this study.

To sum up, in January 2012, half of the universities had language policies in place (8/16), and three more universities announced that they would have such policies available by the end of 2012. Consequently, 69% of Finnish universities (11/16) planned to have prepared a language policy by the end of 2012. The situation in 2013 at the time of revising this chapter, after another merger of three universities to establish the Arts University, is that 71% of the universities (10/14, i.e. excluding the Theatre Academy) have formulated their language policy.

The language policy documents have different names at different universities and are available in one to three languages: Finnish, Swedish and English (FI, SE, EN); Finnish and English (FI, EN); Swedish and English (SE, EN); or a single language, either Finnish (FI) or Swedish (SE). They also differ in content and length.

As far as contents are concerned, the legislation and regulations on the national languages (Finnish and Swedish) were generally taken into account, and the policies emphasised internationalisation and the importance of English. All the university policies highlighted the importance of offering good opportunities for foreign personnel and students to learn the national languages, which was also seen as a way of supporting their integration into the university environment. On the other hand, providing English-language services was mentioned as a way of benefiting international recruitment. Some language policies were very explicit about specific measures for teaching, research, internal and external communication and administration, whereas others were somewhat vague on this point. As regards the publication of research results, the dominant role of English was generally acknowledged, but publishing in the national languages was also seen as important in all the university language policies. There was scant reference to publishing in foreign languages other than English, and at some universities the tone on this point was one of 'tolerance' ('if strategically important'). In January 2012, only at the University of Helsinki was the importance of publishing in foreign languages other than English articulated on a more general level: 'The University also believes in the importance of publishing scientific and other scholarly work in foreign languages other than English' (University of Helsinki, 2007: 47).

Some universities referred to multilingualism and multiculturalism as resources within the academic environment and emphasised competence in foreign languages other than English, as for example in the case of the University of Helsinki and the University of Jyväskylä:

Multilingual and multicultural communities promote creative thinking. (University of Helsinki, 2007: 41)
Since English is not enough to meet the needs of foreign language competence for academically trained Finns, the University will make it possible for students to expand their foreign language skills in other languages. (University of Jyväskylä, 2004: 4)

However, the new language policy of the University of Jyväskylä (2012b) no longer mentions the need to expand foreign language skills into other languages. Instead, it more or less takes multilingualism for granted and emphasises the importance of 'partial language competences' (see also below). Also, most other universities made only vague reference to the importance of 'multilingualism' and 'other foreign languages' without offering any further details. Aalto University (2010: 2), for example, states that it encourages 'linguistic diversity and parallel use of languages'. The concept of 'multilingualism' varied at different universities, from including only three languages (Finland's national languages – Finnish and Swedish – and English as the academic lingua franca) to also encompassing foreign languages other than English. Only at two universities were the languages of students, researchers and other staff with immigrant backgrounds referred to as important resources in the academic context.

Only the University of Helsinki explicitly pointed out the growing impact of English as a foreign language and the related risk of a weakening of users' skills in their first language and in languages other than English. In what is clearly a response to this point, the new language policy of the University of Jyväskylä (2012b: 1) defines 'modern multilingualism' as also comprising partial language competences and parallel use of languages in certain situations. On the one hand, this concept of 'modern multilingualism' is commendable because it might encourage people to use all the resources available to them in their language repertoires as the situation requires. On the other, on its own it does not help to identify strategically important languages other than English. Nor does it help to promote strong skills in these other languages (for example through measures to develop related possibilities for studying languages as major and minor subjects, or for specific academic and vocational purposes at the Language Centre). The 'operational programme' published in June 2012 at the University of Jyväskylä did not include any strategies for promoting foreign languages other than English.

Up until January 2012, only the documents of the universities of Helsinki and Eastern Finland explicitly named foreign languages other than English. The University of Helsinki, for example, listed as strategically important academic languages 'German, French, Spanish, Russian and Chinese, among others'. These were seen as supporting global development and European integration and 'required within academia and in Finnish society at large' (University of Helsinki, 2007: 45). The language policy of the University of Eastern Finland singles out Russian as having a special status within the university's strategy. Apart from Russian, only English was mentioned as strategically important in connection with major subjects ('English and Russian, among others'). This vague expression 'among others' obviously offers the possibility of giving up other languages as major subjects. The possibility of reducing the number of universities that offer certain languages as major subjects is currently under discussion in connection with the university reform. The University of Eastern Finland listed Chinese, English and Finnish for written and spoken communication; Finnish as a second language; and French, German, Spanish, Swedish and Russian as languages offered by its Language Centre. In addition, degrees in French, German and Russian as a minor subject are to be offered by the Language Centre via a new channel (University of Eastern Finland, 2011: 7, 12).

At some universities, there was a special focus on developing communication in Swedish and English to promote internationalisation of the home university and expand academic cooperation with Nordic countries and globally. Here, other foreign languages were not mentioned at all.

An additional analysis of the three language policies published in 2012–2013 (after this first study) showed interesting developments towards a more concrete definition of language policy objectives and measures. All three universities are Finnish-medium, and the role of Finnish for teaching, publication of research results for the local society, and university services is acknowledged. In addition, the role of English in university communication is highlighted in all of these new language strategies. However, there are interesting differences in valuing languages other than English and Finnish between the Universities of Turku and Tampere on the one hand and the Tampere University of Technology on the other.

The language policy of the University of Turku, completed in 2012, describes its approach as being based on the principle of 'parallel lingualism [...] because many other languages are also required in the international academic community, the aim is to teach and use them whenever possible'. All students, except for international students, are expected to have good oral and written proficiency in Finnish. For academic cooperation, the Baltic Sea region (Scandinavian languages, German, Estonian and Russian), the European academic and cultural community (French, Spanish and Italian) and Asian languages (Chinese and Japanese) are mentioned as being specifically important. Also languages offered as a major subject are stated: Finnish, English, Spanish, Italian, Scandinavian languages, French, German and Russian of the modern Indo-European languages, and Greek and Latin of the classical languages. Likewise, the language strategy of the University of Tampere, completed in March 2013, highlights the importance of foreign languages other than English for international collaboration as well as in teaching and publishing research without naming any foreign languages specifically. On the contrary, the new Tampere University of Technology language plan, adopted in 2012, aims primarily to strengthen and support English 'as a medium of instruction and above all as a language of science'. For example, master's level studies are planned in English by 2020, and the publication of 'important scientific articles will be published on international forums primarily in English'. Also, for recruiting new support staff, the candidates' proficiency in English will be one of the recruiting criteria.

In sum, whereas the Universities of Tampere and Turku espouse wider use of different languages, the Tampere University of Technology sees English as the first and foremost important language in teaching and research to become an internationally active and recognised university.

In the next section, the role of different academic disciplines in formulating university language policies will be briefly discussed.

Are academic areas (natural sciences, humanities, etc.) relevant to defining university language policies?

One aim of this study was to look at which academic and occupational areas were involved in defining university language policies. Appendix 4.2 shows the number of participants in the development of university language policies and their working areas.

On average, the groups preparing university language policies consisted of nine members (4–14). Representatives of those concerned with language as an object of study (from language departments and/or language centres), university administration (international relations, public relations and the university's central administration) and students were usually involved in the process. Representatives from other academic fields (natural and technical sciences, business, social sciences and philosophy, theology and the humanities) also participated to varying degrees. Some universities at least had their draft documents reviewed by all faculties to get feedback. Overall, different academic fields were quite well represented. Nevertheless, the documents themselves were written on a rather general level and did not go into detail for different disciplines. Instead, responsibility for concrete guidelines on discipline-specific communicative conventions was passed on to departments or units.

Can we speak of a nationwide university language policy?

As shown in the previous sections, the answer to the question of whether Finland has a nationwide university language policy is both 'yes and no'. 'Yes' is the answer with respect to the national languages, Finnish and Swedish, which are regulated by law as languages of administration, instruction and examination. 'No' is the answer for foreign languages, because by law, universities are guaranteed freedom of choice to decide on the use of languages other than Finnish or Swedish for instruction and examination.

Universities make use of this 'freedom of choice', but English is practically the only language other than Finnish or Swedish that is chosen as a language of instruction and examination, and for administrative use. Other foreign languages were sometimes mentioned in a rather vague manner in the context of exchange programmes or research, and more specific strategies for foreign languages other than English were found only at three universities (universities of Helsinki, Eastern Finland and Turku). Responsibility for more specific language policies was delegated to departments. One thing evident from this study is that the universities clearly did not cooperate in developing their language policies, even though some of the documents contained references to the policies of other universities. Common topics were internationalisation and the importance of English. Attention was also given to legislative regulations concerning the national languages, Finnish and Swedish.

Language Practices at University Level

Which languages are used by students and staff of universities in Finland?

A comparison of two large surveys among students and staff at Finnish universities showed that English has become practically the 'second national language' in academic life (see Figure 4.1). It is used almost to the same extent as Finnish and more than Swedish (one of the official national

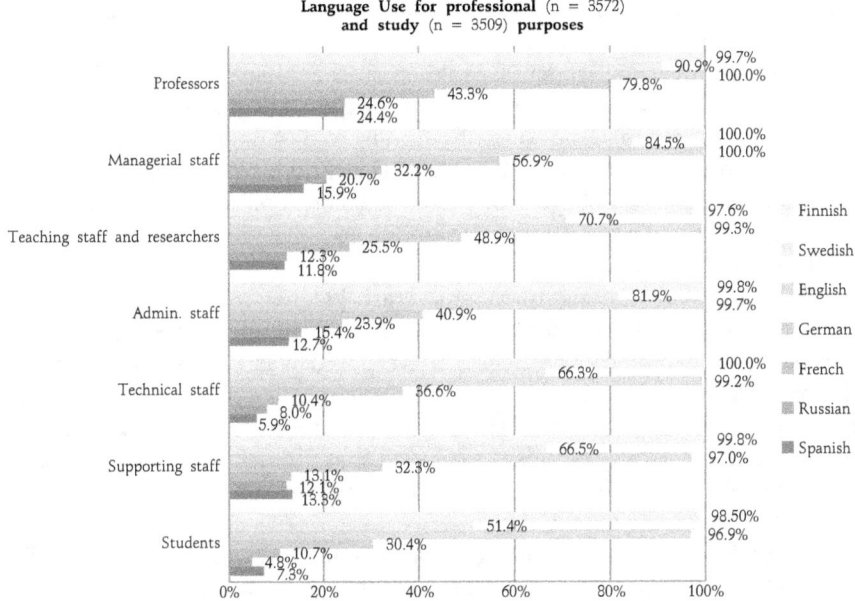

Figure 4.1 Comparison of any language use between different personnel groups and students

languages) when considering any language use. Altogether, we received 3513 valid answers from students in 2008 and 3598 from staff members in 2009 (Ylönen & Kivelä, 2011; Ylönen & Vainio, 2010). Responses to the question 'any language use' were recorded with a frequency ranging from 'daily' to 'seldom' on the staff survey, and in the range from 'mostly' to 'seldom' on the students survey. Responses were given on a five-point Likert scale, with the fifth value corresponding to 'not at all', here combined with no answer. In Figure 4.1, any language use (daily/mostly–seldom) is summarised. However, more detailed analyses of the frequencies showed that in the staff groups, the 'daily use' figures were 90.7% for Finnish, 65.5% for English and 13.1% for Swedish (see Ylönen & Kivelä, 2011: 42). In the student group, 86.6% indicated they used Finnish mostly, 36.5% used English mostly and 3.3% Swedish mostly (see Ylönen & Vainio, 2010: 37).

Whereas Finnish and English were used to about the same extent across professional groups and among students, the use of other languages varied slightly more (again for 'any use'). Professors and managerial staff used languages other than Finnish and English to a greater degree than other groups of personnel. This suggests that versatile language skills enhance career potential at universities.

Among university students, languages other than Finnish and English were used to a lesser degree than in any of the staff groups (except for the technical staff group). Due to the dominant role of English, the motivation to learn and use other foreign languages is clearly lower in the younger age groups. A comparison of age groups showed a clear tendency towards fewer language skills and more limited use among younger age groups of university staff (Ylönen & Kivelä, 2011: 47–50).

In the survey among university staff (Ylönen & Kivelä, 2011), the proportional language use for reading, writing, listening, speaking and other use was also explored. The question we posed was: 'For which purposes do you use the following languages as working languages?' Respondents could select all the answers that were applicable. Considering any use (daily/mostly–seldom), the results showed that Finnish was mostly used for speaking (95%), whereas English was mostly used for reading in academic contexts (96%; see Figure 4.2).

Overall, both Finnish and English were used more or less equally (±90%) for reading, writing, listening and speaking purposes. However, Finnish was the language used most for speaking, and English was used most for reading. Bigger differences in these four core components of language use could be observed for other languages. In these cases, reading was clearly the commonest use and writing was the least frequent. The differences between listening to and speaking languages other than Finnish and English were not as marked. 'Other' – generally less frequently mentioned activities – were, for example, thinking, singing or using some form of sign language. Overall, university staff claimed that they used Swedish less than Finnish

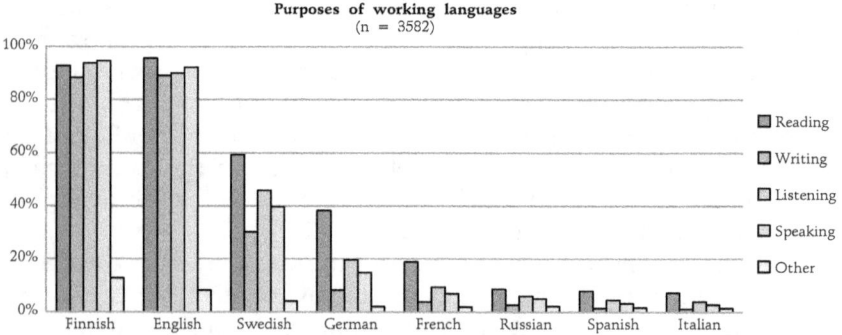

Figure 4.2 Language use at Finnish universities in terms of different skills

and English for oral purposes (46% for listening and 40% for speaking). As for foreign languages other than English, only German and French were mentioned as being used to a higher degree at least sometimes for oral academic purposes (German about 20% for listening and 15% for speaking, and French 9% for listening and 7% for speaking), whereas other languages received only values below 5%. These figures show that Finns are indeed still very plurilingual and obviously value multilingualism highly, which is also reflected in the answers given for a separate question: 'How important are different languages in a university working environment in your opinion?' A large majority of respondents (92.8%) indicated that they regarded multilingualism as very important or important (see Ylönen & Kivelä, 2011: 39). Nevertheless, without a higher education policy that addresses the role of languages more directly and develops appropriate support measures, the future may look quite different.

Which languages are used for instruction at different degree levels?

The constitution of Finland guarantees everyone the right to use his or her own language, either Finnish or Swedish, in dealings with authorities, and to receive official documents in that language. On the other hand, offering degree programmes in 'foreign languages' has become one of the strategic focuses in Finnish higher education.

Undergraduate-level teaching is conducted mostly in Finnish or Swedish, but there are attempts to increase teaching in 'foreign languages', because international degree programmes have become central to the development of internationalisation in Finnish higher education since the start of this century (Garam, 2009: 2). Consequently, departments are expected to offer more undergraduate-level teaching and master's programmes in 'foreign languages', a direction supported by university councils or senates. Undergraduate-level teaching and master's programmes are therefore also targets of strategic financing.

Nevertheless, despite the high percentages of international degree programmes taught in English, the proportion of foreign students is relatively low when compared internationally (see Tables 4.2 and 4.3 and Figure 4.3). According to Wächter and Maiworm's (2008: 25–26) large-scale surveys, in 2007 Finland had the highest number of institutions (66%) offering English-taught bachelor's and master's programmes among 27 European countries, followed by Cyprus (50%) and the Netherlands (42%). In 2008, 275 degree programmes were taught in English (see Table 4.2). Among these degree programmes taught in English at the bachelor's, master's and doctoral levels,

Table 4.2 Degree programmes in Finland taught in English by educational level for 2008

	UAS	Uni.	Total	Total (%)
Bachelor	79	4	83	30
Master	15	156	171	62
Doctorate	–	21	21	8
Total	94	181	275	100

Source: Garam (2009: 13)
UAS: universities of applied sciences; Uni.: universities

most were offered in the field of business (23%), engineering and technology (20%) and information technology (12%) (Garam, 2009: 13). However, there are university-specific differences. At the University of Jyväskylä, for example, the School of Business and Economics ranks first in foreign language teaching, which accounts for 24.7% of all credit points awarded at the bachelor's and master's levels (there are no official doctoral-level programmes taught in English at the University of Jyväskylä), followed by the Faculty of Sports (9.6%) and the Faculty of Arts and Humanities (8%).

However, compared to the figures given in Table 4.2, Brenn-White and van Rest (2012: 8) list a divergent number for English-taught master's programmes in Finland at MastersPortal, and Välimaa *et al.* (2013: 20–21) point to the fact that probably nobody knows the exact number of international degree programmes in Finland or in Europe due to the lack of reliable records running at a given time. They state that the only reliable indication is that the number of programmes taught in English is growing continuously. This tendency is confirmed and vividly illustrated by the updated report of the Institute of International Education (Brenn-White & van Rest, 2013: 4).

The number of foreign degree-level students in Finnish higher education institutions has also grown steadily, reaching about 5% of all students in 2010. This means that the number has practically doubled since the beginning of this century (see also Garam & Korkala, 2011: 34–35). The increase has taken place slightly faster at universities of applied sciences (5.7% in 2010) than at other Finnish universities (4.6% in 2010) (see Figure 4.3).

A more detailed analysis of the data in the KOTA database showed that the number of international doctoral and master's degree students at Finnish universities increased from 2007 to 2009, while the number of foreign bachelor's degree students decreased slightly over the same period (see Table 4.3).

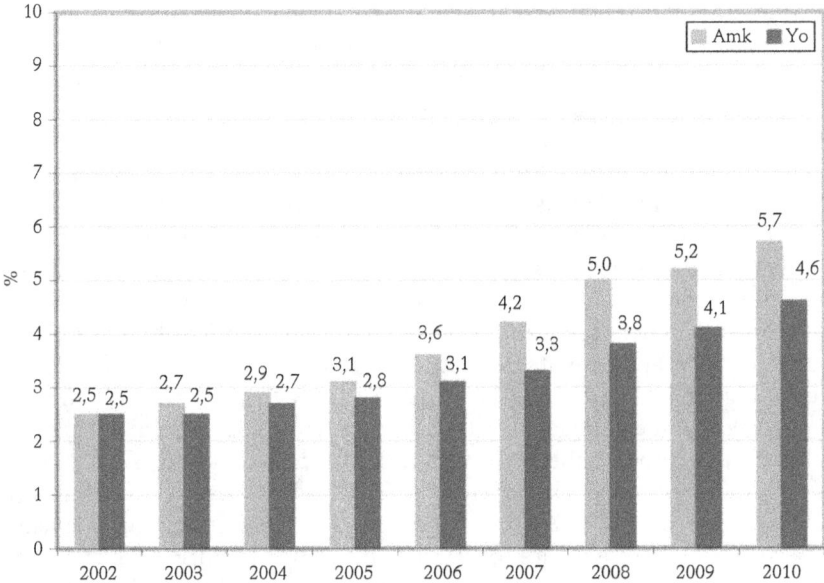

Figure 4.3 Foreign degree students in relation to the total number of students at Finnish universities (Yo) and universities of applied sciences (Amk)

Source: Cimo 2011 (based on Statistics Finland, KOTA and AMKOTA databases)

At less than 4% of all higher education students in 2008, the number of foreign students has been below the Organisation for Economic Co-operation and Development (OECD) average of 6.9% (Garam, 2009: 13). In its 2009–2015 internationalisation strategy for higher education institutions, the Finnish Ministry of Education has set the target of increasing the number of foreign degree students considerably by 2015 (from 11,303 = 3.7% in

Table 4.3 Percentage of foreign degree students at Finnish universities 2007–2009

	2007 (%)	2008 (%)	2009 (%)
Bachelor	1.3	1.1	1.0
Master	3.5	6.9	7.8
Doctorate	8.5	9.3	10.5
Other	3.3	3.8	3.8
Total	3.3	3.8	4.1

Source: KOTA database

2007 to 20,000 = 7% in 2015). These figures include both first-degree and postgraduate students in all higher education institutions. The international student population (and international personnel) is seen as 'a key factor in Finnish higher education institutions' internationalisation at home' (Ministry of Education, 2009a: 10, 29, 30).

In 2009, the Research and Innovation Council of Finland (RIC, 2009: 17) concluded that 'Finnish higher education institutions have not gained a foothold in the rapidly growing global education market' despite the high number of degree programmes taught in 'a foreign language'. Although their tuition fees are high, English-speaking countries (especially Australia, the United Kingdom and the United States) have traditionally attracted the majority of Asian students who study abroad (Hughes 2008). In Finland, where higher education has been free for everyone, the 2010 university reform led to the launch of a trial project that enables universities and polytechnics (now called 'universities of applied sciences') to collect fees from foreign students from outside the European Union/European Economic Area (EU/EEA) who participate in foreign-language master's programmes. A prerequisite for participating in this tuition fee trial is the university grant system, and the trial will be evaluated in 2012 (Ministry of Education and Culture, 2011a: 14). Nine universities and ten polytechnics are taking part in the trial, which started in 2010 and will run to 2014, and a total of 130 degree programmes are involved. The participating higher education institutions are free to decide the amount of the tuition fee. In 2010, half of the trial programmes collected such fees; others intend to start applying them later in the trial period (new programmes may also join the trial). During the trial period, the effects of introducing tuition fees on the internationalisation of universities, the attractiveness of higher education in Finland, student flows and the quality of higher education in a foreign language will be evaluated (Ministry of Education and Culture, 2011a: 20).

As for lifelong learning, no language policy is specified by the Ministry of Education (2009b) in its latest interim report 'Key competences for lifelong learning in Finland'. There are also no registers for continuous education in Finland. However, universities do offer training for their staff in English. At the University of Jyväskylä, for example, four institutions offer staff training in English on a regular basis. These are (1) the Information Management Centre (partly in cooperation with the University Library), (2) the Research and Innovation Office, (3) the International Office and (4) the Language Centre. In 2011, for example, there were courses on the use of computer management systems (CBS: Optima) and on the study register (Korppi), organised by the Information Management Centre. Training on the use of the JyU dissertation template and RefWorks reference manager was also offered in cooperation with the University Library (four courses). The Research and Innovation Office has also offered four courses in English (out of a total of 17), which means that about one fifth (23.5%) of the staff training offered by the office was in English. In addition, annual information events for foreign staff are organised by the International Office. The Language Centre offers courses in Finnish as a foreign language and staff training in English (for example, Teaching Academic Content through English [TACE], Fundamentals in Intercultural and Multilingual Communication and 'What Can I Do for You? – *Asiakaspalveluenglantia*' – Customer Service English). There are no overall statistics concerning [foreign] languages used used in staff training, but the officer responsible estimates that it amounts to about 5% of all staff training organised by the university.

Although strategy documents usually refer to 'foreign languages', in practice all degree programmes in Finnish higher education are taught in English and none are offered in any other non-native language (Garam, 2009: 14). Saarinen (2012: 237) points out that language is rarely mentioned and becomes almost invisible when observed at the micro level of foreign language programmes. She concludes that language is clearly regarded as something so self-evident that it need not be problematised. In my view, the euphemism 'foreign language' may also be motivated by a widespread appreciation of multilingualism among academically trained Finns, who have traditionally been plurilingual (see Ylönen & Kivelä, 2011). Also, Saarinen (2012: 243) suggests that the use of 'foreign language' may be related to the Finnish goal of promoting other languages as well. However, given that the use of languages in the academic context is also linked to power relations, strategic measures are needed if future generations are also to value foreign languages other than English.

To sum up, internationalisation strategies have led to English being favoured without any reflection on the role of language in the cognitive and sociocultural aspects of education and research. According to a survey conducted by the Finnish CIMO, many degree programmes taught in 'a foreign language' (i.e. English) are motivated by the goals set in national and institutional internationalisation strategies. The results of this study also showed that one third of these programmes had not defined their target group (Finnish students, international students or immigrant Finns), and many were vague about the labour markets and target countries for which they were educating students (Garam, 2009: 6, 9). On the whole, the role of language(s) in education and research should be more thoroughly examined. One could also ask whether English is the only key to internationalisation, which facets of this phenomenon could and should be taken into account and supported, and why and how this could be done.

What are the practical language requirements that teaching staff, students and administrative staff have to face?

Teaching staff

As indicated above, teaching staff are expected to master the language of instruction (Finnish or Swedish). At bilingual universities, satisfactory oral and written proficiency in Finnish and Swedish is required. Exemptions may be granted based on university regulations (Government Decree 770/2009, Section 1). When teaching staff are recruited, their language proficiency is verified by a university diploma: a university degree always includes proof of language skills in Finnish, Swedish and one foreign language (Government Decree on University Degrees 794/2004). Members of international staff are usually expected to have competence in English, which must be verified either at the job interview or on the basis of certificates. The types of certificates are not usually specified.

According to the education and research development plan for 2007–2012 issued by the Ministry of Education (2008: 44), universities are expected to require proof of language proficiency from teachers who provide instruction in a foreign language. This may be demonstrated by means of a language proficiency certificate or in some other recognisable manner. However, it seems that such proof is generally not required from non-native teachers, either for teaching in English or for teaching in Finnish. It is up to teachers who are willing to offer classes in a foreign language to judge their own proficiency as sufficient. In my opinion, one reason for avoiding stricter rules concerning official verification of language competences may be that the universities or departments are worried about not being able to recruit enough teachers who are qualified and willing to teach in a foreign language.

Until now, Finnish universities have not applied any measures to assess or support the quality of teaching in a foreign language. Hughes (2008) refers to the risks associated with such a vague language policy. One can only share her opinion that the lack of any concrete preparatory and ongoing support measures may be damaging not only to the quality of teaching and the university's own global brand, but also to learning results, due to constraints on the capacity of individuals to operate in a foreign language and an unfamiliar academic environment.

Students

Finnish degree students have to know Finnish and/or Swedish depending on the university's official language(s). Their language competence is officially verified by the national matriculation examination certificate. From the 1970s until 2004, this matriculation examination was compulsory in both national languages, but since 2005 it has been optional in the second national language due to legislative regulation based on a decision made by the Finnish parliament in 2003. This was a result of ongoing discussions about the state of Swedish in Finnish education and one of the arguments was that voluntariness would increase the motivation to learn Swedish. However, decreasing numbers of voluntary participants in the Swedish matriculation examination proved this argument wrong and the strong aversion against *pakkoruotsi* ('forced Swedish') in school continues to be a topic of debate. An initiative launched in March 2013 to even change Swedish into an optional subject in school collected the needed 50,000 votes to be processed by the Finnish parliament (Helsingin Sanomat, 2013). The opposite opinion is also expressed by arguing that the matriculation examination should be compulsory in both national languages again because it would increase people's opportunities in the labour market. In fact, it is widely believed to be much easier to get a place at a Swedish-medium university than at a Finnish-medium university, as I will show later.

Foreign degree students are usually expected to know English, and in some cases also Finnish and/or Swedish (depending on the university and the study programme). The related language proficiency requirements vary from one university to another. At the Sibelius Academy, for example, detailed requirements are listed for foreign bachelor's and master's degree students, who must provide a certificate for English and Finnish or Swedish. Depending on the study programme, they may also be required to demonstrate sufficient skills in Finnish or Swedish in an entrance examination (Sibelius Academy, 2010). At the University of Jyväskylä (2011), requirements are expressed in more general terms: 'International exchange students have the right to use English for their study completion, unless otherwise provisioned by the curriculum'.

There are also different practices with respect to the language requirements that apply to students who want to study abroad. At Aalto University, for example, Finnish students who apply for university grants to participate in international student exchange programmes have to prove their language proficiency by submitting certificates or taking language tests organised by the Language Centre (Aalto University, 2011). The University of Jyväskylä simply recommends practising or refreshing language skills before going abroad (University of Jyväskylä, 2012b).

There are no explicit requirements for exchange students coming to Finland, although skills in English are usually a prerequisite for participating in courses for foreign students without any knowledge of Finnish or Swedish.

Administrative staff

According to the Universities Act (558/2009, Section 35), the language of administration is Finnish and/or Swedish depending on the university (see Are language practices regulated in an explicit way, pp. 66–67). The language competence of administrative staff is not as clearly regulated as before the 2010 university reform (see Are language practices regulated in an explicit way, p. 67). Generally, they are expected to know the language(s) required to perform their duties, and it is up to the universities to define language requirements. Depending on the position, English may be a prerequisite for employment. However, in many cases, English skills are now tacitly expected of administrative staff. As in the case of teaching and research staff, the language competences of administrative staff are officially verified by their matriculation examination certificate. Universities may also apply their own case-specific regulations.

Which languages are used for research?

Languages of scientific publications

The Ministry of Education commissioned a project to investigate 'Disciplinary Differences in Publishing Practices'. The results are based on an analysis of publication register data for three Finnish universities for 1998–2005 (University of Helsinki, Helsinki School of Economics and Tampere University of Technology), and on 44 interviews with lecturers at nine Finnish universities (Puuska & Miettinen, 2008). Table 4.4 shows the results of an analysis of scientific publication registers. Scientific publications comprise scientific books (i.e. books and special issues or conference proceedings), peer-reviewed scientific journal articles, book sections, papers in conference proceedings, editorials, book reviews, short review articles or non-refereed scientific journal articles in the natural sciences (including the agricultural sciences), medical sciences, engineering, social sciences and the arts and humanities.

Almost 40% of all the scientific publications analysed were published in Finland, but in 65% of cases the language of publication was English and in 30% it was Finnish (see Table 4.4). Of the works published in Finland, 17% were written in a language other than Finnish or Swedish, and most of the works published abroad were written in English (91%). The results also showed that in the natural and medical sciences the language of publication was invariably English. In engineering, in areas closely linked to international industry, such as communications technology, biotechnology and electronics, many articles were published in international refereed journals and, without exception, were written in English. In the social sciences, however, the number of international publications had increased significantly, while the number of domestic publications and publications in Finnish had decreased over 1998–2004. Non-scientific publications were analysed separately; most were published in Finland (95%) and in Finnish (83%) (Puuska & Miettinen, 2008: 26–36). In another comparative study, the number of publications in Finnish was found to be higher for state research institutes than for universities (Puuska & Late, 2010).

Table 4.4 Scientific publications at three Finnish universities for 1998–2005: Country and language of publication

Country	No.	%	Language**	No.	%
Finland	24,111	39	English	39,998	65
USA	11,347	18	Finnish	18,223	30
UK	6,639	11	Swedish	1,272	2.1
The Netherlands	3,421	6	German	794	1.3
Germany	3,219	5	Russian	348	0.6
Denmark	1,319	2.1	French	266	0.4
Sweden	1,227	2	Spanish	142	0.2
Switzerland	776	1.3	Estonian	133	0.2
Norway	736	1.2	Italian	120	0.2
France	726	1.2	Hungarian	56	0.1
Other	5,679	10	Other	267	0.4
Total	59,200	100	Total	61,404	
Not specified*	2,204				

Source: Puuska and Miettinen (2008: 26)
*Not given
**Some publications are multilingual

Languages of PhD dissertations

Universities have their own regulations for public examination of doctoral theses. At the University of Jyväskylä, for example, the language used for the oral defence of a PhD dissertation may be chosen in advance by the *custos* (the chairman of the public dissertation defence) by mutual agreement with the candidate and the opponent. Many language choices are possible, from Finnish or Swedish to some other language, or even several languages:

> The language used in the public examination (defence) of the doctoral dissertation is determined by the *custos* in advance, after he/she has discussed the matter with both the doctoral candidate and the opponent. The language of the public examination shall be *Finnish or Swedish* or *the language in which the doctoral dissertation was published*. It is, however, possible to hold the public examination of the dissertation in *some other language*, if the doctoral candidate agrees to it, or to use *several languages* in the public examination, if it has been agreed upon in advance. (University of Jyväskylä 2011, highlighted by the author)

To explore the languages in which PhD dissertations have been written, my research centre[1] enabled me to purchase the register of all PhD dissertations in Finland from the FENNICA database, which contains 45,592 titles. The Finnish National Bibliography (FENNICA) records publications in Finland (books since 1488, journals since 1771, as well as periodicals, maps and audiovisual and electronic data). The register contained all PhD dissertations from the 17th century on. However, almost 4000 (3924) titles were listed twice (for example, when the dissertation was published in both print and electronic versions). These duplicates were deleted and the publication years were coded in order to analyse the data statistically.

For this chapter, I first looked at the languages in which dissertations were written from the 17th century until the end of 2009 (see Figure 4.4), and then at PhD dissertations in the past 40 years, applying a shorter interval of 10 years (see Figure 4.5).

The first university in Finland was founded in Turku in 1640 (the Royal Academy of Turku, then relocated to Helsinki in 1827). The first PhD dissertation listed in the FENNICA database dates to 1642. The analysis of all PhD dissertations listed in the database revealed that Latin predominated until 1900. Swedish began to be used in the 18th century, and Finnish in the 19th century, but it was only from the 20th century on that the latter retained a relatively stable share of over 20%. The first half

The Position of Finnish and Swedish at Universities in Finland 89

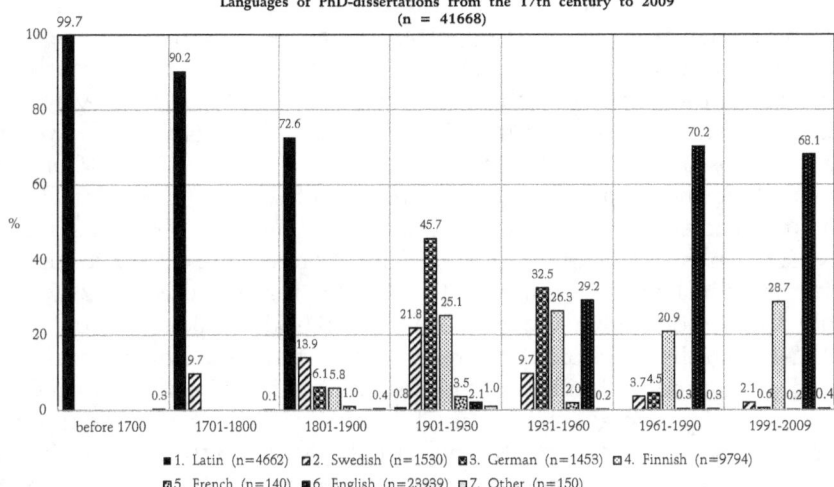

Figure 4.4 Language of PhD dissertations from the 17th century to 2009

Source: Based on data received from the Finnish National Bibliography [FENNICA]

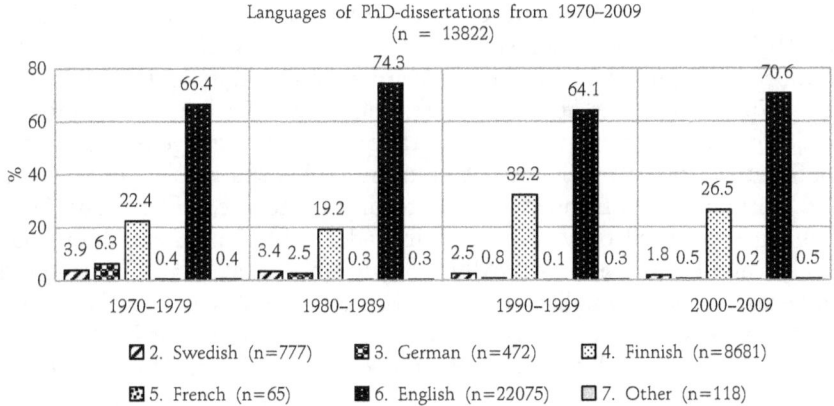

Figure 4.5 Language of PhD dissertations in the past 40 years

Source: Based on data received from the Finnish National Bibliography [FENNICA]

of the last century was the most multilingual. This was also the period when German was the most important language of science. In the first 30 years, five languages were each used for more than 2% of dissertations, with English accounting for the lowest proportion (2.1%), topped by French (3.5%), Swedish (21.8%), Finnish (25.1%) and German (45.7%). However, two world wars and the inhuman policies of the Third Reich led to German gradually losing its popularity as a language of science. A boycott of the language had already begun after World War I (Reinbothe, 2006), and many Jewish scientists had emigrated to the United States, where they continued their work in English. From 1931 to 1960, English was used for 29.2% of PhD dissertations in Finland, but German still held the 'pole position' with 32.5%. From the 1960s on, the number of dissertations in English increased rapidly and it took a clear lead as the most important language. Finnish sank to its lowest percentage, accounting for only one fifth of all dissertations, and Swedish reached 3.7%. In the past 20 years, however, Finnish has regained a bit more ground, and together the national languages (Finnish and Swedish) have been used in almost one third of all PhD dissertations. A more detailed analysis of the languages used to write PhD dissertations in recent years is shown in Figure 4.5.

The results of the analysis of the past 40 years show that PhD dissertations have been written mostly in English since the 1970s, with the language now accounting for over 60% of the total. At the end of the last century, almost one third of all dissertations were written in Finnish, but their number decreased slightly at the beginning of this century. The number of dissertations written in German was only slightly over 6% in the 1970s, which was nevertheless still slightly higher than the figure for Swedish, but the proportion of dissertations in the language fell below that for Swedish from the 1980s on. The number of dissertations in both Swedish and German has continued to fall steadily up to the present day. Other languages are used only to a very limited extent. To sum up, nowadays English and Finnish are practically the only languages used for writing PhD dissertations, with English being used in over 70% of cases. An analysis of discipline-specific language use in dissertations could not be performed within the framework of this study and will need to be carried out in future investigations.

In the next section, I will examine the main discourses about languages policy at university level and look at the social sectors that support each discourse.

Discourses about Language Policies at University Level

Current discourses about language policy at university level focus on two issues: the role of Swedish as an academic language, and the role of English in relation to the national languages.

An extensive discussion of the role of Swedish in Finnish society is currently ongoing in the media. This debate, initiated by the Confederation of Finnish Industries (the leading business organisation in Finland), has also affected universities. Under the new Universities Act, for example, skills in both Finnish and Swedish are no longer a general requirement for university staff. There has also been a heated debate about whether there are better opportunities for native speakers of Swedish compared to native Finnish speakers to study at a university. This debate is unfolding in various online forums especially. The discussion was initiated by news circulated by the Finnish Broadcasting Company (Yle, 2011). They claimed that there were 'controversial estimations' regarding admissions to study at universities and universities of applied sciences. The main thrust of the news story was that only one third of native Finnish speakers were gaining admission as compared to 50% of native Swedish speakers. This article also stated that access to study in Swedish has been possible with eight points less in the entry examination than access to study in Finnish. However, the article also quoted the Finnish Ministry of Education and Culture's permanent secretary who stated that quotas for studying in Swedish and Finnish aim at ensuring bilingualism and safeguarding services in Swedish. After all, such quotas are not made specifically for native speakers of Swedish or Finnish but to ensure that there are opportunities for studying in these languages, independent of one's mother tongue.

The role of English in the Finnish academic sphere is dominant to such a degree that it forces one to reflect on the role of the national languages in higher education. There has even been recent public debate on whether or not to introduce English as one of the primary languages of teaching, and perhaps even administration. This was suggested by Jacobs (2010). The responses to Jacobs have stressed that switching to English in universities in Finland is not only impossible for legislative reasons, but that it would also conflict with the fact that the majority of students will need to operate in the national languages, Finnish and Swedish, in their working environment in Finland after they graduate from university (Hall, 2010; Vänskä, 2010). In addition, Vänskä (2010) criticises Jacobs's attitude as being based on the belief that English is more neutral and natural than other languages. In her opinion, this view is quite naïve and indicates several gaps in Jacobs's education since this is usually the way one feels about a native language. She also points to the fact that language is needed for thinking and the construction of knowledge in the natural sciences too (Vänskä, 2010).

Hakulinen (2009) states that the undeclared policy of Finnish scientific institutions favours the use of English. She continues that the Finnish language can survive if we (i.e. academics in Finland) decide that it must and support this decision in practice. The Research Institute for the Languages of Finland, for example, has published an appeal aimed at defending Finnish as the language of science and higher education (Luukka, 2010), and the CIMO in Finland has recently emphasised the promotion of learning and teaching Finnish as a foreign language, both within Finland and abroad (Ketolainen et al., 2010).

Cases that concern the right to study in one's mother tongue, Finnish or Swedish, have been discussed in the media. For example, at the University of Turku, two lecturers were recently appointed for the subjects of geology and mineralogy. Both were foreigners (one from Sweden, the other from the Netherlands) and both lacked skills in Finnish. Some of the issues considered were the importance of the mother tongue for learning and the right under the Finnish Constitution to study in one's mother tongue, Finnish or Swedish (Saarnisto, 2001). Another case discussed in the media concerned a complaint against the University of Helsinki made by a student to the Office of the Chancellor of Justice about the fact that Finnish students were required to use English in all their studies at the Faculty of Agriculture and Forestry if there was even a single foreign student in the group. The student claimed that this procedure contravened the Finnish Constitution (Yle, 2010). The office ruled against the student, making reference to the Universities Act, which allows universities to use a language other than Finnish and/or Swedish for tuition (OKV/1001/1/2009). A recent complaint to the Office of the Chancellor of Justice was made by a student of the School of Business at Aalto University concerning its decision to teach all master's programmes in English. In his opinion, this contravenes the University Act. Aalto University justified its decision by stating that studies in bachelor programmes are offered in Finnish, and the university aims to enrol more international students at master's level. This decision was motivated by the wish to strengthen internationalisation as a strategic alignment. Furthermore, Aalto University wants to entice promising young researchers. Their aim is an increase in quality through internationalisation (Yle, 2013a). The legal procedure is still underway as I write, but the Finnish

Ministry of Education has gauged that the University Act is possibly in need of change (Yle, 2013b).

At the initiative of Universities Finland, the 'Publication Forum Project' was launched in 2010 (Federation of Finnish Learned Societies, 2010). The project, funded by the Ministry of Education and Culture, aimed at establishing a 'quality classification' for scientific publication channels in all research fields. In principle, it offered the possibility of incorporating language policy considerations in the national policy for assessing the quality of scientific publications. However, the rating results published in January 2012 only reinforced the dominant role of English, because journals classified as Level 3 (top publication channels in their field) and Level 2 (leading scientific publication channels) were mainly in English. Publications in languages other than English made it only to Level 1 (domestic and foreign scientific publication channels). The plan is to take this rating into account in allocating resources (more money to higher-level publications; see Ministry of Education and Culture, 2011b: 41), so the dominance of English is likely to become even stronger. In response, 60 scientific societies signed a declaration in favour of diversified and multifaceted publication principles, questioning both the rating levels and the ministry's plan to use them as a funding criterion (Finnish Youth Research Society, 2012). As a result, the door to Level 2 was opened in principle also for domestic publication channels in spring 2012 (Sintonen, 2012: 6). In contrast, the use of English as the language for research funding applications has not yet been questioned. The Academy of Finland, for example, recommends that funding applicants submit applications in English, despite their basic right to use Finnish or Swedish. This is justified by the practice of recruiting mainly foreign experts as scientific reviewers.

Summary and Conclusions

The status of Finnish and Swedish as national languages in Finland is regulated in the Finnish Constitution and the Language Act, as well as by several acts and decrees in specific societal domains, including the Universities Act. The official bilingual status of the country grants everyone the right to use Finnish or Swedish in matters that concern them, and to obtain documents in the language they use. On the other hand, as medium-sized national languages, neither Finnish nor Swedish are very well suited for the purposes of internationalisation in higher education. This is why foreign language skills have traditionally been very highly valued in Finland. However, growing competition has led to a rapid increase in the importance of English in the Finnish academic sphere, whether as a language of teaching (to recruit more foreign students) or as the pre-eminent lingua franca in research. Like many other countries, Finland also has to address the challenges of internationalisation and competition, which affect national languages as well as the status of foreign languages other than English.

The new government strategy for the national languages of Finland (Prime Minister's Office, 2012) is the first of its kind. Its aim is to safeguard the bilingual nature of the country, and especially to support the minority language Swedish. The growing influence of English is referred to in the context of recommendations to use Finnish and Swedish 'in all walks of life' to 'maintain diverse and nuanced vocabulary and expressions' (Prime Minister's Office, 2012: 9). In terms of foreign languages other than English, the goals to enlarge the language resources of the country, as set out earlier in the programme of Prime Minister Jyrki Katainen's government (Prime Minister's Office, 2011: 51, 53), have not been pursued. The 2011–2016 programme for the development of education and research, for example, emphasised versatile language and cultural competences as being needed in all areas of our increasingly internationalising society. The authors point out that, in line with the requirements of globalisation, the learning of foreign languages at school 'has been overly focused on the English language' (Ministry of Education and Culture, 2012: 18). The Finnish government's language strategy does not touch upon this topic. With regard to science communication, the strategy characterises the use of English as 'a natural development'. Despite the fact that the strategy does not include any proposals for reform of legislation, the Finnish Ministry of Education has gauged that the University Act is possibly in need of change because of the ever strengthening position of English at Finnish universities. The latest complaint from a student against the Aalto University's decision to teach all master's programmes in English is still being processed by the Office of the Chancellor of Justice.[2]

According to the Ministry of Education (2008: 44), universities in Finland are expected to develop language policies for their own purposes. Our analysis showed that half of the universities had developed such policies by January 2012 and 71% by 2013. These language policies were developed by the universities independently from each other, and there does not appear to have been any cooperation. Moreover, the language policy documents have different names and are available in one to three languages: Finnish, Swedish and English; Finnish and English; Swedish and English; or a single language, either Finnish or Swedish. They differ in content and length but all emphasise the role of English for internationalisation, without overlooking the legislative status of the national languages. Foreign languages other than English are usually referred to rather vaguely. In January 2012, only one university (Helsinki) mentioned the importance of publishing in foreign languages other than English, and two more universities (Turku and Tampere) postulated the same in their new language policies developed later in 2012 and 2013. Concrete measures to implement the language policies were included only in a minority of cases and focused especially on strengthening the role of English in teaching, publishing research results, and administration. However, there seems to be a tendency towards more concrete definitions of objectives and measures in the three newer language policies developed in 2012 and 2013. Interestingly, two universities (Tampere and Turku) espouse wider use of different languages, and, in contrast, one other (Tampere University of Technology) emphasises the role of English to promote its internationalisation.

Although Finnish legislation guarantees the status of the national languages for tuition and administration, assessment and auditing procedures at the internal, national and international level clearly favour English in higher education and research. For example, universities are encouraged to offer foreign language teaching to attract foreign students, and today a foreign language invariably means English. At the same time, there are still no concrete measures to ensure the language competence of staff teaching in a foreign language. Also, the use of English in research is clearly favoured and rewarded. As long as concrete measures for valuing and supporting the national languages and foreign languages other than English are lacking, language policies remain no more than bits of paper that articulate good intentions. One university, for example, justified the fact that it did not have a language policy by arguing that it lacked the resources needed to take concrete measures. On the other hand, opportunities to develop concrete measures for promoting the use of the national languages and foreign languages other than English are far too often missed, as shown in the discussion about the national publication forum project. One could ask whether English is the only key to internationalisation and how the use of terms such as 'natural development' could escape critical scientific gaze. A more in-depth reflection on the interdependence of thinking, language and the sociocultural construction of knowledge (see Ylönen, 2011) beyond the vocabulary dimension would advance the status of the national languages and foreign languages other than English.

Acknowledgements

Thanks are due to Elina Laajala for eliminating double listings of PhD dissertations and coding the years of publication, and to Helena Mackay and Marilyn Martin-Jones for proofreading different drafts of the chapter.

Note

(1) The Centre for Applied Language Studies (Soveltavan kielentutkimuksen keskus) at the University of Jyväskylä/Finland.
(2) In November 2013, the Solicitor General decided in favour of student and obliged the Aalto University to define (for example in its degree regulations) the degree to which English can be used instead or in addition to Finnish and the degree to which students may use Finnish in their exams, written assignments or lectures (The Office of the Chancellor of Justice, 2013).

References

Aalto University (2010) *Aalto University Language Guidelines*. Received via personal email (Leena Plym-Rissanen) on 18 October 2011.
Aalto University (2011) *Kansainvälistyminen ja opinnot ulkomailla – Vaihto-opiskelu: Kielitaidon osoittaminen* [Internationalisation and studies abroad – exchange studies: Demonstration of language proficiency]. See https://into.aalto.fi/display/fimasterchem/Kielitaidon+osoittaminen (accessed 17 January 2012).
Act on the Knowledge of Languages Required of Personnel in Public Bodies 424/2003. Original: Laki julkisyhteisöjen henkilöstöltä vaadittavasta kielitaidosta. *Finlex*. See http://www.finlex.fi/fi/laki/alkup/2003/20030424 (accessed 17 January 2012).
Act on the Language Skills of Civil Servants 149/1922. Original: Laki Valtion virkamiehiltä vaadittavasta kielitaidosta. *Finlex*. See http://www.finlex.fi/fi/laki/alkup/1922/19220149 (accessed 17 January 2012).
Amendment 715/2004. Amendment to the Universities Act 645/1997. Original: Laki yliopistolain muuttamisesta 715/2004. *Finlex*. See http://www.finlex.fi/fi/laki/alkup/2004/20040715 (accessed 17 January 2012).
Brenn-White, M. and van Rest, E. (2012) *English-Taught Master's Programs in Europe: New Findings on Supply and Demand*. New York: Institute of International Education. See http://www.iie.org/Research-and-Publications/Publications-and-Reports/IIE-Bookstore/English-Language-Masters-Briefing-Paper (accessed 2 October 2013).
Brenn-White, M. and van Rest, E. (2013) *English-Taught Master's Programs in Europe: A 2013 Update*. New York: Institute of International Education. See http://www.iie.org/~/media/Files/Corporate/Publications/English-Language-Masters-2013-Update.ashx (accessed 29 August 2013).
CIMO (2011) *Ulkomaiset tutkinto-opiskelijat korkeakouluissa suhteessa opiskelijamäärään 2002–2010*. [Foreign degree students in Finnish higher education institutions in relation to the total number of students]. CIMO – Centre for International Mobility, Helsinki. See http://www.cimo.fi/instancedata/prime_product_julkaisu/cimo/embeds/cimowwwstructure/21342_UTO_suhteessa20022010.pdf (accessed 1 February 2012).
Decree on demonstrating proficiency in Finnish and Swedish for public administration 481/2003. Original: Valtioneuvoston asetus suomen ja ruotsin kielen taidon

osoittamisesta valtionhallinnossa 481/2003. *Finlex*. See http://www.finlex.fi/fi/laki/alkup/2003/20030481 (accessed 17 October 2011).

Federation of Finnish Learned Societies (2010) *Julkaisufoorumi* (publication forum) 2010. See http://www.tsv.fi/julkaisufoorumi/ (accessed 29 April 2012).

Finnish Constitution 731/1999. Unofficial translation of *'Suomen perustuslaki* 11.6.1999/731'. *Finlex*. See http://www.finlex.fi/en/laki/kaannokset/1999/en19990731.pdf (Original: http://www.finlex.fi/fi/laki/ajantasa/1999/19990731) (accessed 12 October 2011).

Finnish Youth Research Society (2012) Monipuolisen ja -muotoisen tieteellisen julkaisutoiminnan puolesta. (For diversified and multifaceted publishing). See http://www.nuorisotutkimusseura.fi/sites/default/files/tapahtumatiedostot/Kannanotto_lopullinen.pdf (accessed 2 February 2012).

Garam, I. (2009) *Degree programmes taught through a foreign language in Finnish higher education*. Faktaa – facts and figures 2b/2009. CIMO – Centre for International Mobility, Helsinki. See http://www.cimo.fi/instancedata/prime_product_julkaisu/cimo/embeds/cimowwwstructure/15610_degree_programmes_faktaa_summary.pdf (accessed 1 February 2012).

Garam, I. and Korkala, S. (2011) International mobility in Finnish vocational and higher education in 2010. CIMO – Centre for International Mobility, Helsinki. See http://www.cimo.fi/instancedata/prime_product_julkaisu/cimo/embeds/cimowwwstructure/21273_Faktaa_1b_2011_web.pdf (accessed 1 February 2012).

Government Decree 463/1998. Original: Asetus korkeakoulujen henkilöstön kelpoisuusvaatimuksista ja tehtävistä annetun asetuksen muuttamisesta 463/1998. *Finlex*. See http://www.finlex.fi/fi/laki/alkup/1998/19980463 (accessed 17 October 2011).

Government Decree 770/2009. Original: Valtioneuvoston asetus yliopistoista (Government Decree on Universities). *Finlex*. See http://www.finlex.fi/fi/laki/alkup/2009/20090770 (accessed 17 October 2011).

Government Decree on University Degrees 794/2004. Original: Valtioneuvoston asetus yliopistojen tutkinnoista. *Finlex*. See http://www.finlex.fi/fi/laki/alkup/2004/20040794 (accessed 17 October 2011).

Hakulinen, A. (2009) Kielipolitiikka ja suomalainen tiede. [Language policy and Finnish science] *Academia Scentiarum Fennica*. See http://www.acadsci.fi/tiedostot/vuosikirja_2009/hakulinen_esitelma.pdf (accessed 4 April 2011).

Hall, C. (2010) Suomalaiset yliopistot englanninkielisiksi? *Acatiimi* 6 (10), 23–24.

Helsingin Sanomat (2013) Aloite pakkoruotsin poistamisesta ei saa hallituspuolueiden kannatusta. [The initiative to remove compulsory Swedish does not receive support from the government parties]. Helsingin Sanomat. See http://www.hs.fi/politiikka/a1376273063752 (accessed 5 September 2013).

Hughes, R.(2008) Internationalisation of higher education and language policy: Questions of quality and equity. *Higher Education Management and Policy* 20 (1), 102–119.

Jacobs, H. (2010) United by an uncommon language. *Acatiimi* 4 (10), 28–29. See http://www.acatiimi.fi/4_2010/04_10_11.php (accessed 5 October 2010).

Ketolainen, J., Kopperi, M., Siltala, A., Vehkanen, M. and Daavittila, T. (eds) (2010) *CIMO korkeakoulutuksen kansainvälistäjänä 2009* [CIMO as a Promoter of Internationalization in Higher Education]. Helsinki: Centre for International Mobility CIMO. See http://www.cimo.fi/dman/Document.phx/~public/Julkaisut+ja+tilastot/Esitteet+suomenkieliset/TA2_2009.pdf (accessed 5 October 2010).

Language Act 423/2003. Unofficial translation of 'Kielilaki 6.6.2003/423'. *Finlex.* See http://www.finlex.fi/en/laki/kaannokset/2003/en20030423.pdf (Original: http://www.finlex.fi/fi/laki/ajantasa/2003/20030423) (accessed 17 October 2011).

Luukka, M-R. (2010) Vetoomus suomen kielen turvaamiseksi tieteen ja korkeimman opetuksen kielenä [Appeal for safeguarding the status of Finnish as a language of science and higher education]. Kotimaisten kielten tutkimuskeskus. Suomen kielen lautakunta. (Research Institute for the Languages of Finland. Finnish language board.) See http://www.kotus.fi/files/1429/Vetoomus_lautakunta_2010.pdf (accessed 17 October 2011).

Ministry of Education (2008) *Education and Research 2007-2012. Development Plan.* See http://www.minedu.fi/export/sites/default/OPM/Julkaisut/2008/liitteet/opm11.pdf?lang=fi (accessed 12 October 2008).

Ministry of Education (2009a) *Strategy for the Internationalisation of Higher Education Institutions in Finland 2009-2015.* See http://www.minedu.fi/export/sites/default/OPM/Julkaisut/2009/liitteet/opm23.pdf (accessed 14 January 2012).

Ministry of Education (2009b) Key Competences for Lifelong Learning in Finland, Education 2010 – Interim Report. See http://www.minedu.fi/export/sites/default/OPM/Koulutus/Liitteet/Education_2010._Interim_report_2009._Finland.pdf (accessed 1 February 2012).

Ministry of Education and Culture (2011a) *Korkeakoulut 2011 – yliopistot ja ammattikorkeakoulut.* [*Higher Education Institutions 2011 – Universities and Polytechnics*]. See http://www.minedu.fi/export/sites/default/OPM/Julkaisut/2011/liitteet/okm10.pdf?lang=fi (accessed 2 February 2012).

Ministry of Education and Culture (2011b) *Laadukas, kansainvälinen, profiloitunut ja vaikuttava yliopisto – ehdotus yliopistojen rahoitusmalliksi vuodesta 2013 alkaen.* [High-quality, international, specialized and influential university – proposal for a university financing model from 2013 on]. See http://www.minedu.fi/export/sites/default/OPM/Julkaisut/2011/liitteet/okmtr26.pdf (accessed 2 February 2012).

Ministry of Education and Culture (2012) *Education and Research 2011-2016. A Development Plan.* See http://www.minedu.fi/export/sites/default/OPM/Julkaisut/2012/liitteet/okm03.pdf (accessed 28 September 2012).

OKV/1001/1/2009. Englannin käyttäminen yliopiston opetuskielenä. [Use of English as a language of tuition]. Apulaisoikeuskanslerin päätös (decision of the Deputy Chancellor of Justice): 25.11.2010. See http://www.finlex.fi/fi/viranomaiset/foka/2010/20101621 (accessed 12 October 2011).

Prime Minister's Office (2011) *Programme of Prime Minister Jyrki Katainen's Government.* Helsinki: Finland. See http://valtioneuvosto.fi/hallitus/hallitusohjelma/pdf/en334743.pdf (accessed 28 September 2012).

Prime Minister's Office (2012) *Strategy for the National Languages of Finland. Government Resolution.* Helsinki: Prime Minister's Office Publications 7/2012. See http://vnk.fi/julkaisukansio/2012/j04-kansalliskielistrategia-nationalspraksstrategi-j07-strategy/PDF/en.pdf (accessed 2 October 2013).

Puuska, H-M. and Miettinen, M. (2008) Julkaisukäytännöt eri tieteenaloilla. (Disciplinary differences in publishing practices). *Opetusministeriön julkaisuja* (*Publications of the Ministry of Education*), 33. Helsinki: Helsingin yliopistopaino. See http://www.minedu.fi/export/sites/default/OPM/Julkaisut/2008/liitteet/opm33.pdf?lang=fi (accessed 12 October 2011).

Puuska, H-M. and Late, E. (2010) Julkaisukäytännöt yliopistoissa ja valtion tutkimuslaituoksissa: kolmen tieteenalan vertailu. [Publishing practices at universities

and national research institutions]. Abstract. *Informaatiotutkimus (Information Studies)* 29 (3): Informaatiotutkimuksen päivät 2010 (Conference on Information Studies 2010). See http://ojs.tsv.fi/index.php/inf/article/viewFile/3601/3353 (accessed 10 February 2012).
Reinbothe, R. (2006) *Deutsch als internationale Wissenschaftssprache und der Boykott nach dem Ersten Weltkrieg. Duisburger Arbeiten zur Sprach- und Kulturwissenschaft 67.* Frankfurt am Main: Lang.
RIC (Research and Innovation Council of Finland) (2009) *Internationalisation of Finnish Education, Research and Innovation.* See http://www.minedu.fi/export/sites/default/ OPM/Tiede/tutkimus-_ja_innovaationeuvosto/erillisraportit/liitteet/KVstrategia_ Eng.pdf (accessed 3 February 2012).
Saarinen, T. (2012) Internationalization and the invisible language? Historical phases and current policies in Finnish higher education. In S. Ahola and D. Hoffman (eds) *Higher Education Research in Finland. Emerging Structures and Contemporary Issues* (pp. 235–248). Jyväskylä: Finnish Institute for Educational Research.
Saarnisto, M. (2001) Millä kielellä yliopistossa opiskellaan? [In which language do we study at the university?] Tieteessä tapahtuu *(Science Now)* 2001 (3). See http://www. tieteessatapahtuu.fi/013/paakirjoitus.htm (accessed 15 October 2011).
Sibelius Academy (2010) *Guide for International Applicants 2011.* Helsinki: Sibelius Academy. See http://www.siba.fi/en/c/document_library/get_file?uuid=09a3583b-0bc0-4744-b9a8-a1f3ee201537&groupId=10157 (accessed 24 October 2011).
Sintonen, K. (2012) Julkaisufoorumin tasoluokitusta muutettiin [The criteria for classification in the publication forum were changed]. *Acatiimi* 2 (6). See http:// www.acatiimi.fi/2_2012/02_12_03.php (accessed 23 April 2012).
Statistics Finland (2013) Appendix table 2. Population according to language 1980–2012. See http://www.stat.fi/til/vaerak/2012/vaerak_2012_2013-03-22_en.pdf (accessed 15 August 2013).
The Office of Chancellor of Justice (2013) Anonymisoitu päätös [Anonymised decision] Dnro OKV/727/1/2013. See: http://www.oikeuskansleri.fi/media/uploads/ ratkaisut/ratkaisut_2013/okv_727_1_2013.pdf (accessed 26 August 2014).
Universities Act 645/1997. Unofficial translation of 'Yliopistolaki 645/1997'. *Finlex.* See http://www.finlex.fi/en/laki/kaannokset/1997/en19970645.pdf (Original: http:// www.finlex.fi/en/laki/kaannokset/1997/en19970645.pdf) (accessed 12 October 2011).
Universities Act 558/2009. Unofficial translation of 'Yliopistolaki 24.7.558/2009'. *Finlex.* See http://www.finlex.fi/en/laki/kaannokset/2009/en20090558.pdf (Original: http://www.finlex.fi/fi/laki/ajantasa/2009/20090558) (accessed 15 August 2013).
University of Helsinki (2007) *University of Helsinki Language Policy.* See http://www. helsinki.fi/inbrief/strategy/HYn_kieliperiaatteet.pdf (accessed 12 October 2011).
University of Eastern Finland (2011) *Itä-Suomen yliopiston kielipoliittinen ohjelma vuosiksi 2011–2015.* [Eastern-Finland university language policy 2011–2015]. Received via personal email message (Raija Elsinen) on 7 December 2011.
University of Jyväskylä (2004) *Jyväskylä University Language Policy.* See https://www.jyu. fi/hallinto/strategia/en/JY_languagepolicy.pdf (accessed 2 February 2012).
University of Jyväskylä (2011) *Degree Regulations of the University of Jyväskylä,* Chapter 6, Section 29: Language used in the public examination of doctoral dissertation. See https://www.jyu.fi/opiskelu/degreereg (accessed 24 October 2011).

University of Jyväskylä (2012a) *Jyväskylän yliopiston kielipolitiikka* [Jyväskylä university language policy]. See https://www.jyu.fi/hallinto/strategia/politiikat/Jyvaeskylaen%20yliopiston%20kielipolitiikka%2025012012.pdf (accessed 2 February 2012).
University of Jyväskylä (2012b) Tietoa ulkomaille lähteville [Information for students going abroad]. See https://www.jyu.fi/hallintokeskus/opiskelijoille/oppaat/tietoa_ulkomaille_lahteville/referencemanual-all-pages (accessed 2 February 2012).
Välimaa, J., Fonteyn, K., Garam, I., van den Heuvel, E., Linza, C., Söderqvist, M., Wolff, J.U. and Kolhinen, J. (2013) *An Evaluation of International Degree Programmes in Finland*. Helsinki: Publications of The Finnish Higher Education Evaluation Council 2: 2013. See http://www.kka.fi/files/1822/KKA_0213.pdf (accessed 29 August 2013).
Vänskä, A. (2010) Kieli-imperialismia [Language imperialism]. *Yliopisto* 10, 54.
Wächter, B. and Maiworm, F. (2008) English-Taught Programmes in European Higher Education. The Picture in 2007. *ACA Papers on International Cooperation in Education*. Bonn: Lemmens.
Yle (2010) Englannin kielen ylivalta johti kanteluun Helsingin yliopistosta [Domination of English led to a complaint against the University of Helsinki] Yle uutiset (public-broadcasting/Yle news). 17 March. Helsinki: Yle (Finnish Broadcasting Company). See http://yle.fi/uutiset/kulttuuri/2010/03/englannin_kielen_ylivalta_johti_kanteluun_helsingin_yliopistosta_1537907.html (accessed 2 October 2011).
Yle (2011) Yliopistojen ovet aukeavat helpommin ruotsinkielisille [The doors of universities open easier for speakers of Swedish]. 3 October. Helsinki: Yle (Finnish Broadcasting Company). See http://yle.fi/uutiset/yliopistojen_ovet_aukeavat_helpommin_ruotsinkielisille/2914002 (accessed 19 August 2013).
Yle (2013a) Kauppakorkeakoulu hylkäsi suomen – maisteriopinnot vain englanniksi [The School of Business abandoned Finnish – master studies in English only]. 16 February. Helsinki: Yle (Finnish Broadcasting Company). See http://yle.fi/uutiset/kauppakorkeakoulu_hylkasi_suomen_-_maisteriopinnot_vain_englanniksi/6494336 (accessed 19 August 2013).
Yle (2013b) Opetusministeriö: Yliopistolakia ehkä muutettava englanninkielisen opetuksen takia. [Ministry of Education: Universities act may have to be changed because of teaching in English]. 25 February. Helsinki: Finnish Broadcasting Company Yle. See http://yle.fi/uutiset/opetusministerio_yliopistolakia_ehka_muutettava_englanninkielisen_opetuksen_takia/6508928 (accessed 19 August 2013).
Ylönen, S. (2011) Denkstil und Sprache/n in den Wissenschaften. Mit Beispielen aus der Medizin. *Zeitschrift für Angewandte Linguistik* 55, 1–22.
Ylönen, S. and Vainio, V. (2010) Mehrsprachigkeit und Rolle des Deutschen im Studium aus der Sicht finnischer Studierender. *Apples – Journal of Applied Language Studies* 4 (1), 29–49. See http://apples.jyu.fi/ArticleFile/download/116 (accessed 1 February 2012).
Ylönen, S. and Kivelä, M. (2011) The role of languages at Finnish universities. *Apples – Journal of Applied Language Studies* 5 (3), 33–61. See http://apples.jyu.fi/article_files/Ylonen_Kivela_final.pdf (accessed 1 February 2012).

Appendices

Appendix 4.1 Languages of instruction and examination as regulated by Finnish legislation

Finnish (9+1*)	Swedish (2+1*)	Finnish and Swedish (5)
University of Eastern Finland	Åbo Akademi University	University of Helsinki
University of Lapland	*Hanken School of Economics*	Aalto University (formed by the merger of the University of Art and Design, the Helsinki School of Economics and Helsinki University of Technology)
University of Jyväskylä		*Arts University (in 2013) (before 2013: Sibelius Academy, the Academy of Fine Arts and the Theatre Academy)*
University of Oulu		
University of Tampere		
University of Turku		
University of Vaasa		
Lappeenranta University of Technology		
Tampere University of Technology		
Former *Helsinki School of Economics** of Aalto University	*Swedish School of Social Science** of the University of Helsinki	

Asterisks indicate the existence of separate units with special language regulations; italics identifies specialised universities; shaded: universities situated in Helsinki

Appendix 4.2 Language policies at Finnish universities

	No. of participants in working group	Lang./ LC	Nat./ Tech.	Admin.	Kursiv	Other
Results of the first study (January 2012)						
University of Jyväskylä 2004	14 and smaller 'core group'	x	x	x	x	Cultural politics, Bus.
2012	12	x	–	x	x	Bus.
Hanken School of Economics	11	x	Not applicable	x	x	Four dept.
University of Helsinki	8	x	x	x	x	Soc. Sci.
Åbo Academy	8	x	x	–	x	All fac.
University of Vaasa	9	x	x	x	x	Bus.
Aalto University	2–4	x	–	x	–	–
University of Eastern Finland (University of Joensuu)	8	x	x	x	x	Theol., Bus., Comp. Sci.
	11	x	x	x	x	Soc. Sci., Bus., Philosophy
Theatre Academy (merged with Sibelius Academy and the Academy of Fine Arts to the Arts University in 2013)	11–12	–	Not applicable	x	x	–
Results of the updating study (August 2013)						
University of Turku	10	x	x	x	x	All fac.
Tampere University of Technology	9	x	x	x	x	–
University of Tampere	5	x	–	x	–	–

AAbbreviations: Lang.: Languages; LC: Language Centre; Nat./Tech.: Natural/Technical Sciences; Admin.: Administration; Stud.: Student Union/

5 Challenges for Hebrew in Higher Education and Research Environments

Drorit Ram

Introduction

Hebrew's role as a medium of instruction in higher education in Israel goes back 100 years, and although the recent expansion of English in the world's universities has challenged medium-sized language use (Ammon, 2001), Hebrew has held fast as the medium of instruction in Israeli higher education. This could be the result of the language war that took place in Palestine a hundred years ago, before the foundation of Israel's first university, the Technion in Haifa. At that time, Hebrew was being challenged by German and was not, in fact, the language that university lecturers might have chosen, given that many were not proficient users of Hebrew. Nevertheless, Hebrew won this particular war because of its proponents' firm belief that nation and language should march together, that sustainability should be achieved and that language cultivation should be initiated and practised in the education system from preschool to higher education (Spolsky & Shohamy, 1999). This, indeed, is the conviction that currently obstructs any challenge to the hegemony of Hebrew.

There are currently 62 institutions of higher education in the state of Israel. Its first two universities, the Technion and the Hebrew University of Jerusalem, were founded in Palestine in 1924, when the Technion mainly offered technical and vocational studies such as engineering and the Hebrew University of Jerusalem was multidisciplinary. Following the foundation of the State of Israel in 1948, five new universities were created: Bar-Ilan, Tel Aviv, the University of Haifa, Ben-Gurion University of the Negev and the Weizmann Institute of Science. In the mid-1970s, the Open University of Israel also began to offer courses. Today in a total of eight state-subsidised universities, students' tuition fees are determined by a government-appointed committee, and university programmes in all disciplines require the approval of the government's supervisory body, the Council for Higher Education.

In the 1970s, teachers' colleges became institutions of higher education and in the 1990s an amendment to the law on higher education led to the foundation of various private academic, technical and vocational colleges. A total of 27 of Israel's academic institutions are not universities and a number of these receive government funding. Since the 1950s, public committees have set tuition fees for BA and MA students at the state-funded universities. The universities' executive bodies are their senates, whose decisions are binding on all academic bodies. In most universities, the members of the senate include the rector, the president, the vice-president for research and development, the vice-rector, the faculty deans and senior professors, the heads of faculties, the dean of students and a lecturer's representative.

In 2006, of the 245,000 students enrolled in academic institutions, some 170,000 were studying at the eight universities (Israel Central Bureau of Statistics, 2006). Two percent of these 170,000 were international students and most were enrolled in MA programmes. Currently, some 380,000 students are enrolled in institutions of higher education supervised by the Council for Higher Education (see the document Hizuk sherutei hahaskala hagvoha al basis calcali, [Strengthening higher education services on an economic basis], 2009). Language policies in education in Israel are substantially different as far as primary and secondary education and higher education are concerned. There are two official languages in Israel, Hebrew and Arabic, each serving as a medium of instruction in each of the two separate educational systems from K-12, both under governmental supervision. Although Hebrew has been taught as a compulsory school subject from the second grade in the Arab school system and Arabic-speaking students have to take a matriculation examination in Hebrew (Spolsky & Shohamy, 1999), the teaching of Arabic, literary Arabic or the Palestinian vernacular is limited in the Hebrew school system from the seventh until the ninth grade by law (Ministry of Education, State of Israel, 2012a), and only recently it has been suggested to give Arabic special encouragement in the eleventh and twelfth grades (Ministry of Education, State of Israel, 2012b). Upon entrance to the university, the status of Arabic as an official language diminishes. Knowledge of Arabic is not required, albeit in three teacher training colleges designated for Arab teachers – Al Quasami Academic College of Education in Baqua Al Garbia, Arab College of Education in Israel located in Haifa and Sachnin

Teacher Training College in Sachnin. *De facto* language policy in higher education in Israel requires academic language competence in Hebrew and English as a prerequisite for admission to universities.

According to the policy for language education of 1996, all students in both Hebrew and Arabic systems learn English as the principal foreign language, starting in fourth or third grade or earlier, and continuing to the twelfth grade. In addition, a significant number of pupils learn French, Russian or Yiddish. The place of English as the first foreign language is stated, and new immigrants are to be encouraged to maintain their home languages while acquiring Hebrew (Shohamy, 1994; Spolsky, 1996). This language policy where two languages are official and English serves as the first foreign language is similar to the language policy in Finland where there is legislation that requires the use of the official languages – Finnish and Swedish – and ensures the place of English as the first foreign language (Yiönen, this volume). In Israel, however, no choice is offered at universities between the two official languages. When higher education is at stake, the policy is monolingual and requires the use of Hebrew for all language functions.

All over the world, there is fear that English would replace regional, national and local languages that are currently linguae academicae even in contexts in which English is only taught as a subject (e.g. Latin America). Tollefson and Tsui (2004: 279) claim that 'in a unified Europe, an educational system using Slovene as the medium of instruction may not be able to compete with schools using English or other dominant languages'. In most contexts, it has been shown that the choice of a foreign medium of instruction for dominated groups is, from an educational and linguistic point of view, less than efficient, and often disastrous, except for a privileged elite. Still, this method of instruction through a foreign medium has been preferred in several countries against solid research results and the recommendations of various educational committees (Tollefson & Tsui, 2004).

This chapter is divided into two sections that examine, respectively, the language management and the attitudes, and the language practices that can be observed in the teaching and learning of arts and sciences at three of Israel's biggest universities: the Technion-Israel Institute of Technology, the Hebrew University of Jerusalem and Tel-Aviv University. Most of the data were collected in 2000 and 2001 for the author's doctoral dissertation (Ram, 2006) and were related to the language policy of the time at the universities in question. The documents and theses used as data and written before those years, however, will reflect Israeli language policy on writing in the decades previous to the year 2000. Data collected from interviews, observations and documents will be presented first and data obtained from a survey will follow.

Language Management and Linguistic Ideologies

This section focuses on management and ideologies regarding both the corpus and the status of languages in Israeli universities. The text examines the declared policy, hidden agendas (Shohamy, 2006) and legislation of the authorities responsible for university language management (Spolsky, 2004). To do this, the data collected for the author's dissertation (Ram, 2006) incorporated 12 student newsletters that publish language regulations each academic year, 32 course catalogues, 70 syllabuses, 12 tests, 4 documents describing the minutes of university senate meetings, the details of 3 addresses delivered by university authorities on special occasions (and relating in some way to language management), 13 documents describing the minutes of the Academy of the Hebrew Language (which is assigned the task of corpus planning) and publications by that academy, and interviews with 58 lecturers and heads of departments on the subject of language regulation. Some respondents were university senate members and others were both senate members and members of the Academy of the Hebrew Language. The secretary of the Office of Technological Terminology (OTT) at the Technion was also interviewed about the office's language management role at the university.

Cultivation of Hebrew and Limitations

When the Technion and the Hebrew University of Jerusalem first opened their doors in the 1920s, the Academy of the Hebrew Language created the, OTT to cater to their academic language needs. The OTT's various special committees or work groups began the task of creating Hebrew-language lexicons, coining the terms and words that teaching staff and students would use in lecture halls and in papers, and until the 1970s, the Technion Office's bulletins continued to publish Hebrew word lists, thus contributing actively to the university's academic language.

Between 1970 and 2001, however, the OTT was neglected: its on-campus premises were reduced to a single room staffed by just one secretary, and little work was done to update the Hebrew technical terms that were used in the university's courses. To save the office, the authorities recruited industrial engineer Shabtai Azriel, who gained the support of various governmental agencies, engaged the press and organised an emergency conference of Hebrew-speaking scientists and users of technical language in Hebrew. At the conference, held in 2001, the various threats to the OTT were evaluated and a plan for its recovery was proposed. In the period following this, the Technion's authorities and the Academy of the Hebrew Language reinstated the office, supplied it with new materials and logistic support and supported the activities of its work groups. These prepared a number of new lists of terms and went back to work on several technical dictionaries which had been abandoned in the previous decades and which, eventually, were published at the academy's own website (Azriel, 2006).

The committees' work at the Technion has increased ever since. The group responsible for technological terminology has recently published scientific word lists in Hebrew in the fields of chemical engineering, energy and modern physics (The Academy of the Hebrew Language, 2013). Since 2003, the academy has also created a number of new work groups, including a committee on zoology in 2005 and a committee on communication in 2009. The committee on medicine, for instance, operates within the academy. This group was active until 1999 and was then reinstated in 2003, when its objectives were to continue the work other groups had started in various disciplines that had been brought together in a medical dictionary in 1999. This particular committee aims to set terms in medical professions that were not discussed by previous committees and to propose Hebrew alternatives for academics and professional medics. The group is still active and in 2010 the academy approved a list of 219 new terms that it had compiled in the field of dermatology.

Among the members of the Academy of the Hebrew Language that were assigned by the government to regulate language matters are university staff members who believe that the status of Hebrew should be promoted and who have joined the committee in charge of coining new terms in academic disciplines. These university lecturers teach in Hebrew and some also publish in that language, producing texts that are mostly for instructional purposes (Ram, 2006).

From the policymakers working within universities and the state of play between proponents of Hebrew-only and Hebrew-plus-English language policies, we now turn to the question of policy making in written language.

Hebrew as a Compulsory Medium of Instruction

Ever since they were founded, universities have generally required their staff and students to use Hebrew for all language functions and to be competent readers of English. In the study this author conducted, this was stipulated in advertisements announcing job opportunities in administrative positions and in course catalogues for students. The study also indicated that each undergraduate must also demonstrate a satisfactory level of reading skills in Hebrew and English in standardised psychometric tests (this requirement is stated in course catalogues for students published between 1936 and 2001). Course catalogues typically stated that undergraduates who had not completed their university entrance examinations in Israel were expected to master Hebrew within a year of beginning their studies. Lecturers could teach in English in special programmes for students from the United States who studied in English, trained at Israeli hospitals and were planning to return to the United States upon graduation, and in MA and PhD degree courses at the Weizmann Institute of Science. The Academy of the Hebrew Language, located on-campus at the Hebrew University of Jerusalem, its special committees for terminology and the branch of its OTT at the Technion all catered to language needs so that Hebrew could serve as the medium of instruction.

In recent years, the study showed, pressure from lecturers at university senate meetings has slightly undermined the requirement to use only Hebrew for all language functions in writing, and the minutes of one of the senate meetings of 1982 at the Hebrew University of Jerusalem records the first documented attempt to alter language regulations regarding the writing of theses (*Homer liyshivat senat*, 1982). On that occasion, debate led to the addition of clauses allowing doctoral students to write their theses in 'a foreign language', although no language was actually named. Furthermore, the modification only applied to the dissertation, and research students were still obliged to complete other kinds of paper and also examinations and tests in Hebrew.

The second documented attempt to change language regulations occurred in 1994, again at the Hebrew University of Jerusalem, in the work of one of the senate's permanent committees (Ram, 2006). The committee proposed that students should be permitted to submit written papers in a language other than Hebrew (again, no language was actually named). At the time, further discussion was scheduled, but no resolution of that proposal has been documented either in the committee's minutes or in the minutes of the senate's own meetings. As of 2012, this university's course catalogues have published the original language requirement accompanied by an explanation that language choice may be granted upon a student's request and his or her lecturer's approval (*Shnaton Tahsab*, 2012, clause 8.1.51). Tel Aviv University's 2012 course catalogue republished the original requirement with the original phrasing (*Yedion halimudim lishnat tashab*, 2012), and although the Technion catalogue for the same year did not state that students were required to write in Hebrew (*Yedion musmahim tashag*, 2012: 39, clause 27.03), it did specify that the title of any student's thesis must be submitted in Hebrew and English. In this last case, one might conclude, the requirement to write in Hebrew was unstated but quite clearly there.

The third attempt to change university language policy occurred at a senate meeting at the Technion in 1995, when trends and policies for the coming years were being discussed, and when professor and senate member Dr P. Zinger made the proposal that curriculums should be tailored to suit the ongoing trends in internationalisation and globalisation and suggested, albeit indirectly, that English might be used as a medium of instruction in MA studies:

> The concept of *am levadad ishkon* ['a nation stands alone'] no longer holds. Even the US, which used to believe in this, now wishes to adopt the European plan. That plan requires MA students to take some of their degree subjects in another country. Cornell University is negotiating this idea with the Technion and has already signed such an agreement with Hamburg University so that lecturers there will teach in English. Speaking of internationalization and globalisation, one cannot ignore the fact that we are connected to the European community. (Zinger, 1995: 2)

Although his views were personal, by speaking out in this way Zinger highlighted the tension that existed between two groups of Technion lecturers: those who were in favour of using more English and those who wanted to see the application of a Hebrew-only language policy. Since the time of this meeting, the Technion's language regulations have not been modified as such, but two measures have been implemented: first, the teaching of a new course in academic writing in English, which is designed to improve MA students' English language skill; and second, the reinstatement of the OTT (practically inactive at the Technion since the 1970s due to lack of funds), which aims to improve the status of Hebrew at the university by increasing its use among academics. These two measures of foreign language learning on the one hand and language cultivation of a local, formal language on the other reflect an ecology of language perspective according to which language rights are recognised alongside encouraging the use of a foreign language for particular communication domains (Phillipson & Skutnabb-Kangas, 1996; Spolsky & Hult, 2008; Tsuda, 1994).

The data indicate that while the requirement to use Hebrew as a medium of university instruction has remained constant since the 1970s, the policies determining which language is to be used in written expression have been modified in such a way that English may now be used for writing dissertations.

The text of the regulations for research students published in 1996 at the Hebrew University of Jerusalem and at Tel Aviv University indicates that the requirement to write theses in Hebrew is in line with university senate resolutions of 1982, where an option to write in a recent foreign language was proposed, though under specified conditions (translated from the original):

> The thesis should be written in the Hebrew language, but in special cases the Chairman of the Committee may allow it to be written in a foreign language as well, on the conditions that this is recommended by the thesis supervisor and that there are referees who master the foreign language in question.

The original text, which appeared in *Takanon halimudim letalmidey mehkar* [The regulation of studies for research students] and *Shnaton hafakulta lematematika ulemada'ey hateva tashnaz* [The regulation of studies for the Faculty of Mathematics and Natural Science], both of 1996, and in *Yedion latalmidim tashnu* [The regulation of studies for students], 1995–1996, was particularly significant in one respect. Where other senate resolutions described the conditions in which language choice became possible, this text actually named the authorities on which that choice depended (the committee chairman and the supervisor) and indicated that authority in language matters was effectively in the hands of the lecturers who supervised research students or with the heads of teaching committees. Note, too, that this regulation was not congruent with the senate decisions of 1994, which maintained the requirement to use Hebrew.

Until 2000, the Hebrew University of Jerusalem course catalogue stated that students should write in Hebrew and accompanied this by an explanation of the conditions needed for students to write in English. In 2001, a revised version of the text no longer stated that students should seek permission to write in English, but still required all theses to be submitted in Hebrew (paragraph 1 of the text at *Shnaton hafakulta lematematika ulemada'ey hateva* translates roughly as follows: 'As a rule the thesis should be written in Hebrew. An elaborate abstract in Hebrew should be attached to a thesis written in English.' [*Shnaton hafakulta lematematika ulemada'ey hateva*, 2001: 41]). The revision, we might argue, reflects a basic shift in attitude and a willingness to contemplate both Hebrew and English, even while the two languages remained mutually exclusive. This removal of strictures on English language use in scientific writing could reflect a kind of institutional readiness to facilitate science writing in that language; it could suggest that in the sciences there was no perceived need for restrictions on writing in English and that English and Hebrew were given equal status in MA science studies.

The attempts to change the Hebrew-only policy, and particularly in the written medium, reveal that under the 'still waters' of monolingual policy there are struggles between various agents operating in the field of language management at universities, each holding to its beliefs. The agents and their beliefs are introduced in the next section.

Agents in University Language Management and Their Beliefs

Four different agents manage language use in Israel's universities and they are presented in the order of their proximity to state authorities from the closest to the most remote, the first is an entity of state and the last is an individual agent: the Israeli Ministry of Education, the Academy of the Hebrew Language, the university senates and university lecturers.

Language management and beliefs within the Ministry of Education

The Ministry of Education is not directly involved in setting language policy at universities, yet it is involved in setting admission criteria for universities and managing examinations that are a prerequisite for admission. Admission to universities is currently dependent on achieving required scores in matriculation examinations and psychometric examinations – the latter were recently referred to by the Minister of Education as redundant. Since competence in Hebrew and English is essential for success in the pre-university examinations, the Ministry of Education invests in teaching and testing both Hebrew and English in high school. Moreover, the Ministry of Education has focused its ongoing efforts to promote the status of learning and teaching English as a foreign language in all grades in the school system for the purpose of achieving language competence in English that would serve the academic needs of students and lecturers.

In 2013, education ministers of Israel and Britain signed an agreement to cooperate and promote English studies in Israel. The English curriculum has been changed several times since 1996 in order to adjust the goals of teaching English to the demands of higher education and globalisation (Ministry of Education, 2001). In the updated revised English curriculum as of November 2013 (Ministry of Education, 2013), it is stated that speakers of Hebrew or Arabic will need to be able to use both spoken and written English in order to progress in their professional, business or academic careers. A new component was added to the English curriculum and matriculation examinations in English – higher-order thinking skills related to English literature. This component requires high-proficiency skills in the English language and has been added to the revised curriculum in order to promote learners' understanding and critical thinking skills (Ministry of Education, 2009) and their manifestation in the foreign language. It could be that the addition of higher-order thinking skills in a foreign language is expected to lead to better academic success for learners and better language competence in the written medium in English. Another evidence for the ministry's intent to promote learners' language skills in English is the ministry's attempt in 1998 to teach two school subjects in English: music and gymnastics in several schools, but due to resistance, this initiative hasn't taken place. Recently, under the concept of content language integrated learning (CLIL), which means teaching a school subject in English, the ministry is attempting to have schools teach several school subjects in English, but this initiative hasn't yet taken place in schools.

Language management and beliefs within the Academy of the Hebrew Language

According to the academy's law of 1952, the Israeli Ministry of Education entrusts the academy with corpus planning. As explained in the section 'Cultivation of Hebrew', as reported by Dr Irmay, former OTT head of office and public relations of the Technion during an interview held in Haifa in 2000, corpus planning is currently being implemented, even though a large corpus of Hebrew terms that could be used for modern academic functions already exists. However, because of the increased presence of English in the academic world at an international level, Hebrew terms have to compete with their more widely used English equivalents, and academy members, therefore, point to the need to defend Hebrew and maintain its purity. Minutes of the academy's meetings during the 1980s and 1990s indicate that on several occasions suggestions were made to take action to counterbalance English, and one of these was taken up by an academy member (Ben-Haim, 1992: 142).

Today, however, the academy's members actually consider that their responsibilities should include status planning and language defence:

> Being a member of the Academy of the Hebrew Language does not simply mean having the honour to preside over an institution of higher education; it means attempting to mould language into its proper form and assigning it its proper status in everyday life. (Translated from *Zichronot ha'Academya* [the Academy's proceedings], 1992: 74)

Lecturer and professor members still actively defend the status of Hebrew for two reasons: the increased presence of English in the academic world at an international level and the weakening of Zionist ideology within university senates. University senates are perceived as no longer maintaining an inseparable relation between nation and language, and no longer supporting Hebrew-language use for all language functions as was decided when the first Hebrew universities were founded.

During the 1980s and 1990s, some academy members also felt the need to defend Hebrew from the effects of mass immigration and from what they perceived as the academy's own laissez-faire policy (Martel, 2001, *Zichronot ha'academya*, 1992: 81). These members considered that Hebrew's status was being undermined by internal problems and by the increasing presence in the Hebrew language of foreign words (or *laaz*) (*Zichronot ha'academya*, 1992: 81) and they expressed concern about how English was undermining Hebrew and the little resistance that the supposed guardians of the nation's language were making. No measures against the expansion of English were actually taken, though proposals were made on various occasions (*Zichronot ha'academya*, 1992: 81). In conclusion, the notion of activism in the preservation of Hebrew language rights was present as a group view but not as a line of action.

The question of language rights was raised at the academy's 187th meeting in 1989 (*Zihronot ha'academya*, 1992: 75–81), which discussed at length Hebrew's condition as a language languishing under the shadow of 'almighty English'. International English was declared to be an alien 'force of evil' and a threat to Hebrew, and the increasing presence of English in the academic world was variously described as 'cultural colonialism', 'American cultural imperialism' and the 'Americanisation of language and culture throughout the world' (*Zichronot ha'academya*, 1992: 79). Such beliefs represent a hierarchical model where languages compete, rather than an ecological perspective of networks and connections between languages.

A proposal to take action in the field of status planning was put forward by professor and academy member Mr Dotan, who contended that English was winning the language war and that this was reflected in the diminishing interest in Hebrew taken by the general public, especially the educated public. '*Laaz* is being used everywhere', he said, thus referring to the use of the English language in higher education 'and its fortress is higher education. *Laaz* is winning the language war these days and it is the Academy's task to fight this; it is the Academy's task to direct the growth of the Hebrew language' (translated from the minutes of the *Halashon ha'ivrit* [the Hebrew Language Committee], 1990: 205). On another occasion, it was also proposed that the Israeli Education Minister should be sent a formal memorandum regarding his and the ministry's role in the state's instruction in Hebrew (*Zichronot ha'academya*, 1992: 81).

As the Academy of the Hebrew Language sees it, the Ministry of Education actually promotes the use of English as a medium of instruction at universities and has, in recent years, encouraged its presence in the state's new academic institutions (see the observation made by academy member Mr Broyda in *Zichronot ha'academya*, 1992: 76, on the Israeli deputy prime minister's proposal to found a state-level English-language university).

In fact, the academy considers that both the university senates and the ministry promote 'anglo-bilingualism', and in its 218th meeting in 1998, it condemned a ministry proposal to launch pilot music and gymnastics classes in English in a small group of schools to determine whether students' English language skills could be improved. Instead, it proposed, the government should find ways to improve students' English skill that would not undermine the status of Hebrew, such as additional English language classes in schools or preparatory university courses (see the proposal made by academy member Mr Morag in *Zihronot ha'academya*, 1998: 201).

Finally, the academy also considers that the ministry uses its financial weight to exert greater power, choosing where it allocates money and resources, as this observation on its allocation of money to the Weizmann Institute of Science indicates: 'And it would have been so easy to prevent this [the use of English as a medium of instruction] had the law enforcement authorities allocating most of that institution's budget required Israeli lecturers to deliver their lectures in Hebrew' (Blau, 1988: 39). Budget decisions, especially state or government driven, should reflect language policy and should cultivate Hebrew, according to this view.

Language management and beliefs within university senates

Minutes of meetings and other documents pertaining to university senates have indicated that senates, whose members are senior professors of various disciplines and who meet regularly to discuss academic matters, are active in language management (*Homer liyshivat senat*, 1982): the minutes list the issues discussed and resolutions are then published in course catalogues and informal administrative documents. The regulations published in course catalogues also reflect the involvement of the senates in status planning. Finally, the minutes of their meetings also indicate that this authority, like the academy, discusses language choice.

The data collected suggest that the university senates are, in fact, the authority that most clearly drafts the rules of practice and that each university independently implements language policy within departments and even within degree courses. There is evidence that university senates are active language managers, especially in the field of status planning, and that they discuss choices and issue regulations. Furthermore, university senates are perceived to be an influential authority by the academy.

In terms of their attitudes towards language use, the senates are divided and do not uniformly support the system's traditional monolingual policy. Some senate members support a Hebrew-plus-English language policy and the use of English in writing, and would like to assign autonomy of language choice to lecturers. Observing the period of history that led up to the 1990s, one lecturer at the Hebrew University of Jerusalem proposed that forcing students to write just in Hebrew was unfair because it prevented them from getting practice in real academic writing. Describing the situation, however, the same lecturer also explained the following (translated from the original):

> [There was] conflict and bitter discussion at senate meetings over the subject of the language to be used for writing theses and it was strictly forbidden to write in anything but Hebrew unless the dissertation dealt with another language. In recent years the authorities are bending more and permission to write in English is being granted. (Ram, 2006)

Then, there is the case of a lecturer in natural science at the Technion who wanted to teach in English but was forced to adhere to the regulations of the academy (whose members she referred to as 'those stubborn mules' and whose resistance at senate meetings obstructed the modifications of decisions on language choice). This particular lecturer's report clearly described the two opposing fronts that were present within the senate: on the one hand, the Hebraists, who were either academy members or other, like-minded defenders of language rights; and on the other, those who would favour the complementary use of English as a medium of instruction in natural sciences.

Either way, why should there be this disagreement within university senates? Differing character and conflicting agendas may explain part of it. Differences in age and background may compound the disagreement, given that some lecturers are younger professionals who graduated in English-speaking countries while their older colleagues belong to the generation who founded Israeli higher education and are academy stalwarts and determined defenders of Hebrew. Finally, there are also the ideological factors: according to one party of senate members, the current status of Hebrew in Israel is such that it requires no protection and faces no threat from English, whereas other members wish to preserve the status quo.

Language management and beliefs of university lecturers

Although this group overlaps with the academy and the university senates (some lecturers are also academy members, members of university senates or holders of administrative or academic positions within universities), it should still be considered as a separate force. In the study, this was made clear in interviews with the university lecturers (Ram, 2006).

In the interviews with lecturers conducted during the study, almost three quarters of the respondents (74% of them, see Figure 5.1) favoured Hebrew as a medium of instruction and chose Hebrew when asked which of the two languages they would prefer to teach in. Only 16% expressed a desire to use English as their medium of instruction (the language they

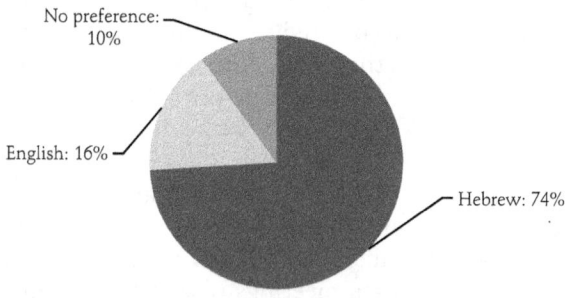

Figure 5.1 Lecturers' language preference (*n*=58)

actually used at the time was Hebrew) and 10% had no language preference at all.

This finding is particularly interesting in the context of a Hebrew-only language policy. If most lecturers chose Hebrew as a medium of instruction, as Figure 5.1 indicates, there may not actually be a need for top-down language management. And as Figure 5.2 indicates, lecturers' choices were not ideological but pragmatic inasmuch as they chose the language that best served the purpose of instruction. If this was Hebrew, then they favoured Hebrew; if English could serve the goals of learning better than Hebrew could, they favoured English. When lecturers were asked to give reasons for their language choice, 38% provided a pragmatic rationale. Of the pragmatists, 12% thought Hebrew would facilitate student learning and the remaining 26% considered Hebrew to be the most prominent and widely used language of the state (comments included 'Hebrew is the language of Israel', 'Hebrew is the native tongue of most students' and 'English would serve students' future needs better'). A total of 22% of lecturers based their language preference on which language they felt more comfortable working in (i.e. on their own level of language skill) and 16% adopted an ideological position from which they defended the symbolic value of Hebrew. Finally, 24% of respondents voiced a combination of several of the reasons mentioned above.

We might conclude that lecturers have a deeply rooted preference for Hebrew as their medium of instruction and that this stems from ideological reasons or from personal or pragmatic reasons regarding their own level of language skills. None related this preference to the fact that university regulations stipulated the use of Hebrew. Nobody's explanation was that they did as they were told or as they were required to do. It is even arguable that these lecturers would have taught in Hebrew even

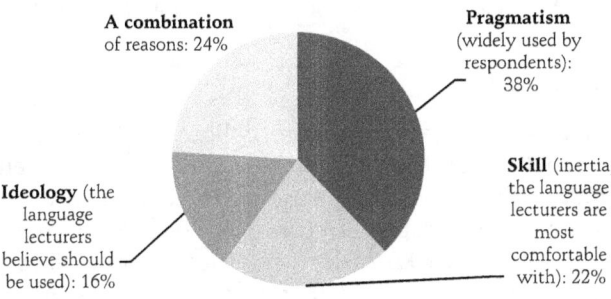

Figure 5.2 Lecturers' reasons for their language preference (*n*=58)

if they hadn't been obliged to. In other words, Hebrew appears to serve pragmatic reasons, is widely used in academic domains and stands as the language that most lecturers and students feel competent in.

It appears that the four language agents of language management do not present a united front. They pose various conflicting interests. The Ministry of Education would like to see English being more widely used, the academy supports a Hebrew-only language policy, and would like the ministry to influence language choice by allocating money to universities that implement a Hebrew-only policy. University senates use their weight to create systems of language choice. Among senate members there are Hebraists as well as globalists who support the use of English to some extent, and most lecturers are pragmatists and would therefore use Hebrew as the medium of instruction.

Language Practice: Results from the Survey

This section analyses a series of data including student examinations, syllabuses, newsletters, information bulletins and other publicly posted material, advertisements and dissertations to determine the language policy actually implemented in Israeli universities. In the study, which was conducted at the three universities, the Technion, the Hebrew University of Jerusalem and Tel Aviv University, a total of 58 lecturers were interviewed, and 200 questionnaires were completed by students enrolled in BA and MA degree courses in the four subject areas of biology, education, medicine and philosophy. Twelve lectures were also observed in those four subject areas.

By and large, Hebrew and English were used bilingually in all subject areas from the first year of studies onwards. Lecturers and students, however, reported in questionnaires that English was only occasionally used, mainly for reading and for writing dissertations and mostly in MA and PhD degree courses in the two sciences, biology and medicine.

Lecturer's practices

Lecturers reported that they were obliged to be bilingual because they needed English for their research and Hebrew for their teaching. This is corroborated by the data below on the extent to which lecturers used English for writing papers, lecturing at conferences and conducting research. Approximately 90% of lecturers also reported that they rarely published papers in Hebrew and three quarters of those interviewed had published at least two English-language papers in international journals during the year in which the interviews were held.

About three quarters of the lecturers interviewed had attended at least two conferences in English in the year 2000 and a similar proportion had lectured in English at international conferences at least twice in that year. Only one third of the total had attended conferences in Hebrew, and in most cases where respondents had lectured in Hebrew, they had done this only once. More than half had reviewed at least two English-language articles. Approximately 90% were collaborating with colleagues in writing and conducting research and about 60% reported an English-language collaboration with more than one colleague. About three quarters of the respondents had collaborated with colleagues from abroad and approximately half had undertaken one or more than one collaborative project with colleagues from abroad in the year leading up to the interview. All those collaborative projects had produced papers written in English.

About 80% of lecturers had read at least three English-language articles in their field in the two weeks before the interview and, in the week leading up to the interview, a similar percentage had received more than 20 work-related English-language email messages. With regard to the medium of instruction in their own studies as students, the 43 lecturers who had studied at universities in Israel were asked about the language of instruction that they had received and about the language they had used to read and write. From their reports, it is clear that much of the reading material in their MA and PhD studies had been in English (all reported that almost all or all of the reading material related to their studies had been in English). About half of the lecturers who had studied in Israel had written their doctoral thesis in Hebrew (these had been written in the 1970s, 1980s and 1990s). Approximately half of the lecturers had written their thesis in English, but most of those who had written their thesis in English had not graduated from an Israeli university.

Turning to lecturers' medium of instruction, the respondents generally reported using Hebrew as the written medium in examinations and assignments. Only 2% of lecturers assigned written tasks in English to BA students while approximately 90% assigned written tasks in Hebrew. Again, in MA courses, few lecturers assigned written tasks in English while about 90% assigned written tasks only in Hebrew. The lecturers' reports would therefore suggest that the common practice was to teach in Hebrew and for students to write in that language.

In examinations, almost all lecturers reported using Hebrew as the medium of instruction and only a few administered examinations in English. Approximately 90% of lecturers assigned end-of-year papers in Hebrew in BA and MA degree courses. Only a few respondents assigned such evaluative tasks in English or in both languages or did not mind whether the papers were written in Hebrew or English.

In class, lecturers used Hebrew as their oral medium. As for teaching practices, only a few reported having taught a BA course in English and about 90% taught in Hebrew. A few lecturers did not teach any BA course and therefore had nothing to report. As for MA courses, few lecturers used English as their medium of instruction; and again, approximately 90% taught only in Hebrew.

Lecturers used Hebrew and English as the written media to compose syllabuses and support thesis writing. Approximately 80% of lecturers reported that most of the texts in the reading lists they gave their BA students were in English, and almost all the lecturers reported that most of the texts in the lists they gave their MA students were in English. The remaining respondents may have been lecturers in the arts and in education, where there sources were in Hebrew. As for the language in which syllabuses were written, approximately 80% reported writing their syllabuses mostly in Hebrew, while 10% wrote their syllabuses in English and the remaining 10% wrote their BA syllabuses in Hebrew and their MA syllabuses in English.

Did lecturers' practices vary by university or was there an overall tendency to use English for writing and Hebrew for speaking? Were practices in the sciences similar to practices in the arts? The practices described above were examined at each of the three universities from which the data had been retrieved and were then compared. A cross tabulation of the universities by each characteristic was computed and a chi-squared test was used to examine the significance of the relationship. No practice was significantly associated with one of the universities and not with the others. For the purpose of the following analysis, the five faculties in each university (medicine, biology, exact sciences, philosophy and education) were distributed in two categories: sciences and arts. The sciences and arts categories were then compared in terms of the practices described above. A cross tabulation of universities by each characteristic was computed and a chi-squared test was used to examine the significance of the relationship. Again, no practice was significantly associated with one of the universities and not with the others.

A further comparison was made between Israeli Hebrew-speaking lecturers who were Weizmann Institute of Science alumni and Israeli Hebrew-speaking lecturers who had studied at other Israeli universities, where there was a difference in the language the lecturers had used to write their dissertation. Approximately 80% of the Weizmann Institute of Science alumni had written their dissertation in English, compared with only 10%

in the case of graduates from other universities ($\chi^2=16.61$, $p<0.001$). This suggests that, as a rule and excluding the Weizmann Institute of Science, theses were written in Hebrew.

As far as oral instruction is concerned, the study collected data from the class activity in 12 BA lectures, all given by respondents who had allowed their lectures to be observed for the purposes of evaluating how far English was spoken in class or how far English-language terms were used. The only moments in which the lecturers engaged in code-switching occurred when a lecturer could have used a widely recognised term in Hebrew. Of the 14 lectures, four were in the subject area of medicine (two such lectures were observed at Tel Aviv University) and four in biology (again, two lectures in this subject area were observed, this time at the Hebrew University of Jerusalem). Rather unexpectedly, in three of the lectures in medicine, English terms were used very little (fewer than 10 were mentioned), while their use in three lectures in biology was much more frequent (more than 15 terms were mentioned). In the lectures in philosophy, there was very little use of English and there was almost no English at all in the lecture on education. Since the sample was rather small, however, the author would prefer to remain tentative in her conclusions.

In the classes observed, the lecturers taught in Hebrew when the students were Hebrew speakers, but in three of the four subject areas used English-language slide and presentation programmes. Administrative staff, it would appear, do not use English for any academic function, even though the on-campus presence of English in some of the publicly posted material addressed to students (see above) indicates that, when it comes to language choices, university administrations take a practical approach to their job and to the student body they serve.

Finally, it should be noted, a small number of academic institutions do use English as their principal medium of instruction. These tend to be institutions that offer MA degree courses, such as the Weizmann Institute of Science and the medical schools at the Technion, the Hebrew University of Jerusalem and Tel Aviv University (the medical school at this last university offers a programme for students from New York). And English is also used as the medium of instruction when visiting lecturers do not speak Hebrew or when universities host research students on exchange programmes organised by the Israeli Ministry of Foreign Affairs (Sher, head of the Office for Foreign Students, 2001, personal communication).

Generally speaking, the lecturers' reports on their language practices and the data coming from observation revealed an overall pattern in which English was used for career advancement and Hebrew was used for instructional purposes and this pattern was visible in all three universities. At the same time, however, lecturers believed that their language choice was determined by the demands of each study area or subject and that English was therefore more widely used in science subjects than in arts. The data obtained from the questionnaires completed by students corroborate this finding.

Students' practices

BA students in their first, second and third year of study in all four subject areas (biology, education, medicine and philosophy) reported on how much reading and writing they were required to do in English. Figure 5.3 describes the frequencies of all dependent variables for the whole sample. The variables that relate to reading describe how much reading English students were required to do, whether they actually read or not and how they handled the reading, and whether they read on their own or sought assistance (see 'Reading'). Thesis papers were also identified in the questionnaire and students were asked about the language of recommended reading lists (see 'R. lists'), written assignments ('Ass. 1' – courses with assignments in English and 'Ass. 3' – use of assistance in written assignments in English), examinations ('Exam.'), lectures ('Lect.') and syllabuses ('Syllab.').

The data in Figure 5.3 indicate that English was prevalent in the reading lists in most subjects for nearly 80% of students, which corroborates lecturers' reports. About half of the student respondents reported a significant requirement to read in English and about half sought assistance

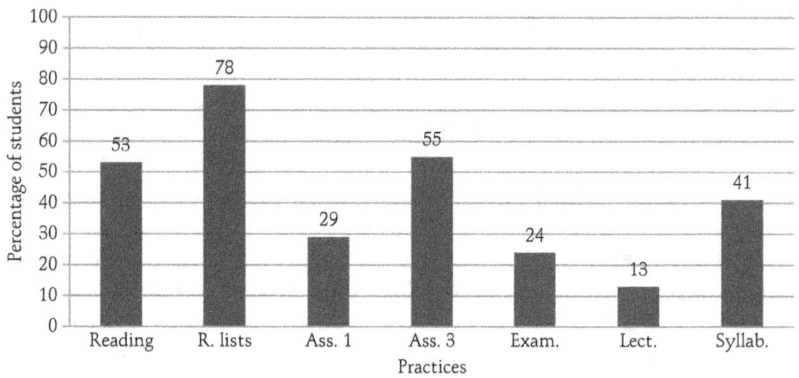

Figure 5.3 The prevalence of English in reading and writing activities

for their English-language reading and writing tasks. Approximately 40% of students reported that English was prevalent in the syllabus in most subjects. Only one quarter of the students received English-language assignments or examinations and only 10% took courses taught in English. These frequencies may suggest that approximately 80% of students encountered English mostly in their reading lists, and about half read without assistance when required to read in English. However, interviews with first-year, BA science students at Tel Aviv University revealed that although English was prevalent in reading materials, students could generally avoid reading in English because the lectures that examined these materials were delivered in Hebrew. Generally, students reported that English was only minimally present in syllabuses, written assignments and examinations; however, they reported that it was more prevalent than lecturers did.

To examine whether language choice and the year of study were related, our study cross-tabulated each measure according to the year of study. The years of study were distributed in two categories: the first three years of study were grouped in the category 'BA' and the fourth and all subsequent years were grouped in the category 'MA and PhD'. Chi-squared tests were used to examine the significance of the relationship and the only measure that yielded a significant result was 'assignment' ($\chi^2=6.74$, $p<0.01$). Courses in which English-language assignments were required were more frequent in MA and PhD degree programs, where they represented 41% of the total, than in BA degree programs/curricula, where they represented only 23% of the total.

To examine whether language choice and subject area were related, our study cross-tabulated each measure according to faculty (as indicated above, the five faculties chosen in all three universities were medicine, biology, philosophy, education and exact sciences). After an initial analysis of frequencies, these were distributed in two categories: arts and sciences (see Figure 5.4).

R1: The percentage of students who were required to read in English (any source – an article or a book) at least one source per course.
R2: The percentage of students who were required to read extensively one source in English every week.
R3: The percentage of students actually handling or performing the reading assignment).
R4: The percentage of students autonomous in reading (not getting assistance).
Requirement: a combination of the amount of reading required and the success in performing the reading assignment in percentages.

The data in Figure 5.4 indicate that the experience of language choice in arts and sciences differed in most aspects. Approximately 40% of sciences students were required to read in English, while only 10% of arts students reported the same requirement (see R1). Approximately half of the sciences students also reported the requirement to read extensively in English, while only one quarter of arts students reported the same (R2). As for the actual handling of reading and writing assignments, more than half of the sciences students were able to complete reading assignments successfully, while this was only true for less than half of the arts students (R3). Approximately 80% of sciences students reported completing written assignments in English on their own, while 70% of arts students reported the same (R4). In the overall measure of reading that calculated measures R1 to R4 all together (Requirement), sciences and arts students differed significantly (60% and 30%, respectively) and this difference related to both the amount of reading required and the degree to which that requirement was successfully handled.

Finally, the linguistic evolution of doctoral theses was also subject to analysis. Recall that in this respect, two different language management procedures had been identified. The first was congruent with the regulation enforcing the use of Hebrew in speaking and writing. The second procedure performed by lecturers was to allow students to write their thesis in English, using the authority that had been granted to them in 1994 (Hafakulta Lerefua al shem Reymond ve Beverly Sackler, 1995). Had this change in policy led to an increase in the number of theses written in English?

The study examined a total of 100 theses written by students in the three universities surveyed (the Technion, the Hebrew University of Jerusalem and Tel-Aviv University) and in the four subject areas in question (biology, education, medicine and philosophy). All the theses that were written in

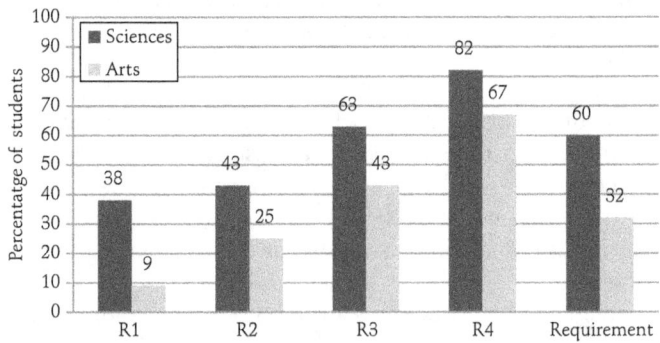

Figure 5.4 Measures of reading in English among arts and sciences students

Hebrew included an abstract in English. A total of 92% of the theses written at the Technion followed this pattern and only 8% were in English. A total of 83% of the theses written at the Hebrew University of Jerusalem were written in Hebrew and 17% were written in English. Finally, 95% of the theses presented in Tel Aviv University were written in Hebrew and only 5% were in English.

To summarise, three major findings relate to student practices. The first concerns the amount of English that students used in their studies, where over half of the students reported both a requirement to read in English and the ability to complete the requirement without seeking assistance. English was used mainly for reading relevant literature, especially in scientific subjects, and reading literature in English increased from one year of study to another. Reading literature in English was most prevalent in the two subject areas in the sciences category (biology and medicine) than in the two subject areas in the arts category (education and philosophy). The second finding relates to the extent to which English was used and the year of study, where the use of English was seen to increase from one year to the next, but only in written assignments (only 20% of BA students submitted English-language written assignments, while approximately 40% of MA students did the same). The use of English for writing theses was minimal and increased in MA and PhD degree courses. The third finding relates faculty (distributed in the categories arts and sciences) and the use of English, where sciences students were observed to use English more than arts students did, and where this more intensive use was mainly exemplified in the requirement to read in English.

Three patterns of Hebrew and English as mediums of university instruction

In addition to the data obtained through lecturers' and students' reports, actual representations of language choice in the written medium were examined. These included sample syllabuses, lecture transcripts, examinations, theses and public announcements. Three patterns of language choice were identified, the most prevalent being the unmarked pattern Hebrew-plus-English, and the other two being the marked patterns in which only English or only Hebrew were used. Table 5.1 describes the three patterns of practice observed and the language functions these patterns were used for.

The Hebrew-plus-English pattern, mostly Hebrew with English to some extent, prevailed in the lecture halls of all three universities in examinations, syllabuses and theses, and in administrative announcements and informative leaflets on the subject of conferences. The Hebrew-only pattern was used in all lectures in the subject area of education and in most lectures in biology,

Table 5.1 Patterns of Hebrew and of English as mediums of university instruction

	Hebrew only	Hebrew-plus-English	English-only
Oracy: the oral medium	Most lectures in biology, medicine, philosophy and education Some lectures at local conferences	[Some lectures in biology and medicine and in philosophy]	Few lectures, mostly given by visiting professors or to students in exchange programmes Lectures at conferences overseas and some lectures at local conferences Special programmes for overseas students (medicine) MA and PhD programmes at the WIS
Literacy: the written medium	Local correspondence A few publications of lecturers	Syllabuses Announcements Posters Theses Examinations	Lecturers' publications Reading lists in some syllabuses in the sciences Lecturers' email correspondence with overseas colleagues Slide presentations in lectures in the sciences and arts Few posters and announcements

medicine and philosophy. Hebrew was used at some conferences held in Israel. Hebrew was also used by administrative staff to correspond with academic staff and among Hebrew-speaking lecturers in Israel. Except in the subject area of education, English was used exclusively in the written medium in lecturers' slide presentations in class (where written materials taken from English-language books were also projected) and in their published research. The following observations corroborate the arguments presented above by providing examples of these three patterns of language choice.

As observed above, the Hebrew-plus-English pattern was the most prevalent across the four subject areas for all degree courses in the written medium. With regard to publicly posted material in the universities themselves, however, this study found that the pattern varied. On the one hand, any visitor entering a building on any of the campuses of the three universities might see posted material that made use of both Hebrew and English, like the poster shown in Picture 5.1 (in which the title in Hebrew translates as 'A rationale for the teaching of sciences as inter-disciplinary academic subjects').

On the other hand, for example, it was also observed that public announcements posted in the Faculty of Humanities and Art at the Technion were mostly in Hebrew and that, at the time of the study, only two advertisements out of 24 were in English. At the Faculty of Graduate Studies at the Technion, however, English was integrated into the Hebrew text of some announcements, with staff notifications being published in Hebrew only but announcements to students combining the two languages. Finally, in the faculty's registration board, all the titles of announcements were written in Hebrew while the announcements themselves were written in English. One of the announcements in English was for a PhD course in scientific writing in English.

In any case, what does seem clear is that in general terms the current practice at universities is for students to use English mainly for reading and for lecturers to use it for reading and for writing their own papers.

Summary and Conclusions

The findings that relate to the oral and written medium of language practice in higher education in Israel implied that Hebrew, one of the two official languages in Israel – Hebrew and Arabic – maintains its status as lingua academica in the local context. Hebrew is widely used in most lecture halls, is the favoured medium of instruction of most lecturers and is widely used in theses. Hebrew has been and is still cultivated by legislation and state support through the Academy of the Hebrew Language, probably a prerequisite for maintaining the status of any medium-sized language as a lingua academica (Vila, 2013). The use of English, the undisputed academic

Picture 5.1 Example of a poster in Hebrew and English. Photograph taken at the Department of Teaching of the Sciences, School of Education, Tel-Aviv University, April 2002. (Title in Hebrew means: A rationale for the teaching of sciences as interdisciplinary academic subjects)

lingua franca in the time of globalisation and scientific dissemination, is limited to academic functions where English is the default case – literature and publications, and communication with scholars worldwide.

At the turn of the 21st century, Hebrew maintains its dominant status in Israeli higher education even while English is gaining ground in the written medium in most academic subject areas. The coexistence of Hebrew and English in the university system is expressed in that system's language management, the attitudes of its language managers and the practices of its lecturers and students. Current practice is multifold, although assessments conflict: the Academy of the Hebrew Language proposes that English has entered almost every academic subject area in all the study cycles (BA, MA and PhD), while lecturers and students contend that Hebrew is the common medium of instruction and that the use of English is mainly restricted to the literature in the sciences and the arts. Lecture observations and sample examinations, theses, syllabuses, written assignments and public announcements point to three patterns of language practice (see Table 5.1), of which Hebrew-plus-English appears to be the most prevalent.

Where might Hebrew stand as a medium-sized language in an 'ecology of language' paradigm? This author argues that Hebrew remains the main medium of instruction and communication in all academic spheres except for language functions that require the use or knowledge of English as a lingua franca, access to and writing for international publications, and communicating with colleagues and students who have not mastered Hebrew. And this functional allocation, where a medium-sized language is used for all local academic functions but not for global academic functions, reflects linguistic sustainability in a globalised academic sphere.

References

Ammon, U. (2001) English as a future language of teaching at German universities? A question of difficult consequences, posed by the decline of German as the language of science. In U. Ammon (ed.) *The Dominance of English as a Language of Science. Effects on Other Languages and Language Communities* (pp. 343–362). Berlin: Mouton de Gruyter.

Azriel, S. (2006) *Mihtav hamlatsa me'et hamerkaz haisraeli leminuah maday technologi* [A letter of recommendation from the Israeli Centre for Scientific and Technological Terminology] (in Hebrew). See www.azriel.co.il/modules (accessed 4 February 2006).

Ben-Haim, Z. (1992) *Bemilhamta shel lashon*. (Language war). Jerusalem. *Ha'Academya Lalashon Ha'ivrit. Hamahon Letipuah Ha'ivrit*. (The Academy of the Hebrew Language, The Institute of Developing Hebrew) (in Hebrew).

Blau, J. (1988) The 186th Meeting of the Academy of the Hebrew Language, In *Zichronot ha'akademya lalashon ha'ivrit lamedhe – Lamedvav – Lamedzayin Lashanim Hatashmah, Hatashmat, Hatashan*. (1992). Jerusalem. *Ha'akademya Lalashon Ha'ivrit Hatashnab, Dfus Graph-Peres*. (Records of the Academy of the Hebrew Language, 36–37 of the years 1988–1990) (in Hebrew).

Hafakulta Lerefua Al Shem Reymond ve Beverly Sakler (1993) *Yedion latalmidim tashnab*. (1993–1994). Tel Aviv: Tel Aviv University (Course catalogue for students, School of Medicine, Tel Aviv University) (in Hebrew).

Hafakulta Lerefua Al Shem Reymond ve Beverly Sakler (1995) *Yedion latalmidim tashnab*. (1995–1996). Tel Aviv: Tel Aviv University (Course catalogue for students, School of Medicine, Tel Aviv University) (in Hebrew).

Hafakulta Lemada'ey Haruah Al Shem Lester ve Sally Antin. Beit Hasefer Lehinuh (1995) *Yedion latalmidim tashnu*. (1995–1996). Tel Aviv: Tel Aviv University (Course catalogue for students, Faculty of Humanities, School of Education, Tel Aviv University) (in Hebrew).

Hafakulta Lemada'ey Haruah Al Shem Lester ve Sally Antin. Beit Hasefer Lehinuh (1997) *Yedion latalmidim tashnu*. (1997–1998). Tel Aviv: Tel Aviv University (Course catalogue for students, Faculty of Humanities, School of Education, Tel Aviv University) (in Hebrew).

Hafakulta Lemada'ey Haruah Al Shem Lester ve Sally Antin. Beit Hasefer Lehinuh (1998) *Yedion latalmidim tashnu*. (1998–1999). Tel Aviv: Tel Aviv University (Course catalogue for students, Faculty of Humanities, School of Education, Tel Aviv University) (in Hebrew).

Hafakulta Lemada'im Meduyakim Al Shem Reymond ve Beverly Sakler (1999) *Yedion latalmidim tashas.* (1999–2000). Tel Aviv: Tel Aviv University (Course catalogue for students, Faculty of Exact Sciences, Tel Aviv University) (in Hebrew).
Hafakulta Leumanuyot Al Shem Yolanda ve David Katz (1999) *Yedion latalmidim tashas* (1999–2000). Tel Aviv: Tel Aviv University (Course catalogue for students, Faculty of Arts, Tel Aviv University) (in Hebrew).
Hafakulta Lemada'ey Hahayim Al Shem George C. Weise (2000) *Yedion latalmidim tashsa* (2000–2001). Tel Aviv: Tel Aviv University (Course catalogue for students, Faculty of Natural Sciences, Tel Aviv University) (in Hebrew).
Hafakulta Lemada'ey Haruah Al Shem Lester ve Sally Antin. Beit Hasefer Lehinuh (2000) *Yedion latalmidim tashsa* (2000). Tel Aviv: Tel Aviv University (Course catalogue for students, 2001/2002, Faculty of Humanities, School of Education, Tel Aviv University) (in Hebrew).
Hafakulta Lehandasa Al Shem Ibi ve Alder Fleishman (2000) *Yedion latalmidim tashsa* (2000). Tel Aviv: Tel Aviv University (Course catalogue for students, 2000/2001, Faculty of Engineering, Tel Aviv University) (in Hebrew).
Hafakulta Lemada'ey Haruah Al Shem Lester ve Sally Antin. Beit Hasefer Lehinuh (2001) *Yedion latalmidim tashsa* (2001). Tel Aviv: Tel Aviv University (Course catalogue for students, 2001/2002, Faculty of Humanities, School of Education, Tel Aviv University) (in Hebrew).
Hizuk sherutei hahaskala hagvoha al basis kalkali (2009) *Hamachon haisraeli letichnun kalkali.* A paper presented at the Hertzliya Conference. (Strengthening higher education services on an economic basis. The Israeli Institute of Economic Planning) (in Hebrew).
Homer liyshivat senat In Takanot letalmidey mehkar (1982) *Yerushalayim: Ha'universita Ha'ivrit Birushalayim. Sivan, Tashmab.* (Material for Senate Meeting, in Regulations for Research Students. Jerusalem: The Hebrew University) (in Hebrew).
Hozer mankal tashsaz (2012) (Director general, 7 July 2012). Jerusalem: Ministry of Education.
Israel Central Bureau of Statistics (2006) Students at universities and at other institutions of higher education. A collection of statistical findings no. 5 (in Hebrew). *Letalmidey Mehkar* (1996) (The Regulation of Studies for Research Students); *Shnaton hafakulta lematematika ulemada'ey hateva tashnaz* (1996) (The Regulation of Studies for the Faculty of Mathematics and Natural Sciences); Jerusalem: The Hebrew University. *Shnaton hafakulta lematematika ulemada'ey hateva* (2001: 41, paragraph 1); Jerusalem: The Hebrew University (in Hebrew).
Martel, A. (2001) When does knowledge have a national language? Language policy-making for science and technology. In U. Ammon (2001). (Ed.). *The dominance of English as a language of science. Effects on other languages and language communities.* pp. 27–58. Berlin: Mouton de Gruyter.
Ministry of Education (2001) *English Curriculum for all grades. Principles and standards for learning English as a foreign language in Israeli schools,* Jerusalem.
Ministry of Education (2009) *Higher-order thinking skills.* Jerusalem (in Hebrew).
Ministry of Education (State of Israel) (2012a) *Hozer mankal tashnaz (Director General).* July 7th, 2012. Jerusalem. (in Hebrew)
Ministry of Education (State of Israel) (2012b) *Pedagogical Secretariat. Arabic Inspectorate.* Jerusalem. (in Hebrew)
Ministry of Education (State of Israel) (2013) Pedagogical Secretariat. Language Department. English Inspectorate. *Revised English Curriculum.* November 2013.

Phillipson, R. and Skutnabb-Kangas, T. (1996) English only worldwide or language ecology? *Tesol Quarterly* 30 (3), 429–452.
Ram, D. (2006) Hebrew and English as a medium of instruction in tertiary education in Israel: Policy, ideology and practice. Unpublished PhD dissertation. Bar-Ilan University.
Shohamy, E. (1994) Issues in language planning in Israel: Language and ideology. In R.D. Lambert (ed.) *Language Planning Around the World: Contexts and Systemic Change* (pp. 131–142). Washington, DC: National Foreign Language Centre.
Shohamy, E. (2006) *Language Policy: Hidden Agenda and New Approaches*. New York: Routledge.
Shnaton Tashab 2011/2012. *Nehaley horaa velimudim.* (2012). *Hauniversita Ha'ivrit biryushalayim. Hafakulta lematematika vlemadaey hateva.* (Instruction procedures for the academic year 2012). Jerusalem: The Hebrew University.
Spolsky, B. (1996) English in Israel after Independence. In J.A Fishman, A.R. Lopez and A.W. Conrad (eds) *Post-Imperial English*. Berlin: Mouton.
Spolsky, B. and Shohamy, E. (1999) *The Languages of Israel: Policy, Ideology and Practice*. Clevedon: Multilingual Matters.
Spolsky, B. (2004) *Language Policy*. Cambridge: Cambridge University Press.
Spolsky, B. and Hult, F.M. (eds) (2008) *The Handbook of Educational Linguistics*. Malden, MA: Blackwell Publishers.
The Academy of the Hebrew Language (2013) *Akadem. Yedion Haacademya lalashon haivrit, 23(2).* June 2003. (Bulletin of the Academy of the Hebrew Language) (in Hebrew)
Tollefson, J.W. and Tsui, A.B.M. (eds) (2004) *Medium of Instruction Policies. Which Agenda? Whose Agenda?* Mahwah, NJ: Lawrence Erlbaum Associates.
Tsuda, Y. (1994) The diffusion of English: Its impact on culture and communication. *Keio Communication Review* 16, 49–61.
Vila, F.X. (2013) Challenges and opportunities for medium-sized language communities in the 21st century: A preliminary synthesis. In F.X. Vila (ed.) *Survival and Development of Language Communities: Prospects and Challenges* (pp. 179–200). Bristol: Multilingual Matters.
Yedion halimudim lishnat tashab (2012) (Course catalogue of studies for the year 2012. Tel-Aviv University). See www.tau.ac.il/humanities/yedion
Yedion musmahim tashag 2012/2013 (2012). The Technion. (Course catalogue for graduate students 2012/2013). See www.graduate.technion.ac.il/heb/Rishum/yedion.pdf
Yedion shvuee mispar 5 (2001) Hatechnion-Mahon Technologi Le'Israel (a weekly bulletin, No. 5. 30 December–6 January, The Technion-Israel Institute of Technology) (in Hebrew).
Zihronot ha'Academya lalashon ha'ivrit lamedheh – lamedvad' lamedzayin Lashanim hatashmah, hatashmat – hatashan (1992) *Yerushalayim, Ha'Academya Lalashon Ha'ivrit, Hatashnab, Dfus Graph-Peres, Yerushalayim*. (Records of the Academy of Hebrew Language of the years 1988, 1989 and 1990, Jerusalem, The Academy of Hebrew Language. Jerusalem: Graph Peres Press (in Hebrew).
Zihronot ha'Academya lalashon ha'ivrit memaleph – membet memgimel lashanim hatshnad, hatshnah - hatashno (1998) *Yerushalayim, Ha'Academya Lalashon Ha'ivrit, Hatashnab, Dfus Graph-Peres, Yerushalayim*. (Records of the Academy of Hebrew Language of the years 1994, 1995 and 1996, The 218th meeting. Jerusalem, The Academy of Hebrew Language. Jerusalem: Graph Peres Press (in Hebrew).
Zinger, P. (1995) in A Discussion: The Technion 1995–2005. Trends and policies (a meeting held on 30 October 1994, Senate Hall, Senate Building, Haifa: The Technion).

6 Challenges for South Africa's Medium-Sized Indigenous Languages in Higher Education and Research Environments

Anne-Marie Beukes

Introduction

It is a truism that language plays a pivotal role in learning and hence in empowering individuals to be both producers and consumers of knowledge. It is likewise obviously true that the choice of the language(s) of instruction has been a thorny issue in Africa since its former colonies gained their political independence. Prejudice and confusion about the role and potential of Africa's indigenous languages to act as suitable languages of instruction persist and have resulted in these languages being viewed as barriers to successful learning and hence relegated to the back seat, with the former colonial languages primarily being the preferred language of instruction. Ouane (2010), drawing on UNESCO's 2004 Global Monitoring Report on Education for All, which underscores the choice of the language of instruction and language policy in schools as critical for effective learning, argues that low-quality education and the marginalisation of the African continent can be linked to its language in education practices:

> Africa's marginalisation is reinforced by its almost complete exclusion from knowledge creation and production worldwide ... Africa has the smallest share in scholarly publishing, which is mirrored by the international Social Science Citation Index which, despite its cultural bias, covers the world's leading scholarly science and technical journals in more than 100 academic disciplines. Only one per cent of the citations in the Index are from Africa. The publicly-accessible

knowledge production of African scholars takes place outside Africa. The UNESCO Science Report of 2005 indicated that Africa is contributing only to 0.4 per cent of the international gross expenditure on research and development, and of this, South Africa covers 90 per cent. (UNESCO, 2010: 5)

Notwithstanding research evidence that challenges current practices and suggests new approaches to language-in-education policies, the pattern on the African continent of favouring a language of wider communication such as English as a language of instruction seems to be a growing one. In October 2011, Africa's newest nation, South Sudan, where some 60 indigenous languages are spoken, announced that it would change the language of schooling to English and phase out Arabic as a national language. This move was inspired by the fact that since 1898 Arabic was imposed from the north as a tool to spread oppression throughout Sudan. As from 2012, South Sudan would teach its national languages at the preschool level and thereafter use English as the language of instruction. Arabic would only feature as a language subject: 'The government hopes the move will unify the new nation … and also bring it in line with neighbouring countries' education systems' (news24, 2011).

As far as South Africa is concerned, English and Afrikaans have served as languages of teaching and learning in higher education for roughly the past century. The aim of this study is to assess contemporary South Africa's higher education landscape with particular attention to the challenges that the medium-sized official languages face in a significantly transformed higher education environment. Notwithstanding the radical political, social and economic transformation of post-apartheid's higher education environment, it is now characterised by the domination of English and the continued marginalisation of the (official) indigenous languages. However, the use of Afrikaans as a language of learning and teaching (LOLT) is rapidly on the decline.

Language-in-Education Policy in South Africa

While the present chapter deals with language issues in higher education in contemporary South Africa, it is necessary to emphasise that any discussion on language in higher education should, of necessity, also involve language in primary and secondary education. South Africa's language-in-education policy (DoE, 1997) is based on the principle that the use of the learner's home language as a language of instruction should be maintained in the early years of primary school, but that the learner must also have access to an additional language.

South Africa is home to a great variety of languages that are used on a daily basis by its population of close to 50 million people. The South African Constitution (RSA, 1996) acknowledges the rich diversity of its peoples by enshrining official status to 11 of these languages, i.e. English, Afrikaans[1] (the former official languages from 1910 to the advent of democracy in 1994) and nine African languages, i.e. Sesotho sa Leboa, Sesotho, Setswana, Tshivenda, Xitsonga, siSwati, isiNdebele, isiXhosa and isiZulu. According to the latest census by Statistics SA, i.e. Census 2011, the majority of South Africans speak an African language as their first or home language. The most commonly spoken home language is isiZulu, spoken by some 22.7% of the population, followed by isiXhosa (16%) and Afrikaans (13,5%), while English is the home language of 9.6% of the population (StatsSA, 2012). The language clause in South Africa's Constitution is supported by the Bill of Rights which recognises language as a basic human right:

> Everyone has the right to use the language and participate in the cultural life of their choice, but no one exercising these rights may do so in a manner inconsistent with any provision of the Bill of Rights. (Section 30)

However, the choice of languages used for learning and teaching in the South African education system does not reflect the above distribution of home languages. A report by the Department of Basic Education to the South African Development Community (SADC) and the Conference of Ministers of Education of the African Union indicates that home language does not feature prominently in the choices that learners and their parents make as regards the language(s) of instruction (DoBE, 2011). In 2007, the great majority of learners in South Africa's school system from Grade 1 to Grade 12 opted not to learn through their home language (cf. Table 6.1). In fact, the great majority (65%) learnt through the medium of English, while only 12% learnt through the medium of Afrikaans and 7% through isiZulu, ironically the most commonly spoken home language.

Language Policy at University Level

The South African Constitution stipulates that higher education is the responsibility of the national government, whereas other levels

Table 6.1 Choice of language(s) as medium of instruction in South African schools (2007)

Language used as medium of instruction	(%)
Afrikaans	12
English	65
isiNdebele	0.4
isiXhosa	6
isiZulu	7
Sesotho	2
Sesotho sa Leboa	3
Setswana	2
siSwati	1
Tshivenda	1
Xitsonga	1
Total	100

Source: DoBE (2011).

of education are a concurrent responsibility of both provincial[2] and national government. The constitution also prescribes that '(e)veryone has the right to receive education in the official language or languages of their choice in public educational institutions where that education is reasonably practicable' (section 29(2)). The constitution makes it clear that the principles of equity and practicability and the need to redress the legacy of past racially discriminatory laws and practices shall limit the right of individuals to receive education in the language of their choice.

Governance of higher education is executed in terms of the Higher Education Act, 101 of 1997 (RSA 1997). Section 27(2) assigns the responsibility for language policy development to institutions' councils 'subject to the policy being determined by the Minister', thereby providing some space for universities to design their own language policies. However, owing to what Alexander (2003: 15) describes as 'an extremely problematic start', the South African government was sluggish in responding to the fledgling democracy's need for a national language-in-education policy, notwithstanding the exponential growth in student numbers after democracy (see Table 6.2). As a result, the Language Policy for Higher Education (LPHE) (DoE, 2002), which regulates the language dispensation in higher education institutions, was published after almost a decade into the new democratic dispensation.

The LPHE gives due recognition to the critical role that language and access to language skills plays 'to ensure the right of individuals to realize

Table 6.2 Comparison of total number of students in 1993 and in 2004 indicating growth in higher education sector

Higher education institution	1993 No.	%	2004 No.	%	Growth
Universities of technology	80,378	17.3	194,981	26.2	
Universities	180,034	38.8	343,321	46.1	62%
Distance education institutions (UNISA/TSA/VISTA)	204,101	43.9	206,187	27.7	
Total	464,513	100.0	744,489	100.0	

Source: Grové (2006).

their full potential to participate in and contribute to the social, cultural, intellectual, economic and political life of South African society' (DoE, 2002: 4). The government's transformation project for higher education has directly impacted on the language dispensation at higher education institutions. It came as no surprise that the imperative of changing the segregated, fragmented nature of the higher education landscape characterised by the apartheid dispensation's 'ethnolinguistic geography' (Hill, 2008: 160), as well as the need to remove barriers to access in higher education, would inform language policy and planning (Beukes, 2010). In addition, the need for South Africa's transformed institutions to compete in an international environment would point to the pivotal role that English would play in a transformed higher education context (Hill, 2008).

The LPHE is committed to the following framework:

- The development, in the medium to long-term, of South African languages as mediums of instruction in higher education, alongside English and Afrikaans;
- The development of strategies for promoting student proficiency in designated language(s) of tuition;
- The retention and strengthening of Afrikaans as a language of scholarship and science;
- The promotion of the study of South African languages and literature through planning and funding incentives;
- The promotion of the study of foreign languages; and
- The encouragement of multilingualism in institutional policies and practices. (DoE, 2002: 15)

The LPHE acknowledges the historical position of English and Afrikaans as dominant languages of instruction and also acknowledges that other

South African languages should be developed for use in instruction. The LPHE articulates government's concern for the future of the study of South African languages and literature and encourages higher education institutions to develop and enhance the study of these languages as part of an overall medium- to long-term strategy to promote multilingualism. Scholars have expressed serious concern over the lack of interest in the study of African languages. Alexander (2012) points to the fact 'that only 0.5% of all undergraduates are enrolled in African Languages departments in South Africa' and argues that it is 'a damning indictment on social and especially educational policy during the past 15 years'.

Language Practices at University Level

The LPHE has been widely commended for its objectives of promoting multilingualism and enhancing equity and access in higher education (Alexander, 2003; De Kadt, 2006; Foley, 2004). However, government's inertia and 'extremely problematic start' regarding language policy matters, or in the words of De Kadt (2006: 41), its 'lack of political interest' and 'because it was assumed that teaching would take place in English', created a policy implementation vacuum in education that will arguably take at least a generation to address. Historically, English and Afrikaans have dominated higher education as languages of instruction, while African languages were seldom, if ever, used in this regard. The government's LPHE points to this legacy that 'has been and continues to be a barrier to access and success in higher education; both in the sense that African and other languages have not been developed as academic/scientific languages and in so far as the majority of students entering higher education are not fully proficient in English and Afrikaans' (DoE, 2002: 4). When democracy was established in 1994, the majority of the 36 higher education institutions (two thirds) offered English monolingual tuition, a quarter offered Afrikaans tuition and three institutions were classified as bilingual institutions (Webb & Du Plessis, 2008) (see Table 6.3).

Table 6.3 Language dispensation at South African higher education institutions (1994)

Type	Afrikaans	English	Bilingual	Total
Universities	5	13	3	21
Technikons	0	8	7	15
Total	5	21	10	36

Language policies in higher education soon became a bone of contention when the change in demographics at these institutions started to accelerate rapidly. Although race and language in South Africa have always been an 'inextricable bind' (Jansen, 2010: 6), it could no longer be used as a base to separate schools and universities. In the words of former South African President Mbeki:

> ... it is when the borderline between one language and another is erased, when the social barriers between the speaker of one language and another are broken, that a bridge is built, connecting what were previously two separate sites into one big space for human interaction, and, out of this, a new world emerges and a new nation is born. (DoE, 2002: 2)

The higher education landscape in the new South Africa clearly had to be transformed and new language policies in these institutions would of necessity play a pivotal role in this process. Two groundbreaking policy documents by the then national Department of Education, i.e. the National Plan for Higher Education (2001) and the LPHE (DoE, 2002), were finally published. Subsequently, a rationalisation process of mergers and the incorporation of existing institutions reduced South Africa's 36 universities and technikons (higher education institutions with a technical focus) to 22 universities (including new categories of institutions, i.e. 'universities of technology' and 'comprehensive universities') (see Table 6.4).

The changed landscape predictably impacted on the choice of language of instruction, with the National Plan for Higher Education (2001) insisting that ethnolinguistic forces such as the need to be an 'English university' or an 'Afrikaans university' would no longer determine the nature of the language dispensation at any given institution. While the LPHE (2002) acknowledges the status quo in cases where English and Afrikaans are dominant languages of instruction, the language policy

Table 6.4 Language dispensation at South African higher education institutions subsequent to a rationalisation process (2004)

Type	Afrikaans	English	Bilingual	Total
Universities	0	7	4	11
Universities of technology	0	5	0	5
Comprehensives	0	3	3	6
Total	0	15	7	22

rejects the need for designated Afrikaans universities since it 'runs counter to the end goal of a transformed higher education system' (DoE, 2002: 12). Higher education institutions are required to respond to 'the simultaneous development of a multilingual environment in which all our languages are developed as academic/scientific languages' (DoE, 2002: 5) so that they 'unabashedly and unashamedly' become 'South African' (DoE, 2002: 12).

Those institutions that were widely known as 'Afrikaans-medium universities'[3] were singularly affected by the provisions of the LPHE in the sense that it put an end to Afrikaans-only institutions. Extraordinary demographic pressures, which will be discussed below, also contributed to the rapid change at these institutions. Table 6.5 gives an indication of the current language dispensation at previously 'Afrikaans universities'. The use of Afrikaans as a fully fledged LOLT in higher education is in sharp decline, a situation that is deteriorating each year.

The issue of 'Afrikaans-medium universities' has become a vexed one in post-apartheid South Africa. Beukes (2010: 210) cautions that the debate on the status and future of Afrikaans as a language of instruction 'should be understood against the backdrop of the reality that very few of the languages spoken in the world are in fact used in institutions of secondary and higher learning'. A significant achievement of Afrikaans as a language of science is the fact that – in the course of the 20th century – it is one of only a few languages (such as Catalan, Hebrew, Hindi, Indonesian) that has been adequately standardised in order to function as a fully fledged language of science and technology and for undergraduate and postgraduate teaching purposes.

The post-apartheid period witnessed a significant increase in the number of monolingual institutions. The status quo at the time of writing in 2013 indicates that all 22 higher education institutions offer tuition through the medium of English, with no previously 'Afrikaans university' in a position to claim that it offers tuition at the undergraduate level through the medium of Afrikaans by default.

From a demographic point of view, the rapid changes in the composition of South Africa's student population have been described as the fastest of its kind in the world (Smit, 2010: 51). This phenomenon satisfies government's transformation requirements which require the increased participation of all population groups in higher education. In this regard, South Africa's Council on Higher Education reports that the proportion of African students in terms of the total enrolment in public higher education as a whole increased from 49% in 1995 to 63% in 2007 (CHE, 2009: 18). In this process, the so-called historically Afrikaans-medium universities

Table 6.5 Current dispensation regarding language of instruction at previously 'Afrikaans universities'

University	Language policy provision on language of instruction	Covert language of instruction practice
1. University of Johannesburg	English, Afrikaans, Isizulu and Sesotho sa Leboa are 'primary academic languages'	English Afrikaans in undergraduate classes in a few selected departments on one campus
2. North-West University	English and Afrikaans 'primary languages of tuition'	English Afrikaans and English (via whispered interpreting on one campus)
3. Stellenbosch University	Multilingual teaching model is followed: Afrikaans and English are languages of teaching: Parallel-medium teaching used primarily in the first year of teaching (class group is divided into two parallel streams) Double-medium teaching from the second year of teaching (both languages are used in same classroom) Study material in both languages	English and Afrikaans (primarily only in the first year of teaching) English (postgraduate)
4. University of Pretoria	Tuition either in Afrikaans or in English or both	English and Afrikaans (primarily only in the first year of teaching) Parallel-medium in some first-year classes
5. University of the Free State	English and Afrikaans on a 'parallel-medium basis'	Afrikaans and English

(i.e. institutions where Afrikaans was used as the primary language of instruction) have undergone – what Du Plessis (2006: 87) refers to as – a 'sociolinguistic metamorphosis' by offering tuition both in English and (increasingly less) in Afrikaans, in the end resulting in the (almost total) abolishment of Afrikaans in higher education institutions.

The University of Johannesburg (UJ) is a case in point. UJ is situated in the Gauteng province, the economic hub of the country, and is one of the largest residential universities in South Africa with close to 50,000 students. Such was the nature of the sociolinguistic pressure on higher education institutions to facilitate access that, four years before the government formally initiated the transformation of higher education, UJ's predecessor, the Rand Afrikaans University (RAU), introduced English as the language of instruction in addition to Afrikaans in order to satisfy the needs of the non-Afrikaans-speaking students who were enrolling at this institution in increasingly great numbers. That said, it is important to keep in mind that this university, right from its establishment in 1967, chose to teach through the medium of Afrikaans, a decision also symbolically reflected in its choice of name, i.e. the Rand Afrikaans University. In fact, one of the founding principles of the RAU was to provide an academic home 'tailor-made' for Afrikaner students (i.e. an institution that would be Afrikaans in spirit and character) in the then English-dominant Johannesburg area. The Afrikaans language was, therefore, the sole language of instruction for three decades before special measures were adopted in the late 1990s to accommodate the language preferences of its then rapidly changing student population. As a consequence, parallel-medium instruction was introduced at the RAU in 1998, which, in practice, resulted in separate classes, study guides and tutoring for English- and Afrikaans-speaking students, making it possible for them to continue studying in the language of their choice.

This dramatic shift in the linguistic profile of students at the RAU saw the university rapidly evolving from a monolingual Afrikaans university to an institution where parallel-medium instruction became institutionalised. As is the case where a dominant world language forms part of a configuration of languages of instruction, English made rapid inroads at the RAU, thus leading to an imbalance in the number of students in Afrikaans and English classes by 2004, with a ratio of approximately 1:4 preferring tuition through the medium of English (Beukes & Pienaar, 2009). This trend continued unabated, resulting in a steep decline at this institution in the enrolment of students who preferred Afrikaans as a language of instruction (see Table 6.6) and also in the enrolment of Afrikaans students (see Table 6.7). Hence, parallel-medium instruction gave way to English-only instruction.

Table 6.6 Enrolment of students at University of Johannesburg who chose Afrikaans as language of instruction (1999–2011)

Year of registration	Students who opted for Afrikaans as their preferred language of instruction
1999	6010
2008	3386
2011	1595

Source: University of Johannesburg Unit for Institutional and Strategic Planning.

The above statistics beg the question, how and where students who seemingly still prefer being taught through the medium of Afrikaans are now being accommodated. Beukes (2010: 206) argues that the UJ's prospective Afrikaans students, notwithstanding the university's concerted efforts – through an integrated marketing campaign in 2008 and 2009 – to publicise its commitment to offering Afrikaans-medium instruction, are 'being lured to institutions such as North-West University's (NWU) Potchefstroom campus and also Stellenbosch University that still offer Afrikaans-medium teaching'. Other researchers also refer to an emerging trend of Afrikaans-speaking students now increasingly preferring English as their medium of instruction. This trend is a function of the globalisation of English which has, as elsewhere, also resulted in South African students believing that studying in a language other than English would pose a barrier to their full participation in 'the global economy' (Van Coller, 2003: 95).

Another reason for the rapid change in student demographics and the dwindling number of students who study through the medium of Afrikaans is related to the opportunities that globalisation offers. With the increased mobility that the processes of globalisation brought about and the transformation of contemporary societal life into new 'scapes' (Appadurai, 1996 in Pennycook, 2011: 514) such as 'ethnoscapes' characterised by the increased flow of refugees, migrants, immigrants and tourists, and 'financescapes' with flows of capital, Afrikaners (who lost political power in the transition to democracy in 1994) have now also become part of 'the neo-diaspora from Africa' (Du Plessis, 2004: 26). According to estimates, some one and a half million South Africans have

Table 6.7 Enrolment of Afrikaans students at UJ (2000–2009)

2000	2001	2002	2003	2004	2005	2006	2007	2008	2009
4958	4963	5069	5116	5119	4736	4242	3917	3490	3285

Source: Rokebrand (2012).

left the country over the past two decades. Du Plessis (2004: 54) argues that 'about 50% of the approximately 20,000 emigrants leaving South Africa annually since 1994 have been Afrikaners. Over a period of ten years this would amount to 150,000 Afrikaner emigrants or 5% of the Afrikaner population of three million plus'.[4]

Language Ideologies and Discourses

The role of languages other than English in 'opening the doors of education' in South Africa (Beukes, 2010: 194) has, to all accounts, not been a priority for the post-apartheid state. Higher education institutions are, first and foremost, political creations and hence the products of unique contexts, traditions and social conditions (Du Plessis, 2008). Current discourses on the strategic efficiency of English in opening the doors of education have impacted negatively on the efforts of African language scholars to promote the intellectualisation of these languages for use in higher education.

In an effort to respond to the transformation imperative and impact on language practices by introducing an African language for teaching and learning purposes in the higher education context, the University of Limpopo launched the first-ever dual-medium programme in 2003 in which an African language, Sesotho sa Leboa,[5] and English are used for tuition and assessment. The bachelor's degree in contemporary English and multilingual studies (BA CEMS) is a three-year undergraduate programme with two major subjects, i.e. contemporary English language studies (CELS), taught and assessed in English, and Thuto ya bolemente (multilingual studies or MUST), taught and assessed in Sesotho sa Leboa. The CELS course includes modules such as English in society, critical language awareness, language and literacy learning in a multilingual context and language and cognition, while MUST include modules such as an introduction to multilingualism, multilingual services in South Africa and researching multilingualism. Alas, this groundbreaking dual-medium programme was not funded by the government, but it materialised only through intervention by, and a generous grant from, the Ford Foundation. The grant was used (a) to employ and train young Sesotho sa Leboa-speaking staff to develop cognitively challenging materials in that language and (b) to translate key scholarly articles from English into Sesotho sa Leboa.

The BA CEMS programme has, however, become a site of contestation: 'Some academics and students believe that African languages cannot be used to teach university-level content and so discourage students from registering for this degree' (*Mail & Guardian*, 2010: 4). Although graduation figures remain fairly modest, the programme has a pass rate of 92%, reportedly one of the highest rates in that university. Table 6.8 gives an indication of the steady increase in enrolment for the BA CEMS degree since its inception.

Another project aimed at 'intellectualising' an African language, i.e. developing the language to be used as a language of science, was introduced in 2008 by the Rhodes University. The BA Xhosa mother tongue programme by the African Language Studies (ALS) section includes a three-year major in isiXhosa[6] with modules in applied language studies such as sociolinguistics, translation studies, literary discourse, syntax, African languages and localisation, taught through the medium of isiXhosa. On average, the course attracts about 50 students in the first year, 20 in the second year and about 10 students in the third year (Kaschula, 2012). The significance of this programme is that – notwithstanding the lack of a metalanguage in isiXhosa – it is illustrating to sceptics that African

Table 6.8 Student enrolment for BA CEMS degree at University of Limpopo (2003–2012)

Modules	2003	2004	2005	2006	2007	2008	2009	2010	2011	2012
CELS 101	12	15	21	39	32	27	30	27	31	44
CELS 102	12	10	19	39	30	24	30	23	37	44
MUST 101	7	7	25	33	28	17	40	27	33	37
MUST 102	7	7	24	33	27	19	40	28	33	37
CELS 201	–	11	7	12	6	9	8	12	18	11
CELS 202	–	11	6	12	5	8	9	12	20	11
MUST 201	–	6	10	14	28	17	9	19	15	18
MUST 202	–	6	9	14	25	19	9	19	14	18
CELS 301	–	–	6	7	7	4	7	6	10	15
CELS 302	–	–	6	7	7	4	7	6	9	15
MUST 301	–	–	4	9	9	8	7	7	13	13
MUST 302	–	–	4	9	10	8	7	7	12	13
Total	38	83	141	230	214	154	203	193	245	276

Source: Ramani (2012).

languages can be developed successfully as scientific languages and hence used to support learning and teaching through the medium of these languages.

The traditional role of the university – as a centre of research and enquiry, and as a source of solutions to problems of the society within which it is located – demands that South African universities look into using African languages to promote the meaningful participation and success of speakers of African languages in higher education (Maseko, 2011). In a bold and significant move, the University of KwaZulu-Natal announced that acquiring isiZulu proficiency would become compulsory for all undergraduate students in 2014 as part of the university's efforts to promote and facilitate the use of isiZulu as a language of learning, communication, instruction and administration (UKZN 2013). The first pioneering phase of this policy initiative commenced in 2014 and requires that students and staff 'develop communicative competence' in both isiZulu and English for the purposes of 'academic interaction'. In a press release, the university states that this 'reflects UKZN's commitment to the development of isiZulu as an academic language alongside English which at this stage remains the main language of learning and instruction' (UKZN, 2013). The juxtaposition of isiZulu alongside English is particularly encouraging since it would arguably facilitate the entrenchment of additive multilingualism as an educational goal in South Africa.

A summary of language practices at higher education institutions as regards the status quo on languages used for teaching and learning is provided in Table 6.9.

Language Competencies Expected of Teaching Staff, Administrative Staff and Students

It is general wisdom that it would be well-nigh impossible to find a university classroom in the South African context where students all share the same home language. Likewise, the language profile of teaching staff at higher education institutions also reflects a wide diversity of linguistic proficiency. However, against the backdrop of higher education institutions increasingly moving towards monolingual education through the medium of what Beukes (2010: 197) labels a 'standardized LOLT', i.e. using English exclusively for tuition purposes, it is a *de facto* policy that teaching staff should be proficient to teach in English.

One exception, though, is the system of spoken-language educational interpreting services offered on the Potchefstroom campus of the NWU since

Table 6.9 Summary of current language practices at South African higher education institutions as regards languages used for teaching and learning

Level	English	Afrikaans	Other language(s)
Undergraduate	At all universities	Only at five previously 'Afrikaans universities' Selected faculties Sharp decrease since 2002	Two courses partially using African languages as languages of instruction: University of Limpopo Rhodes University
Senior undergraduate (third and fourth year – honours)	At all universities	Only at five previously 'Afrikaans universities' Selected faculties Sharp decrease since 2002	Two courses partially using African languages as languages of instruction: University of Limpopo Rhodes University
Master's	At all universities	Few enrolments (insignificant)	None (except a few in language subjects)
Professional	At all universities	Few enrolments (insignificant numbers)	None
Doctoral research	At all universities	Few enrolments (insignificant numbers)	None (except a few in language subjects)

2004. This campus has traditionally offered tuition primarily in Afrikaans because the majority of students are Afrikaans speaking. However, through providing educational interpreting into English, the language needs of English-speaking students are now also being catered for. This service has grown over the past eight years: the NWU offered educational interpreting using the services of 69 interpreters in approximately 1680 periods per week in the 2013 academic year, a far cry from its modest start in April 2004 when only 22 contact periods per week were interpreted (Blaauw, 2006, 2013). In addition, these services are now also available on its other two campuses where interpreting is offered from English into Afrikaans.

In view of a number of pivotal legal imperatives, among which are the constitutional provisions on language and the government's LPHE, as well as South Africa's post-apartheid transformation project, higher education institutions are seemingly committed to promoting multilingualism. As a consequence, most universities' language policies make provision for the necessary support to improve their staff and students' language skills where required.

Research in Afrikaans

In a study on journal articles published in Afrikaans during the period 1990–2002, Mouton (2005) finds that Afrikaans scholars are increasingly shifting to publishing in English titles. In this period, articles written in Afrikaans comprised only 8.2% of all articles published. Mouton's findings,[7] moreover, point to a significant decline from 14% in 1990 to 5% in 2002 of articles produced in Afrikaans, a decline of almost 300%. These Afrikaans articles were accepted by a small number of so-called accredited journals that primarily publish in the humanities and also, to a lesser degree, in the social sciences.

This decline should arguably be understood against the backdrop of the anglicisation of higher education underpinned by the political and economic objectives of post-apartheid South Africa. It is important also to bear in mind that scholars are increasingly responding to the government's policy objectives as set out in South Africa's National Development and Research Strategy (DST, 2002) that promotes innovation. Strategically, human resource development and knowledge production and dissemination are increasingly taking place through the medium of English. These trends are clearly enhanced by the requirement for higher education institutions to function in an international environment and to compete in a global market for the production of knowledge.

Publishing in the digital age has, however, opened up new avenues for scholars wishing to publish through the medium of Afrikaans. A new online accredited[8] journal in Afrikaans, *LitNet Akademies*,[9] has benefitted from 21st-century information and communication technologies and from so-called open dissemination models. This journal has – as its central drive – the objective of encouraging research in the Afrikaans language. The journal started off with articles that cover the humanities, and in 2010, science and law, and in 2012, religion studies, followed.

Conclusion

Effecting political, social and economic transformation has been a hallmark of the post-apartheid period in South Africa, also as far as the higher education environment is concerned. The particular ideology requirements and attendant policy objectives that have characterised this environment has resulted in the encroachment of English and the abolishment of Afrikaans universities. Given the important role that higher education plays in the national economy, South Africa is now faced with what Webb (2010: 373) refers to as the challenge of 'revitalising' Afrikaans in higher education. The past achievements of Afrikaans as an LOLT and as a language of science could provide a gateway for the meaningful introduction of South Africa's other indigenous languages in higher education. In the words of De Kadt:

> The story of Afrikaans highlights not just the importance of a committed state, but also the importance of cultural bodies and universities in language development. ... Until African languages become an important part of tertiary education, these languages are likely to remain invisible and unusable in government and business. (De Kadt, 2006: 54)

Notes

(1) The Afrikaans language is viewed as an indigenous language of Africa. Afrikaans has multiple roots: it originated at the southern tip of Africa from a 17th-century Dutch dialect with significant influences from indigenous languages such as Khoekhoen, and also Portuguese Creole and Malay varieties. Owing to these influences, the Dutch dialect became Africanised over a period of some 300 years. The language is primarily spoken in South Africa and its immediate neighbour, Namibia, and to a lesser extent in Botswana. It is also spoken in smaller pockets in countries such as Australia and New Zealand which boast significant South African immigrant populations (cf. Barkhuizen, 2006; Hatoss *et al.*, 2011).

(2) South Africa has nine provinces.
(3) Universities, which in the past offered tuition primarily through the medium of Afrikaans, are the North-West University (NWU) – the former University of Potchefstroom (PU), the University of Johannesburg (UJ) – the former Rand Afrikaans University (RAU), the University of the Free State (UF) – the former University of the Orange Free State (UOFS), the University of Pretoria (UP) and the University of Stellenbosch (US). The University of South Africa (Unisa) has offered parallel education in English and Afrikaans since 1946. Unisa is one of the world's 'mega-universities' with more than 350,000 students, of which about 10% are Afrikaans speaking, resulting in it boasting more Afrikaans students than any other South African university (Bornman et al., 2013).
(4) Statistics from StatsSA indicate that South Africa's professionals are emigrating at an increasing rate: the total number of economically active emigrants increased from 4,794 in 1999 to 10,540 in 2003 (*Finance Week*, 2004: 53).
(5) Sesotho sa Leboa is a medium-sized language in the South African context with approximately 7.6% of South Africans who claim to use the language as their home language, compared with 13.5% who use Afrikaans and 9.6% who use English as a home language (StatsSA, 2012).
(6) IsiXhosa is part of the large Nguni group of languages and is spoken as a home language by 16% of the population, second after isiZulu, spoken by 22.7% of the population (StatsSA, 2012).
(7) Mouton's findings are based on an absolute decline in the number of articles published in Afrikaans.
(8) Accreditation of scholarly journals is managed by the Department of Higher Education and Training in terms of the government's Policy and Procedures for the Measurement of Research Output of Public Higher Education. Journals must meet a set of minimum criteria. Authors who publish their research in these accredited journals collect a publication subsidy. According to Gray and Willmers (2009), 210 journals are currently accredited.
(9) *LitNet Akademies* is published by LitNet, an independent journal that went live on the internet on 11 January 1999. The *LitNet Akademies* journal, sponsored by the Dagbreek Trust and PSG Fund Management, was accredited by the Department of Education in 2008. Etienne van Heerden, professor in the School of Languages and Literatures at the University of Cape Town, is the editor-in-chief (LitNet, 2013).

References

Alexander, N. (2003) *Language Education Policy, National and Sub-National Identities in South Africa*. Strasbourg: Council of Europe. See http://www.coe.int/t/dg4/linguistic/source/alexanderen.pdf (accessed 27 January 2012).

Alexander, N. (2012) The centrality of the language question in the social sciences and humanities in post-apartheid South Africa. Inaugural EB van Wyk Honorary Public Linguistics Lecture at the University of Johannesburg, 22 February 2012. See http://www.litnet.co.za/Article/the-centrality-of-the-language-question-in-the-social-sciences-and-humanities-in-post-apar (accessed 1 March 2012).

Barkhuizen, G. (2006) Immigrant parents' perceptions of their children's language practices: Afrikaans speakers living in New Zealand. *Language Awareness* 15 (2), 63–79.

Beukes, A-M. (2010) 'Opening the doors of education': Language policy at the University of Johannesburg. *Language Matters* 41 (2), 193–213.
Beukes, A-M. and Pienaar, M. (2009) Simultaneous interpreting: Implementing multilingual teaching in a South African tertiary classroom. In J. Inggs and L. Meintjes (eds) *Translation Studies in Africa* (pp. 223–244). London: Continuum.
Blaauw, J. (2006) Interpreting with limited training: Experiences in the interpreting of academic lectures at the North-West University, South Africa. In J. Kearns (ed.) *Translation Ireland. A Special Issue. New Vistas in Interpreting Training* 17 (1), 7–22.
Blaauw, J. (2013) Head: Language directorate, North-West University. Email communication 5 February 2013.
Bornman, E., Potgieter, P.H. and J.C. Pauw (2013) Taalkeuses en –opinies van Afrikaanssprekende studente aan Unisa. *Tydskrif vir Geesteswetenskappe* 53 (3), 361–376.
Council on Higher Education (CHE) (2009) *Higher Education Monitor. The State of Higher Education in South Africa*. HE Monitor No. 8, October. See http://www.che.ac.za/documents/d000201/Higher_Education_Monitor_8.pdf (accessed 12 June 2012).
De Kadt, J. (2006) Language development in South Africa – past and present. In V. Webb and T. du Plessis (eds) *The Politics of Language in South Africa* (pp. 40–56). Pretoria: Van Schaik Publishers.
Department of Basic Education (DoBE) (2011) *South African Country Report: Progress on the Implementation of the Regional Education and Training Plan (Integrating the Second Decade of Education in Africa and Protocol on Education and Training)*. South African Development Community (SADC) and Conference of Ministers of Education of the African Union (COMEDAF V), May 2011. Pretoria: Department of Basic Education, South Africa.
Department of Education (DoE) (1997) Language in Education Policy. Pretoria: Department of Education.
Department of Education (DoE) (2001) National Plan for Higher Education in South Africa. Pretoria: Department of Education.
Department of Education (DoE) (2002) Language Policy for Higher Education. Pretoria: Department of Education.
Department of Science and Technology (DST) (2002) South Africa's National Development and Research Strategy. Pretoria: Department of Science and Technology.
Du Plessis, J.A. (2004) Globalisation and cultural transformation: African and South African perspectives. *International Area Review* 7 (1), 37–62.
Du Plessis, T. (2006) From monolingual to bilingual higher education: The repositioning of historically Afrikaans-medium universities in South Africa. *Language Policy* 5, 87–113.
Du Plessis, T. (2008) Perspectives on managing Afrikaans and English as 'equal' languages of learning and teaching at the University of the Free State. *South African Linguistics and Applied Language Studies* 26 (3), 315–332.
Finance Week (2004) Brain drain. Bad form. *Finance Week*, 21 April, p. 53.
Foley, A. (2004) Language policy for higher education in South Africa: Implications and complications. *South African Journal for Higher Education* 18 (1), 57–71.
Gray, E. and Willmers, M. (2009) Case Study 3: LitNet Akademies and OnScreen. Report of the Opening Scholarship Project funded by the Shuttleworth

Foundation. February. University of Cape Town: Centre of Educational Technology.
Grové, N. (2006) 'n Volhoubare plek vir Afrikaans in hoër onderwys en regeringsteun daarvoor I & II [A sustainable place for Afrikaans in higher education and government support for this I & II]. See www.litnet.co.za (accessed 10 February 2007).
Hatoss, A., Starks, D. and Janse van Rensburg, H. (2011) Afrikaans language maintenance in Australia. *Australian Review of Applied Linguistics* 34 (1), 4–23.
Hill, L.B. (2008) Language and higher education in South Africa. Unpublished PhD thesis, University of Warwick.
Jansen, J. (2010) The politics and prospects of Afrikaans, and Afrikaans schools and universities. The 29th DF Malherbe Memorial Lecture, 12 August 2010, University of the Free State.
Kaschula, R. (2012) Head: School of Languages, Rhodes University. Email correspondence 11 May 2012.
LitNet (2013) LitNet Akademies. See http://www.litnet.co.za/Article/litnet-akademies-godsdienswetenskappe-bekendstelling (accessed 2 February 2013).
Mail & Guardian (2010) With many tongues. *Mail & Guardian*, 16–22 April, p. 4.
Maseko, P. (2011) Looking in all the wrong places for real learning. *Mail & Guardian*, 26 April. See http://mg.co.za/printformat/single/2011-08-26-looking-in-all-the-wrong-places-for-real-learning/ (accessed 26 October 2011).
Mouton, J. (2005) Afrikaans as wetenskapstaal in Suid-Afrika [Afrikaans as a language of science in South Africa]. *Tydskrif vir Geesteswetenskappe* 45 (3), pp. 370–385.
news24 (2011) South Sudan to end Arabic schooling. See http://www.news24.com/Africa/News/South-Sudan-to-end-Arabic-schooling-20111026 (accessed 27 October 2011).
Ouane, A. (2010) Lifelong learning for all in multilingual Africa. In UNESCO (eds) *Why and How Africa Should Invest in African Languages and Multilingual Education. An Evidence- and Practice-based Policy Advocacy Brief* (pp. 4–7). Hamburg: UNESCO Institute for Lifelong Learning.
Pennycook, A. (2011) Global Englishes. In R. Wodak, B. Johnstone and P. Kerswill (eds) *The SAGE Handbook of Sociolinguistics* (pp. 513–525). London: SAGE Publication.
Ramani, E. (2012) BA CEMS course coordinator, University of Limpopo. Email correspondence 14 May 2012.
Republic of South Africa (RSA) (1996) *Constitution of the Republic of South Africa, 1996*. Pretoria: Government Printer.
Republic of South Africa (RSA) (1997) *Higher Education Act, 101 of 1997*. Pretoria: Government Printer.
Rokebrand, L. (2012) Afrikaans in higher education. Unpublished BA honours research essay, Department of Linguistics, University of Johannesburg.
Smit, F. (2010) 'n Demografiese ontleding van studentegetalle aan Suid-Afrikaanse universiteite. In *'n Studie oor Afrikaans op Universiteitsvlak* (pp. 59–75). Plattekloof: FW de Klerk Foundation.
StatsSA (2012) *Census 2011 Results*. See http://mobi.statssa.gov.za/census/First%20Language.html (accessed 2 February 2013).
UKZN (University of KwaZulu-Natal) (2013) UKZN pioneers the introduction of Isizulu In undergraduate degrees. Media release, 15 May 2013. See http://www.ukzn.ac.za/docs/media-releases/ukzn-pioneers-the-introduction-of-isizulu-in-undergraduate-degrees.pdf?sfvrsn=2 (accessed 17 November 2013).

UNESCO (2010) *Why and How Africa should Invest in African Languages and Multilingual Education. An Evidence- and Practice-based Policy Advocacy Brief.* Hamburg: UNESCO Institute for Lifelong Learning.

Van Coller, H.P. (2003) Die medium van onderrig aan Suid-Afrikaanse universiteite: die geval van Afrikaans. *Koers* 68 (1), 87–105.

Webb, V. (2010) Afrikaans in higher education in S.A. *Alternation* 17 (1), 355–381.

Webb, V. and du Plessis, T. (2008) Preface. *South African Linguistics and Applied Language Studies* 26 (3), iii–xxii.

7 The Position of Catalan in Higher Education in Catalonia

Eva Pons Parera

Introduction

Catalan in Catalonia seems a relevant case to observe because it provides an example of how a medium-sized language that is not the dominant language of an independent state can achieve and maintain an extensive use and a relatively comfortable position in the field of higher education, although not without tensions arising from various factors that push for the use of Castilian or, more recently, English as academic languages.

The Catalan-speaking community, with over 10 million speakers and spread across eastern Spain, 'Northern Catalonia' (in France), Andorra in the Pyrenees and l'Alguer (the Sardinian town of Alghero/s'Alighèra, in Italy), is by far the largest linguistic minority in Europe. In the case of Spain, these speakers are distributed in various political-administrative divisions, referred to in the constitution as 'autonomous communities': Catalonia, the Balearic Islands, Valencia, Aragon and Murcia. The established legal-linguistic system differs considerably across regions, not only because of sociological factors (e.g. the number of languages in contact, the demographic significance of each language, the extension of the use of each language or the sense of community among its group of speakers), but also, and especially, because of political factors, i.e. the political will of states and substate authorities to recognise and protect, to varying degrees, the plurality of languages present in their territory, and, consequently, legal factors. Although their language is medium sized in global terms, Catalan speakers have no officially recognised rights in the eastern strip of Aragon, Northern Catalonia and l'Alguer. Catalan has no official status either in the central institutions of Spain, France and Italy or in those of the European Union, where only some semi-official uses are recognised.

Since at least the time of the creation of the unitary Spanish state at the beginning of the 18th century, language-in-education policy in

Catalan-speaking territories has rested on the principle that Castilian should become the common language of all subjects/citizens. Language-in-education policies have been key in achieving the supremacy of Castilian in Catalan-speaking territories over the course of the last 100–200 years. In certain periods, these policies have been applied in a strictly linguicidal way. In others, they have been more varied, with more players and more pluralist, leaving more room for the Catalan language (Vila, 2011: 143).

In any case, the proclamation of the Spanish Constitution (SC) of 1978 (see Article 3 SC, about languages[1]) and the subsequent devolution of powers in the form of autonomous self-government to substate institutions were the starting point of the legal and political process of *linguistic normalisation*, i.e. the planned implementation of a gradual process aimed at extending the knowledge and use of the Catalan language so that it improved its preceding sociolinguistic situation. The Catalan language, always together with Castilian, is recognised as an official language by the Statutes of Autonomy of Catalonia (SAC; which also recognises the official status of Occitan), the Balearic Islands and the Community of Valencia (in the last named as 'Valencian'), which identified the language to be protected as their *own language* in an explicit way.

In contrast with the past, self-government of autonomous communities implies that language policies no longer depend exclusively on the Spanish government. Above all in Catalonia, but also, to a lesser degree, in the Balearic Islands, societies and authorities have taken decisive action to win back ground for the local language in many domains. Education has been the field most open to intervention, to the point that both territories have school language policies in which Castilian has effectively lost the supremacy it had enjoyed for many years (Vila, 2011: 144). These policies had significant results, for instance, in terms of extending the knowledge of the Catalan language among the population that, because of the year of birth, has been schooled under them (Table 7.1).

Nevertheless, the existence of a degree of autonomy does not imply that the analysis of (higher) education language policies in Catalan-speaking territories should limit itself to the action of the autonomous administrations and institutions. This restricted vision would ignore the crucial fact that the autonomous authorities and other social actors must act within a framework that is severely limited by other players: namely the state and globalisation forces.

In this chapter, we will focus on language policies in higher education in the Catalan-language territory that has developed the most dynamic measures in favour of its historical language, which is Catalonia. Unlike other state or institutional experiences documented in this volume, the

Table 7.1 Proficiency in Catalan in Catalonia according to age groups in 2013 Percentages

Age groups (years)	Can understand (%)	Can speak (%)	Can read (%)	Can write (%)
15 to 19	100.0	95.6	95.0	93.1
20 to 24	98.2	95.3	96.1	95.0
25 to 29	92.7	86.8	88.4	80.5
30 to 34	94.3	81.5	84.1	70.3
35 to 39	95.2	82.1	84.4	73.5
40 to 44	96.1	83.9	87.0	73.2
45 to 49	93.5	81.5	86.4	66.7
50 to 54	96.8	85.7	87.7	56.2
55 to 59	95.1	79.8	81.6	47.1
60 to 64	95.4	75.3	82.4	39.7
65 to 69	92.8	70.1	72.6	33.6
70 to 74	92.0	69.5	70.6	29.1
75 to 79	90.4	59.5	58.6	25.5
80 to 84	89.4	66.6	61.1	27.6
85 to 89	79.3	59.8	52.7	21.4
90 and more	85.1	73.7	68.8	41.9
Total	94.3	80.4	82.4	60.4

Source: Idescat and Direcció General de Política Lingüística. Enquesta d'usos lingüístics de la població (2013). See http://www.idescat.cat/territ/BasicTerr?TC=5&V0=3&V1=3&V3=3103&V4=49 45&ALLINFO=TRUE&PARENT=25&CTX=B (accessed 27 July 2014).

case of Catalan allows us to 'examine the role of higher education language policies in mediating the tension between on the one hand the centralising forces of state-mandated policies and globalisation and demands for language rights for ethnic and linguistic minorities on the other'(Arzoz, 2012: 5). It should nevertheless be borne in mind that the linguistic rights of the minority (in the Spanish context) tend to be viewed and claimed in Catalonia as majority rights, which is usually associated with demands for a strong self-government or secession (Poggeschi, 2010: 38).

Language Policy at University Level

Historical antecedent

In ways akin to those that led to the introduction into higher education of several other languages reviewed in this volume, like Afrikaans, Finnish or Hebrew, the contemporary presence of Catalan in the university appears linked to the demands for the autonomy of Catalonia and the issue of granting official status to its language in the last third of the 19th century. Previously, and as a consequence of the abolition of Catalan institutions and the annexation to Castile after the War of Succession (1701–1714), Catalan had been legally pushed out of teaching institutions in primary, secondary and higher education. An order issued by the Council of Castile in 1773, for instance, prevented the University of Cervera from publishing books in Catalan, and the first Public Education Act in 1856 (Moyano Act) introduced universal compulsory education in Castilian. In the midst of growing linguistic claims, the practice of offering a university education outside university classrooms started in October 1903 as a result of the First University Catalan Congress, in response to the refusal of the president of the University of Barcelona (UB) to accept Catalan as a language of instruction. Official entrance to public university still took some three decades. On 1 June 1933, a decree signed by the president of the Second Republic approved the autonomy of the university designed by the Catalan government of Catalonia (*Generalitat*) under the Statute of Autonomy of Catalonia of 1932 (Article 7). The UB was renamed the 'Autonomous University of Barcelona' (UAB) with the aim of initiating a movement to reform the education system in Catalonia, converting it into a modern university. Among its new features was that Catalan was declared the official language of the university, along with Castilian (Nadal 1993).

But contrary to what happened with the rest of the languages analysed in the previous chapters, the official status of Catalan was not to last. Not long after it had been achieved and after a cruel civil war, Franco's dictatorship (1939–1975) banned all official use of Catalan and its teaching within the educational system for almost four decades. The new authorities effectively ousted Catalan from the university's official life, but as soon as circumstances permitted, the languages started to come back. The process began during the dictatorship itself: first in the form of clandestine language courses and a lexicographical commission in the 1950s; then by official courses on language, literature, history and culture supported by the first chair on Catalan language and literature since 1965. By 1968, some pioneers were already giving biology lectures in Catalan and, in August 1969, the first Catalan summer university developed – obviously, entirely in Catalan – in Prada de Conflent, in French Catalonia. During the 1969–1970 academic years, many more courses were being taught in Catalan in Catalonian universities. The continued rise in the following years and the dictator's death in November 1975 only spurred the process to the extent that, by 1978–1979, before the new constitution and the Statute of Autonomy were passed, a majority of university courses were already being given in Catalan: 52% in Catalan and 11% bilingual at the UAB and 57% totally or partially in Catalan at the Polytechnic University of Catalonia (UPC) by 1977–1978, and around 50% of courses in Catalan at the UB by 1978–1979 (Oliva & Vinent, 1980).

Catalan was reintroduced into higher education in a comparatively short time, mostly due to the addition of innumerable personal decisions of individuals which did not have any official support; on the contrary, they faced a hostile political regime. One after the other, Catalan-speaking professors and students dared to publicly use their language in domains where it was previously forbidden – in class, in department sessions, in institutional meetings, etc. – and most non-Catalan speakers did not object to that process. In fact, many non-native speakers explicitly adopted Catalan as a form of adhesion to the new times. The spread of Catalan was favoured by the fact that a large percentage of professors and students were Catalan native speakers. Indeed, the process did not take place in the same way in departments with a high percentage of non-Catalan professors. In the beginning, neither professors nor students were literate in Catalan and virtually no written texts were available, so Castilian texts were used instead. Instead of deterring the process, lack of terminology stimulated specialists to join the ranks and contribute by creating it.

In 1977, Catalonia's president in exile was allowed to return by the post-dictatorial authorities, the Francoist decree abolishing Catalan institutions was itself derogated and a provisional Catalan autonomous government was re-established. The approval of the SC in 1978 and of the Statute of Autonomy of Catalonia in 1979 created a new legal, political and institutional framework for the development of Catalan as a lingua academica.

Contemporary basic legal framework

In legal terms, the current linguistic organisation of higher education in Catalonia differs from that of primary and secondary education, because it is not so subject to detailed provisions for the use of official languages as 'a key factor in the promotion and protection of regional or minority languages'.[2] Under the SC of 1978, at least three kinds of competence and spheres of legislation are involved in the regulation of language policy at university level (Arzoz, 2012; Pons, 2012):

Firstly, higher education is a competence shared by the central state and the autonomous communities. In theory, the former establishes the basic legislation and the latter develops and executes it (Article 149.1.30 SC; Article 172 SAC). In practice, however, basic state legislation tends to be very detailed. In 2001, the central parliament passed the University Organic Act (amended in 2007) that abrogated the first law passed in the democratic period (Organic Act 11/1983). According to this law, all Spanish public universities are subject to the authority of regional administrations with only two exceptions, namely, UNED – Spanish distance university – and UIMP – a postgraduate university. Private universities need to be authorised by regional authorities. The University Act of Catalonia, adopted in 2003, regulates the 'Catalonia university system', as a subsystem within the general system.

Secondly, officially bilingual autonomous communities have the competence to establish the legal status of official languages other than Castilian to rule their use and promote their *normalisation*, as expressed, for instance, in Article 143 SAC. This horizontal competence permeates all other competences and binds all regional and central state authorities placed in a bilingual autonomous community (Vernet, 2003: 96–101). At the same time, though, the state has the competence to regulate linguistic aspects of various areas subject to its jurisdiction, whence the distribution of powers on language issues becomes variable. The main piece of legislation in this field in Catalonia is the 1998 Language Policy Act (LPA).

Thirdly, universities have constitutionally entrenched autonomy (Article 27.10 SC). The content of this autonomy, which must be exercised according to law, includes the use of official languages both in internal and external relations, as a matter belonging to the organisation and functioning of public administrations. Catalan universities have ruled upon the use of languages in their university constitutions (*estatuts*) or in specific language regulations.[3]

Summing up, in Spain, whereas there is a rather uniform higher education system, the explicit general university language policy is more diverse. In fact, since 1978 the state legislator has rarely ruled on the linguistic aspects of higher education. But lack of explicit policies does not mean that no policy is applied (Tsu & Tollefson, 2004). Indeed, it can be argued that, in practical terms, the central administration's apparent 'linguistic neutrality' usually redounds in favour of Castilian. At the end of the day, this is the only language which is official throughout Spain, the only one whose knowledge is constitutionally prescribed (Article 3.1 SC) and the only one whose use is implicitly guaranteed at all levels. Remember that the central authorities control numerous crucial aspects of the university system such as the processes of recruiting teaching staff, the existence of a Spain-wide 'single district' that facilitates the free mobility of students without linguistic considerations and most of the funds for research constraints (see also section 4). Indeed, it was only in 2007 that a linguistic clause was included in the Spanish University Act to give some protection to languages other than Castilian. The new Article 6.2 stipulates that public authorities and universities, through their statutes, must introduce mechanisms to endow members of the university community with sufficient knowledge of 'co-official languages' (the term applied to languages other than Castilian) through adequate instruction and initiation processes in order to foster the use of these languages. Note that this provision, which is due to the amendments proposed by regions with two official languages, does not foresee any duty with regard to these languages, thus showing the asymmetry respect of Castilian (Arzoz, 2009).

The distribution of competences in higher education between central and regional government is reflected, for instance, in the Kingdom of Spain's 2001 ratification of the European Charter for Regional or Minority Languages. In that case, the Spanish central government was willing to subscribe to the highest standards as far as minority and regional languages in compulsory education was concerned, which was not its immediate responsibility, but not in higher education, which was (Nogueira, 2012: 197).[4]

The Catalan university linguistic model

The Catalan university system embraces 12 institutions: 7 public universities: the universities of Barcelona (UB), Autònoma de Barcelona (UAB), Girona (UdG), Lleida (UdL), Pompeu Fabra (UPF), Politècnica de Catalunya (UPC) and Rovira i Virgili (URV); 4 private universities: Ramon Llull-Esade (URL), Vic (UVic), Internacional de Catalunya (UIC) and Abat Oliba-CEU; and a distance university, Universitat Oberta de Catalunya (UOC), with a mixed nature both public and private that was created to guarantee the presence of Catalan in this area, since the UNED works in Castilian. As already stated, autonomous communities may opt for different linguistic models within the legal frameworks established by the central government. In this respect, the Catalan legislator has paid special attention to the linguistic dimension of higher education (LPA, Articles 22 and 24; Catalan University Act, Article 6, whose basic principles were raised in 2006 to the SAC, Articles 6 and 35). From these laws, we can draw five main principles on which the university languages policies are based:

- Catalan as Catalonia's *own* language is the language of normal and preferential use in universities as administrative bodies and the normal vehicle for their educational activities.[5]

- The linguistic *normalisation* of Catalan is a goal of the university system, and government and higher education institutions must take appropriate measures to ensure the use of Catalan in all spheres of teaching activity, non-teaching activity and research.
- The *double official status* of Catalan and Castilian means that legal acts and formal communications have full validity and effects in both languages, without translation to the other needed, throughout the territory of the Catalonia.[6] Regarding linguistic rights and duties, the official status means a right of language choice between both official languages in academic tasks and, in more general terms, that the citizens' linguistic rights must be respected by universities as public bodies (Article 33 SAC).
- The principle of *language conjunction* postulates the joint education of students of different native or initial languages and implies the right of students 'not to be separated into centres or different class groups on the basis of their habitual language of use' (Article 35 SAC). But beyond that, the non-separation has become a structural principle of the educational system, their implementation varying in higher and basic levels of education.[7]
- A principle of *internationalisation* that allows universities to establish specific criteria for language use in activities related to international commitments, to promote knowledge of third languages and to foster the use of these languages in academic activities.

The resulting language model can be defined as one of conjunction, with two official and one 'own' territorial language, and speakers' freedom to use the official language of their choice. The legislation of the 1990s has allowed the building of a globally unique linguistic model, despite geographical location, public or private dependency or the legitimate interests of each of the institutions involved. Therefore, inside the Catalan university system there is no distinction between 'Catalan' and 'Castilian' universities, and even the existence of linguistic 'streams' in a given university is the exception rather than the rule. That makes a main feature of this university system, taking into account that, in a comparative perspective, bilingual or multilingual universities as formal institutions are very rare (Arzoz, 2012: 5).

Another phenomenon developed especially in the 1990s was interuniversity cooperation. First in an informal way, this cooperation took place at meetings of university leaders to formulate plans of action for issues of common interest (such as legislative reforms, judicial challenges to university regulations or the implementation of the European higher education standards) and through meetings and constant exchanges between linguistic services of universities. Later, this cooperation was institutionalised with the creation of the Language Policy Committee of the Interuniversity Council of Catalonia.[8] In a broader context, cooperation in linguistic matters is carried through the Xarxa Vives, a network created in 1994 to promote relations between the universities of the Catalan language area, which extends to Catalonia, Valencia, Balearic Islands, Northern Catalonia (in France) and Andorra.[9] This institutionalised collaboration tries to foster regular academic exchanges and students and faculties' mobility, pooling of linguistic resources (http://www.llengua.info) and the establishment of common guidelines on language policy. The strategic plan of the association establishes the linguistic unity of the academic community members as a value to promote.

Since 2009, the Catalan government has opted for a strategy of management by objectives and established a number of annual indicators conditioning the allocation of funding between public universities. Some of these indicators are linguistic, 15% of the 35% corresponding to the teaching sector and the rest being distributed in percentages of 20% for good management and 45% for research and development. These indicators refer to the following goals: implementing a language plan appropriate to the specifications defined by the government; enhancing the linguistic quality of academic and institutional written communications; improving language skills in Catalan and English by academic and administrative staff; implementing linguistic transparency, i.e. making public the language of instruction of each group before enrolment; increasing teaching in Catalan and English; and improving knowledge of Catalan among foreign students and faculty members. As is clear from these indicators, the government has identified the 'third language' with English. Therefore, when one speaks of a 'Catalan model of multilingual universities', the three languages that are contemplated are Catalan, Castilian and English, and the role reserved for other languages is unclear.

Universities' Linguistic Regulations and Plans

In general terms, the linguistic content of the universities' statutes in force is quite similar, since they ratify the legal principles and may specify some linguistic rights and obligations arising from them. It is also common that the statutes and regulations of the faculties or centres provide for bodies responsible for framing the guidelines for language policy (Language Policy Committee) and for language services, and also for administrative units responsible for the linguistic training and multilingual advice aimed at the university community.

Differences between universities appear more important at the regulatory substatute level. Firstly, not all universities have adopted the linguistic regulations called for in 1998 for Article 9 (3) LPA to 'regulate the use of Catalan, within their respective powers', after some of these regulations were challenged in the courts of justice. Secondly, since 2008, all public universities have adopted multilingual plans approved by the board of trustees, approval being a necessary condition for the provision of competitive funding from the Catalan government. Through these plans, language stands as a strategic element in university policy (Table 7.2).

In general terms, these plans introduce some changes in comparison with policies applied in the previous decades. Whereas language policy activities in the 1980s and 1990s were mostly aimed at promoting Catalan, the new strategy expressed in the 2000s through university plans of multilingualism seeks to reconcile two goals: the continuity of policies to support Catalan as the 'own' language and the management of multilingualism within the framework of the European Area of Higher Education (EAHE) and globalisation forces. The general structure and content of these documents tend to be similar: mission and vision, general and specific objectives for different areas of language policy. The content of the documents reveals, however, that the attention or focus on issues and proposed actions are not identical, depending of the size and traits of each institution (e.g. a greater focus on English in the polytechnic university – UPC). Thus, the current trend seems to point to a more marked differentiation between university multilingual models, through which universities will be able to define their own profile in a more competitive context, driven by the need to secure funding and to attract students from abroad.

Although regulation has changed, it is not at all evident to what extent new language planning goals have resulted in a real change of language uses into a more multilingualism context – at least in the sense of adding English to the two official languages. At the end of the day, this is not simply a top-down process but one conditioned by the attitudes and practices of the university community (Armengol et al., 2013: 10).

Language Practices at University Level

Regarding language practices at universities, both oral and written, we must distinguish at least three facets of university activity: teaching, institutional communication and administration (the research sector will be discussed in Research section, page 171.

Table 7.2 Language policies at Catalan universities

Institution	Year	Name	Document language(s)	Length (pages)
University of Barcelona (UB)	2010	Plan for Languages	CAT, CAST	28
Autonomous University of Barcelona (UAB)	2008 2011–2015	Plan for Languages	CAT, CAST, EN	9
Polytechnic University of Catalonia (UPC)	2010	Languages Plan	CAT, CAST, EN	18
University Pompeu Fabra (UPF) (Barcelona)	2009–2013	Action Plan on Multilingualism	CAT, CAST, EN	32
University Rovira i Virgili (URV) (Tarragona)	2009–2011 2012–2014	Language Policy Plan	CAT	30
University of Lleida (UdL)	2008	Language Policy: towards a multilingual reality	CAT	7
University of Girona (UdG)	2009–2013	Language Policy Plan	CAT	28

Concerning teaching, the political and administrative organisation of language use at the universities of Catalonia has been largely based on the principle of language conjunction (see above The Catalan university linguistic model). Catalan and Castilian are used interchangeably in Catalan universities. The official status of both languages is manifested in an emissive freedom, according to which 'the teaching staff and pupils of universities have the right to express themselves, orally and in writing, in the official language of their choice' (Article 35.5 SAC). Certainly, with regard to the language of instruction, teacher language choice – according to their status as public servants – can be modulated by institutional decisions, which can be based on various criteria: to preserve Catalan as a means of instruction, or to offer courses in the languages most widely spoken (Castilian or English) in order to attract mobility students or to foster internationalisation at home. In practice, departments or faculties, as well as structures in charge of the organisation of teaching, are concerned with the practical implications of this issue. In brief, the linguist choice of the teacher remains the general rule but it has limits which are not always clearly identified (only some language plans address the planning question of the language of instruction, e.g. UPF) nor consistently applied.

With regard to students, the linguistic 'conjunction' system involves a double exposure to Catalan and Castilian as a means of instruction. Consequently, students have no right to linguistic choice between the two official languages as teaching languages (despite the existence in big faculties of different class groups where the same academic subject is taught in Castilian and Catalan). Likewise, students are allowed to express themselves, orally or in writing – in exams, presentations, assignments, papers or participation in university life – in the official language of their choice. In principle, possible exceptions to the students' linguistic choice should connect with academic arguments, e.g. the use of content and language integrated learning methodology (CLIL). Thus, the objective of guaranteeing dual language skills can only be achieved if institutions provide the necessary conditions for studies in Catalan, especially in some areas historically Castilianised (e.g. in some faculties of law, pupils study Catalan legal language). Syllabus, notes, diagrams and other teaching materials are available in Catalan or/and in Castilian (and also other languages), depending on the subjects. In this respect, the position of Catalan is less severe than other non-state languages due to institutional factors: on the one hand, Catalan scientific terminology is continuously standardised and updated by Termcat (official agency of the government) and the different language services of the universities; and on the other, a certain number of textbooks or reference books written or translated into Catalan are regularly published by universities or private publishers with the support of a programme of public subsidies (DILL Programme, which in 2011 had a budget of 180,000 euros).

The model applied in Catalan universities has allowed the solid and central position of Catalan as the language of instruction to be preserved. According to a systematic and updated sociolinguistic survey, during the 2011/2012 academic year,[10] overall Catalan was the official language most commonly used as a vehicle of education in undergraduate studies (83.7% of class groups) and official master studies (66% of class groups) within the public universities of Catalonia; Castilian was the second language most used in undergraduate (12.6%) and master studies (19%); and the use of third languages (namely, but not exclusively, English) attained 3.7% in undergraduate and 15% in master studies. While the differences in percentage of use of Catalan in the degree varies little between seven public universities (78.1% UB to 94.3% URV, except UPF with only 55%), the oscillations are clearer in the master (with Catalan percentages of 32.8% UPF, 51.7% UPC, 63.3% UdL and 83.6% UdG), where Castilian has a stronger position (28.9% UdL, 25.4% UPF, 21.4% UB, but only 14.3% URV and 6.4% UdG). In general terms, there is a difference between public and private universities: according to data from 2006 to 2007, while Catalan was used in 72.5% of class groups in public universities, the average was 51% in private universities, with a high internal variation ranging from 23% in Abat Oliba University to 92% in the University of Vic, excluding the distance university UOC with a rate of 84%. These differences can be explained, among other sociological or ideological reasons, by a weaker adherence of such institutions to the legal linguistic provisions.

The model of linguistic conjunction has the advantages of reducing costs, since it avoids having to systematically duplicate all the courses. Additionally, as has been said, this structure discourages the formation of ethnolinguistically homogeneous class groups. Nevertheless, this model also has a number of disadvantages that should be borne in mind. Firstly, freedom of teaching language implies the *de facto* possibility of one of the languages having scant presence in a field, or not at all (this is relatively common in subjects that only have one lecturer and group). If this happens in too many subjects, it may lead to one of the languages not being used in a certain field of knowledge. This is of course a minor problem for an international language such as Castilian, but for Catalan, it is a crucial one. If a field is taught only in Castilian in Catalonia (and the Balearic Islands or Valencia), it is unlikely to be taught in Catalan anywhere else in the world.

A second challenge for the conjunction model involves the integration of 'outside' students, both from the rest of Spain and from the rest of the world. Barcelona and other cities are an important focus of attraction for European and Latin American students. The vast majority of these students tend to choose Castilian as their lingua franca, and often ask for their classes to be given in Castilian, placing in doubt the official nature of Catalan. To manage the impact of mobility students, some big faculties organise new groups taught by means of a lingua franca; but on other occasions, the solution involves the abandonment of Catalan and switching to Castilian, especially at the master level, or even creating new programmes taught entirely in English (also with the main aim of 'internationalisation at home'). Since the 1990s, universities and government have developed strategies of previous information or specific training for these students so that they can follow the courses in Catalan, such as free language courses, online resources, phrase books, self-learning centres and language exchange services. Recent language plans have put the emphasis on the so-called principle of 'linguistic transparency': the language used as a means of instruction of each subject/group has to be made public before the course starts, and it cannot be renegotiated or changed later by participants. This is intended to prevent disagreements about language choice that create an atmosphere of conflict among the class participants and end up denying those students who wish to study in Catalan their right to do so.

The distribution of the role of academic lingua franca between Castilian and English is, and will be in the future, a key issue, the former having so far virtually monopolised this role. Driven by the intertwined desire of enhancing universities' international projection and attracting foreign funds, since 2009 the Catalan authorities have set the goal of increasing the use of English as a means of instruction. However, concerns about the possible negative side effects of this measure have also led to the introduction of some compensatory considerations for Catalan. Achieving an agreement was, however, no easy task, and goals such as an overall minimum 10% of use of English had to be dismissed. Nevertheless, the use of English has continued to grow in undergraduate studies: UPF (with 12%) is the only institution that exceeds the 10% use in the undergraduate studies, where rates tend to be around 5% (UAB, UPC) or less (UdL, URV, UdG and UB). In master studies, English is approaching Castilian – which was for a long time more widespread than Catalan – across the whole public system (15% English, 19% Castilian). In three public universities, English has already passed Castilian in the master level (UPF 41.8% English vs 25.4% Castilian; UPC 29.6% English vs 18.7% Castilian; UdG

10% English vs 6.4% Castilian). These differences regarding the use of English comply with both the intensity of the institutional policies applied (e.g. in UPF and UPC) and the type of disciplines offered. In the UB, the biggest university, while the use of English tends to increase in highly internationalised areas, as an instance, it is the medium of instruction in 8.9% undergraduate medicine courses and 7.4% undergraduate economics; and the medium of instruction in 31.2% and 19.2% master courses in chemistry and pharmacy, respectively. On the other side, the presence of English remains almost symbolic in some areas of social sciences, as proved by its scarce presence in undergraduate studies in the faculties of law (0.8%), philosophy (0.4%) or history and geography (0%).

The internationalisation of universities is also promoted in institutional presentation and communication. Language plans recently approved establish a general pattern of multilingual uses in communications addressed outside the Catalan territory and a series of concrete measures, for example, more detailed websites accessible in English, publication of university reports, etc. In practice, references to institutional multilingualism tend to be equated with the hegemony of English, without excluding the uses of other languages depending on the sociolinguistic context – as French in Girona or Occitan in Lleida – or the wish to make visible the different languages and cultures that provide international students from exchange programmes. The legal principle of Catalan as the 'own' language has an institutional effect, identifying it as the first or the default language in all other written institutional communications and in the speeches of university officials. The daily running of the university administration is in Catalan, although the increase of students' mobility and the requirements of the European Higher Education Area (EHEA) have led to the translation to Castilian and other European languages, supported by languages services, of a certain number of administrative documents: agreements, contracts, academic degrees (European Supplement to the Degree, SET), certificates, syllabi, etc.

Language Competence

Ideally, and historically, higher education is an area characterised by the possession of a large linguistic repertoire by members of the university community. But the regulation of language skills has traditionally been absent from Spanish legislation, with the exception concerning foreigners who access permanent public employment in the areas of education and research, which are required to prove their proficiency in Castilian.[11] Scarcity of explicit regulation may be explained because, as it has already been shown, the Spanish university system is structured such that there is a general *de facto* prerequisite for linguistic knowledge of Castilian for all its members (see Contemporary basic legal framework).

With regard to the academic staff faculty, in spite of the fact that in 2001 and 2007 the legislation bestowed certain powers on the autonomous communities, the central state retained the power to establish regulations over their general status. In practical terms, that means the need to use Castilian in many procedures of professional carrier and university life. That is the case, for instance, in proceedings to access to permanent employment. Since the commissions responsible for assessing the suitability of the candidates are elected among the teaching staff from all over Spain and most often than not at least some of them cannot understand Catalan, the oral and written examinations must almost always be done in the Castilian language. This is also the case for official forms to request funding for research projects or to assess the research conducted, both of them decided by the central authorities. Another important point is the lack of explicit criteria for recognition of the multilingual character of the university system in the composition and operation of state agencies. This is the case of the Agency for the Evaluation of Educational Quality (ANECA), charged with assessing the suitability of teaching and research done by personnel in permanent public employment and employed by public universities, granting supplements to the income of the above-mentioned personnel and evaluating the quality of teaching staff at private universities. Under this set of elements, a large number of teachers perceive that the state system discourages the use of official languages other than Castilian (Catalan and also Basque and Galicia), and even harms the career of those using them (Nogueira, 2013). The general organisation of higher education, thus, clearly favours Castilian. In fact, as mentioned before, the only reference to the other official languages was only introduced in the 2007 University Act and refers to mechanisms to endow members of the university community with sufficient knowledge of 'co-official languages' in order to foster the use of these languages (see Contemporary basic legal framework).

In this framework, what are the possibilities of autonomous communities and universities by themselves to evaluate the knowledge of their own official language in exercising their powers over academic staff, as provided in the general legislation for civil servants?[12] In Catalonia, Article 6 (4) University Act states that:

> In accordance with Law 1/1998, of January 7, on language policy, university teaching staff, except visiting professors and other similar

cases, has to know both official languages in accordance with the requirements of their academic tasks. The Government, in accordance with current legislation and through the Interuniversity Council of Catalonia, must ensure that in the selection, access and assessment processes sufficient linguistic knowledge has been demonstrated. (Our translation)

In juridical terms, this requirement can be justified in the necessary respect for the language rights of students to receive instruction in Catalan and to use both official languages in the learning process.[13] It should be borne in mind that according to the Catalan conjunction model there exist no linguistically separate sections for teachers. Therefore, it is not uncommon that one teacher is required to give either lessons in Catalan and in Castilian depending on the subjects or during different academic years (for example, to balance linguistic offer of a department in both official languages) or because a non Catalan-speaking teacher step towards the use of Catalan, etc.

Pending approval of the regulation mentioned under Article 6 (4) UAC, some universities regulated through specific norms the requirement of knowledge of Catalan and applied it as a prerequisite to fill a vacancy (UB, UVic, UdL), while others have established linguistic accreditation *a posteriori* (UAB, UPF, UdG). In June 2008, an agreement by the Interuniversity Council of Catalonia on the 'accreditation of language knowledge in the selection and access processes of faculty to the universities in the Catalan university system' provided linguistic requirements for university teachers, with some exceptions related to the timing (post certification for non-permanent teachers), teaching in third languages or the need for attracting talent from abroad. Finally, in 2010, a decree with similar content was edicted by the Catalan government,[14] which allows the universities to specify the level of linguistic knowledge required to carry out academic tasks. Measures taken to preserve the use of Catalan in this area have not been proved incompatible with the process of internationalisation, as evidenced by the UB, an institution that has implemented the linguistic requirement more strictly (Matas and Planas, 2008). The administrative staff of public universities has the same status as staff from other Catalan administrations, and that implies a general requirement of knowledge of Catalan language to gain admittance to the post (Article 11 Linguistic Policy Act).

Regulation of students' language competence is yet another area of concern. With regard to students, those who have completed primary and/or secondary education in Catalonian schools 'have the right and obligation to have sufficient oral and written knowledge of Catalan and Castilian upon completing compulsory education' at 16 years old, 'whatever the habitual language [of pupils] at the beginning of their education' (Article 35.2 SAC). Indeed, the statistical data furnished in the Introduction suggest that most pupils end compulsory education being reasonably bilingual and biliterate. However, according to Spanish legislation, any student who has passed baccalaureate studies and the exam previous to the entrance to university is guaranteed equal access to any Spanish university by virtue of the 'open university district' principle, in total disregard of the students' linguistic capacities. In fact, according to the the Spanish Ministry of Education and Science, this legislation prevents the use of language tests of regional official language to regulate the access of students from other territories of Spain or from Europe. Interestingly enough, the central administration has applied a different, more protective criterion regarding Castilian when implementing European directives that require the promotion of student mobility. In these cases, the new official conditions for access to Spanish universities for students from EU states and from other states explicitly state that universities may require an adequate knowledge of the language in which the different academic subjects will be taught and set, if necessary, a test to assess the language proficiency of foreign transfer students. In fact, Andalusian universities have actually set up tests to evaluate the proficiency in Castilian of prospective students from abroad in order to regulate access to higher education. In any case, due to their aspirations to internationalisation as well as to the presence of students on mobility programmes, Catalan universities are often required to find practical solutions for students from outside who have no prior knowledge of Catalan (nor often of Castillian), as seen previously in Language Practices at University Level.

Consistent with actions that promote education in third languages, universities' language plans define different strategies to foster the English competence of their academic and administrative staff, such as generalisation of the merit of proficiency in third languages in recruitment processes; identification of a vacancy where knowledge of English is required; assessment of knowledge of third languages in scales that confer bonus for teaching activity; or reduction of course load to those teachers that start giving lessons in English. At the same time, the availability of English courses for academic and administrative staff has increased and universities have implemented homogeneous mechanisms to certify the level of competence in third languages. All these actions benefit from the previous experience regarding Catalan linguistic training (both through courses and through e-learning) and certification carried out for non-Catalan-speaking teachers by linguistic services.

Regarding students' linguistic repertoire to enable them to act in a more multilingual context, various actions have been taken by the Catalan government and other institutions in recent years, including the integration of the third language (namely English, French, German or Italian) in the conditions for governmental approval of new degrees within the framework of EHEA, and an enlarged offer of language courses and tests and certifications of proficiency in a third language according to uniform models. Since 2010, some universities regulate the procedures to accredit students' proficiency in a third language with similar alternative criteria: certificates, minimum of credits ECTS received in third language, use in the final degree academic work, passing of exams of linguistic subjects included in some degrees, or specific test or participation in mobility programmes. There are, nevertheless, some differences concerning the level of knowledge required by different universities (e.g. a minimum of B1 in UdL, B2.1 in UPF or B2.2 in UPC) or the deadline to accrediting, which is generally at the end of first degree (*but in the UPF by the end of the second year*). These differences should attenuate due to the *Generalitat*'s decision in 2013 to regulate the knowledge of a third language as a general requirement for obtaining the degree. At the end of 2013, state minister of education announced a reduction in a half of the state aid – funded by the EU – to students that were *at that time* abroad with an Erasmus scholarship. This reckless decision was never applied, but for the year 2014–2015, the minister has announced an important reduction in the budget for Erasmus that entails, among other measures, the limiting to four months of the stay in the foreign country, hindering the learning of the language.

Research

The concept of a knowledge society undoubtedly requires that higher education establishments should not only supply training but also produce research products (according to Article 1 of the Spanish University Act, universities perform the public service of higher education through teaching, study and research). The general problems surrounding scientific research in Catalan, as a non-dominant language, are complex and cannot be analysed here in depth. The current situation of the Catalan language in this area is also conditioned by the Spanish system of science and by the universities' efforts, supported by the *Generalitat*, to participate in the European and international forums expressive of the global nature of science. Subject to these factors, as well conditioned by the structure of research funding programmes, favouring the use of

Castilian and progressively English as languages of science (Barraclough, 2009: 27–31), the situation of Catalan in the field of research presents some promising aspects – at least in comparison with other linguistic realities of non-state languages – that should be emphasised and evaluated appropriately.

Catalan universities, often through their institutes or research centres, participate in numerous European or transcontinental research projects that must be conducted in languages other than Catalan or Castilian. English is also the language most used in international conferences and scientific meetings and in general for scientific dissemination. However, this does not imply that both official languages are excluded from the process of doing research in Catalonia. This is evidenced by some of the findings of a study on the use of languages in the Barcelona Science Park, one of the most active scientific, technical and economic hubs in Spain linked to UB: firstly, the existence of a number of sociolinguistic trends coincident with the general Catalan society; and secondly, a trilingual work environment based on a functional distribution between Catalan as the prevalent language for internal questions (i.e. administrative tasks) and relationship with Catalan society, English as a language for international commitments and scientific dissemination (although an intensive use as working language the biomedical centre) and Castilian occupying an intermediate position, as a language used in internal and external relationships, especially in areas with a stronger state connexion (Vila *et al.*, 2012).

Moreover, according to the Spanish legal framework, the increasing efforts of universities to disseminate research results and transfer know-how to the rest of society should, in the first instance, address their most immediate social environment, as should their research efforts themselves. In practice, however, methods used by the state to assess research seem quite inconsistent with those objectives in regard to both the lines of research that are pursued – specially in items of regional or local interest – and the language in which results are presented (Nogueira, 2012: 207). The criteria employed by ANECA, as the body reporting the Ministry of Education, practically boil down to the examination of citation index impact factors. It is necessary here to consider the problems of linguistic under-representation of commonly accepted international indices (Van Leeuwen *et al.*, 2001: 335–346). Among the inequities of this system is the sidelining of research published in languages other than English. Although the evaluation system discriminates against publication in Castilian as well as against Catalan, it is the last language that is most affected. This effect is particularly pernicious in the area of social sciences, in which many of the most demanding journals have to continue to be published in languages other than English, and has a translation in the highest percentage of negative decisions in the evaluation of merits research of faculty by contrast with scientific areas where statehood or regional element is much more relative.[15]

In Catalonia, a number of institutional factors support a significant presence of Catalan in the field of research. "If we look at doctoral dissertations, Catalan maintains a remarkable position: 25% of all theses defended in 2012 at Catalonia's universities were in Catalan. Nevertheless, more doctoral dissertations were written in Castilian (37%) or English (37%), while only 1.2% were written in other languages. 30% of theses written in Catalan were presented at UB, 25% at UAB, 10% at UPC, UdG an URV, and 5% at UPF, UdL and URL. (Source: RACO, HYPERLINK "http://www.raco.cat" \t"_blank" www.raco.cat, personal communication, 26 February 2013). However, a chronological overview helps to highlight some decrease, not spectacular but steady, of the percentage of theses written in Catalan, in favour of English (the UPF provides 6.2% of the total in English and only 1.2%, respectively, in Catalan and Castilian) and the maintaining of a strong position of Castilian in some areas, which cannot be dissociated from state assessment and accreditation criteria that, either implicitly or explicitly, damage or undervalue the research done in the Catalan language. The *Generalitat* maintains a line of financial support for doctoral theses written in Catalan (in 2012 were allocated 80,000 euros, which funded 180 theses, with a fairly consistent presence in all areas of knowledge).

Regarding the publication of scientific results, it is important to emphasise the existence of a significant number of journals, supported by the Catalan government and other public or semi-public institutions, through which scientific research is disseminated. As for books, institutional publishers and editorial services of universities also publish scientific research in Catalan. Private publishers are more reluctant to use Catalan, a language that has an almost anecdotal presence in some areas, given that Castilian is the prevalent language for accessing the Spanish and Latin American markets. The results of the use of Catalan in articles published in journals in Catalonia (usually multilingual) can be considered quite good, especially if we consider that the assessment and recognition of research linked to journal rankings tend to undermine the position of Catalan journals, which have additional difficulties in fulfilling criteria set at state or international levels (Bordons & Gómez 2004). More recently digital versions tend to replace paper versions, both in books and in reviews (Table 7.3).

Table 7.3 Language of the articles that appeared in Catalan scientific journals

	Catalan (%)	Castilian (%)	English (%)	Others (%)
2006–2007	52	36	8	4
2008	62	31	4	3
2009	52	34	6	8
2010	50	32	5	13
2011	34	48	5	13
2012	48	33	5	14
Accumulated	50	36	5	9

Source: RACO (http://www.raco.cat, accessed 26 February 2013)

The government of the *Generalitat* maintains a programme of scientific documentation managed by the Agency for Administration of University and Research (AGAUR) that realises, among other purposes, bibliometric analysis of scientific results, to measure the impact and the level of internationalisation of the Catalan language and the spread of Catalan science and scientific terminology and nomenclature.

Language Ideologies and Discourses

The higher education sector is prone to the development and expression of a plurality of linguistic ideologies, understood as cultural systems of ideas about social and linguistic relationships, together with its cargo of moral and political interests (Woolard, 1998). The autonomy enjoyed by universities (with its components of shared or consensual governance of the university community) and the complexity of the demands projected by surrounding societies favour the intensity of the debates about the use, utility and value of languages that are often masked by sociopolitical, economic or moral considerations. Within the Catalan universities, this debate has been focused since the 1980s in the dichotomy Catalan–Castilian, being the first language subject to a normalisation process which should logically result in a partial displacement of the only official language until then (Cercle 21, 2006). Lately, and without having closed the previous debate, the position of the third language (understatement of huge ideological cargo to refer to English) is the issue causing most ideological questions inside the university community (Armengol *et al.*, 2013: 45–53).

The current state of this debate is conditioned by the management of the linguistic impact of the EAHE on the university system of Catalonia. Initially, the marginalisation of linguistic diversity in the founding documents that designed the main objectives of the Bologna process, launched by the states and the European Union, gave rise to concern about the future of Catalan in the new European framework. The Spanish legislator has followed the same trend observed in previous legislation when incorporating the criteria derived from the Bologna process: no specific mention of languages was made in the norms containing the principles which underpin the new undergraduate and postgraduate programmes, with only two exceptions regarding the need to register the language of writing and defence of doctoral theses and the issue of European Supplement to the Degree in Castilian and another official language determined by universities. While subsequent documents of the EAHE have formally taken into account 'linguistic diversity' as an objective and a value to promote, the regional government and the universities have adopted a more pragmatic approach with regard to the introduction of multilingual criteria through language planning (see above Catalan university linguistic model). At the same time, political and university leaders are conscious of the vagueness of linguistic discourse developed within the EAHE, where the messages in favour of multilingualism are often directed to favour the spread of English as a lingua franca which facilitates mobility within the European area, a role that the Castilian language can also play to some extent.

An analysis of the discourses of universities language plans shows a distinct emphasis on the need and usefulness of English (maximum in UPC and lower in UdG, URV or UB). The explicit intention of influencing favourable attitudes of members of the university community regarding the status of English as a university working language can be found in UPF. The penetration of this discourse among the different sectors of the university community is not possible to determine in general terms, given its internal pluralism, although there are some marked profiles (de Rosselló & Boix, 2003: 4–5): firstly, older members of faculty are usually less inclined to introduce a third language in their academic tasks; secondly, young researchers conceive as a necessary condition for their academic career a good knowledge of English; and, finally, a majority of students distrust changes in the medium of instruction, largely due to their poor security in using English or other languages. A vast majority of the academic staff increasingly perceive the incentives and requirements of the system to acquire language skills in English despite the lack of institutional support in times of economic constraints, which may reduce the gap detected between multilingualism theory and linguistic practices (Armengol *et al.*, 2013). In these circumstances, English is not usually perceived as a killer language, but according to a functional distribution its hierarchical superiority is recognized as lingua franca for the dissemination of knowledge in a vast number of scientific communities (Alcón & Michavila, 2012: 32; Vila *et al.*, 2012: 61). The valuation they deserve other languages in that multilingual context is much more diffuse, although the promotion of French, German and Italian among students is well regarded.

The Catalan–Castilian dichotomy still has a central role in the ideological debate on languages at university. After three decades of a 'normalisation' process, the initial attitudes of commitment and volunteerism of a significant part of staff and students are leading to a more normal inertia in the use of Catalan. However, one can doubt whether, in the absence of current institutional support, this inertia would be enough to maintain a strong position of Catalan as an academic language, given the need to counteract negative factors such as the perceived disadvantages of its use in research or the convergence towards more widespread languages in master studies among others. Another important key is the fact that the professional environment is strongly a state-regulated, and the unitary organisation of some professions (i.e. in the legal area), that foster the historical inertia of use of Castilian. Indeed, a minor percentage of the academic staff feels uncomfortable with some of the proactive language policies and, for instance, distrusts or even rejects the linguistic requirements in recruiting policies. And among students has been detected the lack of a solid discourse to oppose the shift in the language of instruction promoted by the demands of students' mobility (de Rosselló & Boix, 2003: 5).

In short, based on a fairly broad general consensus around official languages built during the last 30 years, which was altered by the ongoing process of acceptance of English as a working language, the ideological struggle around the use of languages in universities doesn't seem to have ended. Conditional on the success of policies to promote polyglot individuals, the current role of lingua franca developed by English and Castilian can vary, so the first gains ground under the 'anonymity' versus the 'authenticity' of the second, with a more marked status for the state (Woolard 1998). The position of the Catalan university will remain strong based primarily if it is also in the overall Catalan society that supports it.

Conclusion

If bilingual higher education can be defined as that which takes place in an environment where two or more languages are normally used and that aims to ensure the training of graduates in both languages, the

Catalan university system is surely one of its most perfect expressions (Purser, 2003). This is at least the aim of the organisation of language use at the universities in Catalonia which is largely based on the principles of language conjunction (joint education of students of different native or initial languages) and emissive freedom in both official languages, Catalan and Castilian. Despite this, the legal and practical position of the two official languages is not identical within the Catalan university system, where other languages, namely English, are increasingly present as working languages, making the system evolve into a multilingual one.

Two circumstances can be identified as positive elements of the current situation of Catalan as compared to other non-state languages: on the one hand, a majority use of Catalan as a language of instruction in undergraduate studies and a significant presence in master's and postgraduate studies; on the other, the institutional support for the dissemination of research and the interuniversity cooperation alongside the Catalan area. The management of the linguistic impact of EAHE, which under its vague linguistic discourse promotes the incorporation of English, has led to a more central role for linguistic policy in the governance of universities through new instruments of language planning and management through objectives. The previous existence of a consistent legal framework and a long experience on language management, assumed by a complex organisation within universities, has facilitated the entry into the new multilingual stadium.

Thus, the current trend seems to point to a more marked differentiation between multilingual university models, as opposed to the precedent linguistic homogeneity, through which universities can try to define their own profile. The results of new instruments and measures to promote multilingualism are not predictable since it is not simply a top-down process but is conditioned by the attitudes and practices of the university community. Language can become a differentiating feature for singular universities in a more competitive context.

Notes

(1) Article 3 (1) of the Spanish Constitution establishes that 'Castilian is the official language of the Spanish state' and that 'all Spaniards have the duty to know it and the right to use it'. Article 3 (2) stipulates that 'the other languages of Spain will also be official in the respective autonomous communities, in accordance with their Statutes', defined as their basic institutional legislation.
(2) Council of Europe, the Committee of Expert's interpretation and evaluation practices concerning the articles on education of the European Charter for Regional or Minority Languages (Strasbourg, 6 October 2005/MIN-LANG (2006) 3 Strasbourg, 6 March 2006.

(3) According to Judgment 75/1997, 24 April, of the constitutional court, these linguistic provisions may be included in the 'ordinary content' of university autonomy, which is not explicitly determined in Article 2 (2) OLU.

(4) Whereas the paragraphs of Article 8.1 that it applies to preschool, primary and secondary education are, respectively, a.i, b.i and c.i (the highest level of protection), the paragraph applied to higher education is e.iii, which was originally conceived for private universities and, according to the 'Explanatory Report on the ECRML' (http://www.conventions.coe.int/Treaty/EN/Reports/Hhtml/148.htm) constitutes a further solution (alternative to teaching in the regional or minority language and teaching that language as an object of education) 'for those cases in which the public authorities have no direct competences for the type of education concerned'.

(5) It must be said that Judgment 31/2010, 28 June, of the constitutional court on the 2006 reform of the Statute of Autonomy has overruled the adjective 'preferential' to qualify Catalan language as Catalonia's own language, to preserve the official status of Castilian, but the concrete consequences of this decision are uncertain at present.

(6) This nuclear content of the officiality principle was formulated by the constitutional court in Judgment 82/1986 and later it was included in Article 32 of the Statute of Autonomy of Catalonia.

(7) The same 'conjunction' system is applied in the University of the Balearic Islands. By way of contrast, universities in Valencia follow a 'streams' model (similar to that of primary and secondary school), where the Catalan streams are even more a minority and very often courses in Catalan cover neither all the demand nor all the education options.

(8) Resolution IUE 135/2007, of April 27, which established the standing committees of the Interuniversity Council of Catalonia. The composition of this body includes one representative from each university, both public and private, with the rank of vice-chancellor or general secretary (and also two students appointed by the Commission of Students of the same Interuniversity Council of Catalonia) and is headed by a university chancellor appointed by the government. Among its functions, this committee proposes political guidelines in linguistic matters and ensures the coordination of various university models for managing multilingualism.

(9) Currently, the Xarxa Vives includes 20 universities, representing a collective of more than 440,000 people: 400,000 students, 30,000 teachers and 10,000 administrative and services staff. Two committees are responsible for the promotion of the language activities: the Language Commission, made up of the directors of language boards at the universities; and the Language Policy Committee, made up of vice-chancellors responsible for language policy.

(10) Data about language of instruction are systematically recorded by public universities (as an indicator linked to conditional funding) and statistics are produced by the Secretary for Universities and Research (independent from government). Regarding the results of the academic year 2011/2012, the percentage of the data known was 90.4% and the margins of error were no more than 3%. See http://www20.gencat.cat/portal/site/ur/menuitem.7f9c2004924f29cf642d3010b0c0e1a0/?vgnextoid=0a5e7ff1301bd310VgnVCM1000008d0c1e0aRCRD&vgnextchannel=0a5e7ff1301bd310VgnVCM1000008d0c1e0aRCRD&vgnextfmt=default.

(11) Royal Decree 800/1995, of 19 May, for regulating access to certain sectors of public administration of nationals of other member states of the European Union.
(12) Law 7/2007, of 12 April, on the basic statute of public officials, establishes that public administrations, in their respective powers, should provide for the selection of adequate personnel to cover public work posts in the autonomous communities with two official languages.
(13) Linguistic choice is not covered by the fundamental right to academic freedom guaranteed by Article 20 (1) (c) of the Spanish Constitution, and consequently, the decision on this subject may be conditioned in order to protect other principles or legitimate interests.
(14) Decree 128/2010, of 14 September, on the accreditation of linguistic knowledge of faculty of universities of the Catalan university system.
(15) *Informe sobre los resultados de las evaluaciones de la CNEAI. La situación en 2009*, published by the Ministery of Education, where data appear distributed by scientific areas and universities. http://www.mecd.gob.es/dctm/ministerio/horizontales/ministerio/organismos/cneai/2009-info-v5.pdf?documentId=0901e72b8008d9ff.

References

Alcón, E. and Michavila, F. (2012) *La Universidad multilingüe*. Madrid: Tecnos.
Armengol, L., Cots, J.M., Llurda, E.I. and Mancho-Barés, G. (2013) *Universitats internacionals i plurilingües? Entre les polítiques i les pràctiques a les universitats de Catalunya*. Lleida: Edicions de la Universitat de Lleida.
Arzoz, X. (2009) Universidad y pluralismo lingüístico. In J. González García (ed.) *Comentario a la Ley orgánica de universidades* (pp. 1125–1192). Madrid: Civitas.
Arzoz, X. (2012) *Bilingual Higher Education in the Legal Context*. Leiden: Martinus Nijhoff.
Barraclough, F. (2009) La 'lingua franca' de la ciència. El predomini de l'anglès en les publicacions científiques'. *Mètode* 62, 27–31.
Bordons, M. and Gómez, I. (2004) Towards a single language in science? A Spanish view. *Serias* 17 (2). See http://www.adawis.de/admin/upload/navigation/data/English%20 as%20a%20single%20language%20of%20Science%20-%20A%20Spanish%20view. pdf (accessed 27 July 2014).
Cercle 21 (2006) El català a la universitat. Anàlisi i propostes per a la normalització social de la llengua catalana a la universitat. *Butlletí virtual* 4. See http://www.cercle21.cat/butlleti/04/index.html (accessed 27 July 2014).
de Rosselló, C. and Boix, E. (2003) Les ideologies lingüístiques de l'alumnat de la universitat de Barcelona. *Enxarxa't* 3. See http://www.ub.edu/enxarxat/3/enxarxat-3.pdf (accessed 27 July 2014).
Matas, J. and Planas, C. (2008) La capacitació lingüística del professorat de la Universitat de Barcelona, *Llengua i ús*, 41: 49–54.
Nadal, O. (1993) Cooficialitat i bilingüisme a la Universitat Autònoma de Barcelona (1933–39). *Revista de Llengua i Dret* 19, 129–169. See http://www10.gencat.net/eapc_rld/revistes/revista.2008-09-18.1622650712/Cooficialitat_i_bilinguisme_a_ la_Universitat_Autonoma_de_Barcelona__1933_1939_/ca (accessed 27 July 2014).
Nogueira, A. (2012) Living in borrowed time: Bilingual law teaching in Galicia or the urgent need to recover prestige. In X. Arzoz (ed.) *Bilingual Higher Education in the Legal Context* (pp. 193–214). Leiden: Martinus Nijhoff.
Nogueira, A. (dir.) (2013) *Investigación e Lingua. Ciencia en galego*. Santiago de Compostela: Comisión interuniversitaria de política lingüística (unpublished report).

Oliva, L. and Vinent, A. (1980) El català a la universitat. Entre l'esforç i la passivitat. In J. Misser (ed). *L'Hora de Catalunya* (pp. 1–13). Barcelona: Editorial Pòrtic.
Poggeschi, G. (2010) *I diritti linguistici. Un'analisi comparata.* Roma: Carocci editore.
Pons, E. (2012) Bilingual legal education in Catalonia. In X. Arzoz (ed.) *Bilingual Higher Education in the Legal Context* (pp. 167–192). Leiden: Martinus Nijhoff.
Purser, L. (2003) L'Université bilingue – Réflexions générales sur ses origines, sa mission et son fonctionnement. In S. Bergan (ed.) *Les politiques linguistiques dans l'enseignement supérieur* (pp. 25–35). Strasbourg: Council of Europe Publishing.
Tsu, A. and Tollefson, J.W. (2004) The centrality of medium-of-instruction policy in sociopolitical processes. In J.W. Tollefson and A. Tsu (eds) *Medium of Instruction Policies: Wich Agenda? Whose Agenda?* Abingdon: Lawrence Erlbaum Associates.
Van Leeuwen, T., Moed, H., Tijssen, R., Visser, M. and Van Raan, A. (2001) Language biases in the coverage of the Science Citation Index and its consequences for international comparisons of national research performance. *Scientometrics* 51 (1), 335–346. See http://www.cwts.nl/TvR/documents/AvR-Language-Scientometrics.pdf (accessed 27 July 2014).
Vernet, J. (coord) (2003) *Dret lingüistic.* Valls: Cossetània.
Vila, F.X. (2008) Language-in-education policies in the Catalan language area: Models, results and challenges. *AILA Review* 21, 31–48.
Vila, F.X. (2011) Language-in-education policy. In M. Strubell and E. Boix (eds) *Democratic Policies for Language Revitalisation: The Case of Catalan* (pp. 119–149). Basingstoke: Palgrave Macmillan.
Vila, F.X., Bretxa, V. and Comajoan, L. (2012) Llengües i globalització en el món de la recerca: Els coneixements i els usos lingüístics al *Parc Científic de Barcelona. Caplletra* 52, 35–64.
Woolard, K.A. (1998) *Language Ideologies: Practice and Theory.* New York: Oxford University Press.

8 Medium-Sized Languages as Viable Linguae Academicae

F. Xavier Vila

On the Goals of this Volume

We started this volume trying to find some answers to a simple question: what is actually going on in terms of language practices, ideologies and management in medium-sized languages (for the concept, see Vila & Bretxa, 2013) which have achieved the status of lingua academica? Irrespective of the authors' personal interest in each particular case, we all shared the feeling that focusing on these types of languages was both academically and practically relevant. Academically, the sociolinguistic weaker position of these languages in comparison to the big, hypercentral and supercentral languages, to put it in terms of de Swaan (2001), made them ideal laboratories to analyse the actual impact of globalisation and internationalisation on higher education. At the end of the day, if English were to become dominant in this sphere of life, it is more than logical that its hegemony would be achieved first and faster at the expense of its weakest competitors. On the contrary, if these languages were to retain their status as a lingua academica, even if only partially, that would suggest that the otherwise undeniable spread of English as the main academic lingua franca was not necessarily leading to a loss of status and domain for these languages. Analysing these societies was, in many respects, quite akin to concentrating on one of the most complex aspects in the process of sociolinguistic globalisation. As a consequence, the languages studied for this goal were not randomly selected, since the sample was not intended to be representative of all medium-sized languages in the world. On the contrary, the chapters focused on a selection of societies which were known to have introduced at least some of these languages into their university life, some for years, others more recently.

The project appeared relevant in other, more practical terms. Managing transnational, multilingual universities has become an urgent task for many campuses and governments around the world, but to date most of the available literature on multilingualism in higher education has focused on how to introduce English as a means of instruction, while very few has focused on the rest of the linguistic ecosystem. This book was intended to target the other side of the coin, and has therefore provided university language policymakers and language managers with both general reflections and comparative data that might be of help in their immediate tasks. The volume had also an added practical value for language activists all over the world. Many speakers of so-called 'minority languages' become convinced of the scarce practical utility of their languages on the basis of general references to globalisation and internationalisation. At the end of the day, linguistic minorisation is to a large extent an ideological construct, and minority status is first of all a state of mind. Showing that at least a number of languages with a medium-sized demographic basis 'have made it', i.e. have become complete languages that serve all purposes of daily life and are not threatened with ineluctable extinction, may be good news for those concerned with the fate of multilingualism in higher education. Or so we hope. Therefore, whereas 'minority languages' were not systematically dealt with in this volume, we hope the substance of these chapters may be of use to them.

The previous chapters have explored the sociolinguistic situation of a number of higher education systems. In the following sections, we will summarise some of the conclusions that can be reached after comparing these cases.

A Medium-Sized Language may be Viable as a Lingua Academica

Several chapters in this book have proved that the field of higher education has historically experienced tensions between two poles that we may term 'the international and the national orientation'. In linguistic terms, the former orientation has encouraged the use of academic linguae francae, while the latter has promoted the elaboration of local languages and their development into linguae academicae. The use of a lingua franca is by no means only dependent on an international orientation: use of Latin in medieval and modern times was also encouraged by the intellectual capital accumulated in that language, by its association with extremely powerful institutions such as the Catholic Church, and by the fact that Latin also worked as a social boundary that protected the interests of some elites. Alternatively, not all nation-building processes have sought the promotion of local vernaculars to the status of lingua academica. Latin American, African and many Asian nation states have rarely promoted their local languages to the status of lingua academica; on the contrary, they have adopted colonial languages for the purposes of higher education. This volume has shown that the sociolinguistic landscape of higher education does not remain still. In the last decades, not only has English spread hand in hand with the post-national university model, but some other languages have declined, like Afrikaans, or they have (re)gained a place in higher education, like Catalan.[1]

In this context of change and limited access to the status of lingua academica, one of the first conclusions, if not the very first, after reading this volume is that at the beginning of the 21st century, most of the medium-sized languages analysed here have proven to function reasonably well as the main means of communication for university systems. In other words, in spite of globalisation and the purported 'stampede towards English' (de Swaan, 2001, 2010), medium-sized languages remain a viable means of instruction in higher education.

Granted, several of the medium-sized languages historically present in the societies analysed had virtually no presence at all in university life. This was the case, for instance, for most of the languages spoken in South Africa. But irrespective of how one values it, their exclusion from higher education is hardly a surprise, since this exclusion is the norm rather than the exception among medium-sized languages – indeed, among languages in the world – especially in the African context. On the contrary, the relevant point here was not that some medium-sized languages were excluded from higher education, but rather that a significant number of these languages were indeed in wide and vibrant use for academic purposes. Even more important was the confirmation that most of these languages do not seem to be in immediate peril of losing their status or of becoming marginalised. On the contrary, these languages were found to be widely used not only as vehicles of private interpersonal communication, but also as the predominant means of instruction and administration of whole university systems. This was not only the case for languages such as Danish, with a strong multisecular history as a vehicle of higher education and research, but also for languages like Czech, Finnish and Hebrew, with a shorter presence in this sphere, and even for Catalan, which only four decades ago was officially banned from university spheres. In fact, among all the languages under scrutiny, only Afrikaans has clearly lost much ground as a lingua academica during the last decade and is in actual danger of being marginalised in the university scene. But the reasons for

Afrikaans' retreat derive from national rather than international causes: a loss of its institutional position in post-apartheid South Africa, a reduction in its demographic basis due to emigration and a concomitant rise in English as the *de facto* national lingua franca. None of these factors can be immediately generalised to the rest of the medium-sized languages which have reached the status of lingua academica. In truth, the actual evolution of all these other languages does not match that of Afrikaans.

Although at first glance this conclusion may seem a trivial fact to some, it implies a powerful corollary for language policy and language management all over the world. What these data suggest is that, faced with the dilemma of adopting a language for academic purposes, the decision of either an international language or a medium-sized language is an open one. The evidence gathered in this volume suggests that nothing seems to preclude the use of these languages as vehicles to teaching and learning beyond secondary education. In other words, medium-sized languages – and their speakers – need not be excluded from professional and highly intellectualised spheres. The choice is out there.

Of course, a number of conditions must be satisfied to make such a choice possible. To start with, it appears reasonable that only languages which have previously occupied the rest of the cultural and economic spheres of modern life will succeed in becoming fully fledged academic languages. In principle, the widespread presence of the language in higher education does not seem possible unless it is solidly established in the rest of the education system. Nevertheless, the case of Catalan furnishes a very interesting counter-example where the language was adopted as a means of instruction in higher education even before it was generalised as a subject matter in schools, not to mention as a means of instruction. In Catalonia, universities spearheaded the process of linguistic normalisation, with teachers and students learning to write the language simultaneously, so to say. The conviction that conquering higher education was crucial for language survival was also evident in the case of Hebrew: other language might have been a more pragmatic option for Technion, but Hebrew needed to occupy the highest positions of education to become viable, or so it was felt. Both cases make it clear that support from an independent state may not be prerequisite to gain the status of lingua academica, but strong political support by a significant segment of the population *is* inescapable. And, in the long run, this commitment needs to transform itself into state support (Vila, 2013). The retreat of Afrikaans bears witness to this need.

In any case, a lesson to be learnt from the previous chapters is that the demographic limits to attain the status of lingua academica seem much more affordable than might be thought at first sight. This volume has focused on languages that have at least three million speakers, but the fact that several smaller communities like Slovenia, Estonia and Latvia, to mention but three, are using their languages as a viable means of communication within the university sphere suggests that this is by no means the lowest demographic threshold for viability (see Bitenc, 2013; Ozolins, 2013; Skerret, 2013). A glimpse at the University of Iceland's website[2] confirms that Icelandic, a language with fewer than 400,000 speakers, is widely used as a means of instruction. Indeed, the case of the Swedish-speaking minority in Finland reviewed in Chapter 4, endowed as it is with a number of higher education institutions, or those of Sami, Faeroese or Scottish Gaelic,[3] suggests that the lowest demographic threshold for a language to function as a viable means of instruction in higher education may be even smaller, provided that the right socioeconomic and political conditions are established.

The Foreseeable Scenario: Institutional Completeness in Plurlingual Ecologies

The second main conclusion that can be drawn from the previous chapters is that medium-sized languages that achieve the status of lingua academica do not enjoy it on their own, i.e. they coexist with other languages in the academic setting. In fact, this has probably been the case ever since universities were created. Consider the case of the Danish universities. In the course of more than half a millennium, these universities have used not only Danish, but also Latin, German, French and English extensively. In Finland, apart from Finnish, universities have also used Latin, Swedish, German and English extensively. Something similar could be said of the rest of the universities under scrutiny. Even in the less multilingual universities, such as the Czech and the Israeli ones, other languages are in use. Indeed, at some historical periods, universities have been less multilingual than at other periods; as Haberland and Preisler point out in Chapter 2, universities are multilingual environments, although they are not necessarily *stable* multilingual environments – if stability and multilingualism can really go together.

At this point, it is important to distinguish between universities located in societies which are rather homogeneous in ethnolinguistic terms, like Denmark and the Czech Republic, and those composed of different linguistic groups, like Finland, Israel, Catalonia and South Africa, because the latter have to cope simultaneously with two different sources of multilingualism: external and internal. In this respect, internal multilingualism is dealt with differently in each society. Some of the systems analysed here have been built on the assumption that the survival of different languages as linguae academicae depends crucially on the existence of some degree of institutional autonomy for each language group. This is the case of Finland, whose network of higher education institutions includes some universities which are monolingual in Finnish, others in Swedish and a number of bilingual institutions. In this sense, Finland is especially concerned with the reproduction of the Swedish language within its society, to the extent that its legislation foresees that several universities have the responsibility to educate 'a sufficient number of persons proficient in Swedish for the needs of the country' (Universities Act 558/2009: Section 12/1, quoted by Ylönen, this volume). The view that institutional completeness should be obtained on the basis of institutional autonomy – which, in the end, is akin to the territoriality principle – is widely supported around the world, as testified by examples such as the Canadian, the Swiss and the Belgian ones (see Arzoz, 2012). On the other hand, the difficulties experienced by South-African languages in this respect in the last decades bears testimony to the difficulty for medium and smaller languages to flourish in the shadow of a giant — namely, English. Nevertheless, the case of Catalonia, where Catalan has achieved a considerable degree of completeness without totally dislodging Castilian or creating parallel institutions, and without an independent state of its own, provides a remarkable case study (see more below).

In any case, the particular sociolinguistic arrangements of universities are obviously dependent on the nature of the societies that host them. In Chapter 2, Haberland and Preisler insist that the significant role of English in Danish universities cannot be fully understood if one fails to recognise the role that it plays in the whole of Danish society. The promotion of this language is steered not only 'from above' – i.e. from public institutions – but also 'from below', and one is tempted to say not only 'from outside', but also 'from inside' Danish society. Danish contemporary culture, from cultural consumption habits such as subtitling, to the alternative young subcultures, values English enormously and has made much social room for it. This is a point that should be taken very much into consideration by those engaged in comparative language policies: rather than the educational system on its own, it is the societal pervasiveness of English in Denmark that explains the high levels of second language proficiency acquired by Danish students. On the other hand, university sociolinguistic realities are not just a mechanical reflex of their societies. As the South African case proves, not all the languages that are used in the university surroundings find their way into these institutions. Universities use languages which are not necessarily (so) widely used outside its gates.

On the whole, universities in medium-sized language communities have a particular linguistic ecology and have developed their own solutions in terms of language management and language policy to their own particular sociolinguistic challenges. These solutions are based on:

(1) A distinguishable pattern of functional specialisation.
(2) A singular configuration of its linguistic repertoire.
(3) A concomitant ideological and discursive arrangement as far as languages are concerned.

Distinguishable Patterns of Functional Specialisation

Most of the languages analysed in this volume were clearly predominant in their campuses. But this predominance has to be nuanced, for the languages analysed here were not predominant in all academic functions. We can explore the patterns of functional allocation step by step, looking at the language of administration, the means of instruction and their use as a language of scientific production and diffusion.

Institutional and administrative purposes

Most of the languages analysed in the volume have proven to be able to function as a means of administration. Admittedly, monolingual Afrikaans-medium universities were turning into bilingual or even monolingual English-medium universities, and no South African university had ever worked extensively on the basis of an African language. But this process of shifting to English for administrative purposes was not detected in the other contexts, which did not show any sign of a shift towards English or to another language in this sphere. Of course, instances of the use of English for auxiliary purposes – for instance, for advertisements addressed to foreign students – were not rare, but this does not equal a shift.

Means of instruction

If we turn to instruction, most of the languages reviewed in the chapters seem to be working relatively well as the *spoken* means of instruction, especially in undergraduate courses. Indeed, with the exception of South Africa, a majority of the undergraduate courses in the university systems were taught by means of a medium-sized language. A case in point is

Finland which, according to a 2007 large-scale survey, had the highest number of institutions (66%) offering English-taught programmes at bachelor and master levels among 27 European countries. In 2008, the percentage of bachelor programmes in English in Finland was 30%. Or consider the case of the Copenhagen Business School, probably one of the Danish universities with the highest number of courses in English. In 2009, 76% of its students followed a Danish-medium bachelor programme, whereas 24% attended an English-medium one. In 2012, only 14% of the bachelor programmes in the Czech Republic were locally accredited – but not necessarily offered – in a language other than Czech (mostly English). Figures for undergraduate courses were similar or even lower in the rest of the systems analysed.

Granted, things were indeed different for masters and doctorates. In 2008, the percentage of programmes in English in Finland was 62% for masters and 8% for doctorates. At the Copenhagen Business School, 43.6% of students followed a Danish-medium programme, whereas 56.4% followed an English-medium one; in the Czech Republic, in 2012, 23% of two-year master's and 39% of PhD programmes were locally accredited in a language other than Czech (mostly English).[4] But before accepting these courses as evidence of a language shift, one should consider two factors: on the one hand, to a large extent, these courses are designed to attract foreign students; on the other, most of these programmes did not previously exist. In other words, since most of these postgraduate courses are an answer to the appearance of an international system of postgraduate education, speaking of a language shift would not be totally accurate: they tend to be more an example of the *addition* of new programmes, rather than the *replacement* of old ones. In this respect, as pointed out by several authors across the volume, we badly need reliable quantitative and qualitative research about language practices in higher education to clearly evaluate, for instance, the spread of English as an instructional lingua franca, and beyond this role.[5] But as long as masters and doctorates are conceived as transnational courses, it is rather predictable that they will not be taught in the local lingua academica but rather in an academic lingua franca. In this respect, it is interesting to point out that even in Catalonia, the divide between undergraduate and postgraduate courses also exists, although with a remarkable difference, since there the role of English is fulfilled by Castilian. On the contrary, this trend is not detected in Israel, where the use of languages other than Hebrew hardly goes beyond 10%. In South Africa, on the contrary, languages other than English are much less used.

All in all, three main conclusions as far as oral language practices can be reached. First, most of the medium-sized languages analysed in the current volume were widely used in higher education. Second, a significant divide was detected between undergraduate and postgraduate courses. A final trend that was perceptible in some chapters pointed to a higher use of English in the areas of the natural and physical sciences in comparison with the social sciences and humanities, although this trend was not so readily demonstrable.

Practices turned out to be quite different as far as written language is concerned. A distinction between receptive and productive uses is pertinent here. On the one hand, students and scholars alike tended to use their local languages more than English in their assignments, syllabi, tests and other written materials. In fact, unless a course was defined as English-medium, or explicitly included the learning of English as one of its goals, productive written practices coincided with spoken ones. On the other hand, almost all the university systems studied relied heavily on materials written in English for reading, due to the need to turn to this language for specialised, updated materials, such as reference books and articles. Again, in Catalonia, Castilian played the role of English, although in this case English was also clearly on the increase, especially in the hard sciences and technology. This global predominance of English does not mean that teaching materials were not available in the medium-sized languages analysed in this volume; in fact, these materials were often available particularly in the disciplines of the social sciences and the humanities and for teacher training. Some university systems, such as the Czech one, appeared to show a stronger trend towards producing original materials for instructional purposes in their own languages, and towards translating versions of canonical works. Of note is that several chapters mentioned that there was little willingness among students to read academic stuff written in third languages, i.e., in languages other than their own or English. Only in cases of strong linguistic proximity and intense vicinity – for instance, Czech and Slovak – were other languages easily accepted.

Research and Academic Publication

The language practices in research and academic publications were probably the area where most coincidences were found across countries. Two main themes appeared repeatedly in this domain. On the one hand, none of the medium-sized languages studied in the volume has ever been the predominant vehicle for the dissemination of scientific research; therefore, some degree of plurilingualism has historically been a normal requirement for academics from these communities. The linguistic evolution of PhD dissertations shown in several chapters beautifully illustrates this trend. The predominant language of doctoral dissertations in Finland, for instance, was Latin until the 20th century, German during the first half of that century and English since then. Finnish only became the second most used language after independence in the 20th century, and in fact has only enjoyed this position without competition since the fall of the rest of its competitors (basically, Swedish and German) during the last 50 years. Patterns not so distant from this, although obviously nuanced by the local historical factors, might be identified for several other languages like Danish and Catalan. Again, Israel stands out as a different case, with a solid majority of doctoral dissertations – around 80–90% – in Hebrew, but it must be borne in mind that the use of Hebrew for PhD dissertation has historically been virtually compulsory.

On the other hand, all authors reported a trend towards the increase of English as the language used for the dissemination of research production in scientific spheres, especially in journals. Data from Finland indicate, for instance, that nearly two thirds of all scientific publications were written in this language, even though 39% of the scientific publications appeared in Finland itself. On their side, 90% of the Israeli scholars interviewed declared that they never published articles in Hebrew. Data about Afrikaans were extreme in this respect, with a 300% decrease between 1990 and 2002. In several countries, a number of journals previously published in other languages have adopted an English name and include more and more articles in this language. It is interesting to note that there was a greater predominance of English in the physical and biological sciences, whereas the humanities and social sciences were more open to other languages, to the extent that publication in the local languages could be more important than in English, for instance, in Danish universities. One finds some bilingual dual publishing, that is, publications that include two versions, one in English and the other in the local language, such as Czech – where it is called 'building parallel discourses' – or Catalan, with or without small adaptations. The language choices for oral presentations in conferences and similar scientific events closely resemble these behaviours.

However, the predominance of English in academic publication does not equal the idea that it is the predominant language of science *tout cour*. On the one hand, we did not gather information about the non-academic dissemination of scientific knowledge and science transfer to the immediate society, but nothing suggests that this is necessarily done in English (see Hamel, 2013). On the other, systematic observation in scientific settings in Denmark, Finland and Catalonia shows that, in the process of *producing* research, the local languages are widely used for oral and written communication between colleagues, management, etc. In fact, it is the local languages rather than English that were by far the preferred languages to communicate among local scientists. To put it briefly, at least in the settings reviewed here, English was used for scientific publications not because it was more appropriate as a lingua academica, but rather because it was the lingua franca – the academic lingua franca – that helps overcome linguistic barriers. If the barriers are not there, English is not needed.

Singular Linguistic Repertoires

In order to operate in multilingual environments such as those described in the volume, individuals have to acquire multilingual repertoires that fit their needs. For centuries, mastery of Latin was both a necessity and a hallmark of belonging to academic circles. It was the language of scientific written production, the academic lingua franca and the language of instruction, all of which meant that oral and written proficiency in this language was essential for members of universities. The progressive retreat of Latin gave way to competition between several alternative languages, which meant that science had to be accessed by means of different vehicles. Elite plurilingualism became a distinctive feature of university life: proficiency in the language which aspired to the status of *the* academic lingua franca was not only a valuable cultural capital that permitted access to knowledge, but also an element of symbolic capital. Some authors in the volume (e.g. Chapter 5) pointed out that, even today, many academics tend to possess plurilingual repertoires.

But the rapid ascent of English in the last decades to the status of academic lingua franca has implied a significant change in the configuration of academics' linguistic repertoires. While proficiency in English seems to be on the increase in all the academic circles analysed, proficiency in other foreign languages, including former linguae francae, is reported to be declining. This reconfiguration is especially resented among students. As Sherman (Chapter 4) puts it for German in the Czech Republic:

> In the higher education sphere, then, expectations that students will read in German has gone from general to field- and region-specific, i.e. German is still expected in fields such as History or Philosophy or at regional universities near the German and Austrian borders, though in some cases, the students are openly reminded of this expectation by their teachers. (Sherman, Chapter 4, this volume)

Similar evolutions are evoked in other chapters (e.g. Denmark and Finland), and, on the whole, might be more the norm than the exception. In other words, traditional expectations about academic plurilingualism may no longer be shared by new generations of students, and may be in the process of being replaced by almost mandatory bilingualism (local language+English), a language pairing in which English plays a pivotal role and third languages are more secondary than they used to be. Increased mobility in higher education may in fact be encouraging this reconfiguration. In Chapter 2, Haberland and Preisler speak about the 'paradox of internationalization', i.e. 'the more international the programs become, the fewer languages are used in them' (see also below). Although it was not mentioned explicitly by any author, it may well be that the differences in quantity were also paired with differences in quality: in the past, basic competences in several languages were probably enough to cope with the most common academic needs, namely reading scientific literature, whereas current academic research probably requires a higher proficiency in one single language because occasions for oral academic interactions are probably higher now than in the past. In other words, a decrease in scholars' range of plurilingualism may be paired with an increase in their mastery of one single L2.

Concomitant Linguistic Ideologies

Although too simplistic to catch all nuances – and much to the regret of most of the contributors to the volume – it can be argued that the majority of linguistic ideologies described in the volume could be synthesised by means of a 'winner' vs. 'loser' languages dichotomy based on their usefulness. The distribution of languages along this hierarchy of evaluation was quite similar, although the position of the local medium-sized language was crucially different according to the context.

The first and most unanimously agreed on element of the hierarchy was that English was valued as a language of the utmost importance in higher education. Irrespective of the continent and of different cultural traditions, all authors agreed that, in their societies, English was perceived as the language of internationalisation and the language of scientific dissemination, 'the language of science' and even 'the language of the future' as expressed in a rather grandiloquent form. No other language compared to English in this respect, which justified the urgency in many sectors to acquire control of this language. English was, in this respect, a clear winner, a highly valued capital in the academic market and the undisputed academic lingua franca, although recognition of this role was reported to be disguised in several contexts by resorting to euphemisms such as 'plurilingualism' or the ambiguous 'foreign languages'. Open recognition of the primacy of English was often resisted by some academic circles. Some of them, for instance in the Czech Republic and Israel, fiercely vindicated the primacy of the national language and expressed concerns about the 'dangers of Americanisation'. But in general terms, reluctant sectors appeared to have lost their capacity to manoeuvre in the last decades. Others still vindicated the role of former competitors to English, but they seemed even weaker.

The position of the different local languages within the hierarchy of academic languages was very diverse, depending crucially on the status of the language in the society as a whole. In those societies where one language was regarded as the undisputed means of social integration, mastery of such language received the highest value, not in the sense that it could compete with English as an international language but rather in the sense that acquiring mastery of the language was crucial for professional success within the country. Czech, Danish, Finnish and Hebrew were clearly included in this category. At the other extreme, African languages in South Africa appeared to be valued very low, and even their intrinsic capacity as a means of instruction – something that, in principle, should be presupposed from any natural language – was questioned in some circles. In between these two poles, Catalan, Swedish in Finland and Afrikaans occupied different positions, and probably followed contradictory paths, depending on their particular value in their respective national, local and sectorial markets, both in absolute terms and in connection with their local *complementary* languages (i.e. Castilian, Finnish and English). Interestingly enough, and leaving aside the case already mentioned of African languages, only in Israel was distrust detected towards the capacity of its medium-sized language, namely Hebrew, to cope with academic and scientific life, and then only marginally.

As a logical corollary to the previous lines, all other languages that had on occasion in the past aspired to the rank of academic lingua franca had been put clearly in a secondary position. French, German and Russian were no longer perceived as competitors to English. Indeed, the perception that proficiency in these languages had decreased among the younger generations was widespread. This is not to say that they were considered irrelevant, but their position was clearly secondary to English, and depended much more on factors like vicinity and practical connections. English enjoyed another advantage in comparison to these languages: in several contexts it was perceived as neutral, whereas other languages suffered from historical connotations that were not necessarily positive for them, like German in Finland and the Czech Republic. Languages of emerging countries were not even mentioned, suggesting that their increasing importance as languages of trade has still not made any impact on the academic world.

Neighbour, linguistically similar languages formed another category which was often mentioned in the case studies presented in the volume, like Scandinavian languages in Denmark, Slovak in the Czech Republic and perhaps French or Italian in the case of Catalonia. These languages enjoyed a particular status which was close to that of former academic linguae francae. As they were widely understood, they seemed to be usable for several academic functions – by visiting professors, by foreign students, as bibliographic materials – and tended not to be perceived as conflictive, in a practice that has received different names: passive or receptive bilingualism in the Catalan context, semi-communication in the Czech context and sequilinguism in the Scandinavian one. However it is called, it is worth mentioning that academic spheres did not suffer from the increasing lack of understanding of neighbour languages that has been detected in several medium-sized communities (Vila, 2013).

Finally, non-official autochthonous and immigrant languages were placed at the lowest level of the hierarchy of evaluation, to the extent that they were not even mentioned in most cases, apart from the logical exception of the Departments of Languages and Cultural Studies. Immigrants were conceived in some contexts not as 'speakers of other languages' but rather as bilinguals (local language+immigrant language). Interestingly, the languages of foreign students were not given any relevant place. In short, they seemed to have no role whatsoever in the academic sphere.

Language Policies in Higher Education: Between National and International Agendas

Universities were created as institutions with autonomous governance which, to a certain extent, escaped the laws that applied to the rest of the society that hosted them, and they have traditionally enjoyed some degree of self-control in their organisation, including language policy. Over the centuries, they organised their language policies rather autonomously from the local powers, leaning especially on Latin, a language that facilitated mobility and transnational interconnectedness, and functioned as the group marker.

But during the 19th and 20th centuries, universities became deeply involved with the processes of nation-building that were occurring in their societies and, in a sense, they acquired a number of national missions.

Universities were charged with (re)producing social groups that could play a crucial role in the fate of the country, including the national élites who should obviously be able to speak the official language and use it for all purposes. Of course, wherever the state's national project was not universally supported, i.e. where national minorities supported an alternative national agenda, political movements fought to bring their languages into higher education as well, as evidenced by the continued efforts to introduce Finnish, Czech, Hebrew, Afrikaans and Catalan into the universities, and the resistance deployed to block their entrance in many cases by state institutions. In time, borders and demolinguistics changed, and language policies in higher education adapted to changing national agendas, but language policy in higher education became intimately interconnected with nation-building policies. It appears that this interconnection continues today. At least in the eyes of national collectivities of European origin as most of those studied here, higher education has become the hallmark of linguistic completion and an irreplaceable institution as far as language elaboration and intellectualisation are concerned. When voiced, the mere possibility that these national missions could be seriously threatened triggers heated public debates and is perceived with anxiety by many social sectors. In this respect, universities' language policies are still deeply conditioned by national agendas including both the continuous formation of the nation's professional, scientific, academic and political elites and cadres that are fully capable of working by means of the national language, and the contribution to the permanent cultivation and elaboration of this language. It is surely no coincidence that medium-sized languages established in contexts which are not demolinguistically challenging – like Denmark or the Czech Republic – tend to have less explicit linguistic regulation, while those in more challenging environments – namely Finland, Israel and Catalonia – are more explicit in their national language policies. The bigger the threat perceived – even if it may not be regarded as tangible by foreigners – the more compelling the need to legislate.

While virtually none of the societies reviewed in the volume has really given up these national agendas – again, the case of Afrikaans must be analysed in the local context – all of them are now faced with the challenges imposed by globalisation, which include among others, variegated forms of internationalisation, commodification of education, and research and privatisation of higher education. Universities are increasingly encouraged to compete for international resources, talent and recognition. These new challenges are impacting on language policies and are transforming the old paradigm, designed to serve national agendas, into a complex one that should simultaneously achieve national and international goals. The need to cope with both old and new challenge seems to be leading to experimentation and to more instances of discrepancies between higher education and general national language policies. The volume has reported several cases of such contradictions. In the Czech Republic, for instance, scholars find themselves forced to develop *ad hoc* strategies to cope with foreign students who spend some time at their universities without knowing Czech. In Finland, on the contrary, where English has spread to foster internationalisation, students are reported to have taken their universities to the courts because they are denied the right to follow their studies in the national languages. Some Catalan universities have tried to further develop their conjunction principle by giving a sort of 'official' status to English in the campuses. These and many other instances have revealed that the gaps and contradictions between national and transnational agendas are not always solved to universal satisfaction. Willingly or not, universities are forced to develop their own language policies. Indeed, although subject to national agendas during the last centuries, universities always retained some degree of autonomy vis-à-vis their administration: for instance, at some level they would encourage the learning of some foreign and/or classical languages and also accept the use of languages other than the official ones in events such as doctoral dissertations and PhD defences. This degree of autonomy, though, may have increased in the last decades, at least in the cases studied here.

What are current language in higher education policies like in the societies reviewed in this volume? As a matter of fact, all universities have their own language policies and management, although their degree of explicitness and their orientation vary enormously depending on a variety of factors such as their degree of autonomy vis-à-vis the state, their primary local or international orientation, their situation within the Bologna Process, etc. It is interesting to note that a majority of the societies described in the volume did not possess an *explicit*, global national higher education language policy, and most did not have organisations explicitly charged with the task of solving language problems and organising language issues. On the contrary, these problems were usually handled in a local way, be it at the level of individual staff or even in specific university departments, as in the Czech case, for instance. In other cases, like Israel, Finland and Denmark, some general university legislation and/or explicit global strategies do exist, although universities enjoy some degree of autonomy. Catalonia has probably the most sophisticated language policy in higher education among the cases analysed, including its central and autonomous legislation as well as a complex system of university linguistic services that assist in the analysis and implementation of the national and institutional language policies.

On the whole, the language policies in higher education presented in this volume seem to face two different issues: on the one hand, promoting and protecting the local languages; on the other, dealing with language needs derived from internationalisation. These two issues can be broken down into four challenges:

(a) Defining the working languages.
(b) Guaranteeing adequate language skills.
(c) Dealing with corpus-related needs.
(d) Building consensus around higher education language policies.

Defining the universities' working languages

The selection of what languages are to be used for each function is one of the areas defined by the language policies explored in this volume. When they mention languages, most university ordinances analysed here make explicit reference to the local language as the basic means of communication, some of them in stricter terms than others. As pointed out in 'A medium-sized language may be viable as a lingua academica' section of this chapter, when universities are found in demolinguistically heterogeneous societies, ordinances were found to be broadly based on two alternative principles: the principle of linguistic separation, which supports the existence of language-specific institutions, as in Finland; or, alternatively, the opposite principle of linguistic conjunction, which does not foresee such separation, as in Catalonia and contemporary South Africa.

Each solution showed its particular advantages and shortcomings. Separation may help in reproducing societal distances and make it difficult for speakers of dominant languages to gain fluency in the other languages; on the other side, the comparison between Catalonia and South Africa suggests that linguistic conjunction in particular seems to require widespread bilingualism or multilingualism to prevent massive convergence towards the most predominant lingua franca is prevented, although alternative systems such as interpreting services are explored in South Africa.

The internationalisation process causes a dilemma between separation and conjunction when it comes to coping with foreign students. A number of strategies were detected to deal with this issue: allowing foreign alloglot[6] students to take regular courses expecting that they will eventually pick up passive competence in the local language; giving them particular support by means of individual attention or *ad hoc* seminars; switching to a lingua franca; creating new groups taught by means of a lingua franca; or even creating new programmes entirely taught in this language. Whereas the management of local languages tends to derive from national legislation, the challenge posed by alloglot students is faced locally, and often left to face-to-face, on the spot negotiation between the participants. This apparent freedom of choice is nevertheless not without its toll. Take the case of Catalonia as an extreme example. During the last decades, several of its universities have attracted significant numbers of students from abroad.[7] Many of these students travelled to Catalonia assuming that the courses they would follow would be taught in Castilian – or English – only to discover on their arrival that the undergraduate courses were customarily taught in Catalan. Before the courses started, a number of these students would ask the teachers to switch to Castilian, and this is what often took place, even with the initial approval of local students, feeling sympathetic towards their 'poor and lost uninformed classmate'.[8] But as this phenomenon spread, and more and more foreign students showed up in the classes, the need to switch languages was increasingly resented by many local students and teachers alike, because they encountered themselves deprived of the right to use their preferred language. The solution to this conflict was making public *and not negotiable* the means of instruction for each group. Similar conflicts derived from the loss of the right to learn in the local language due to accommodating foreign students are recorded in other places, and has even led to judicial issues, for instance, in Finland.

Apart from the language of instruction, other academic activities are also often regulated in higher education. The assessment of written assignments and exams is taken up as a relevant issue for language management in several contexts. Some countries make special legal provisions regarding these issues – guaranteeing, for instance, that the official languages may be always used in exams – whereas others leave these issues to the actors who are directly involved with the examination process. Doctoral dissertations appear as a conflictive area. On the one hand, doctoral dissertations are placed at the peak of the *national* system of evaluation and are therefore regarded in many places as especially symbolic, and it is not uncommon to expect them to contribute to the elaboration of the national language as a language of science, for instance, in the field of specialised terminology. The requirement of Hebrew in Israel for this purpose derives from these considerations. On the other hand, dissertations are intrinsically dependent on the available specialised literature; they are often produced by expatriate students and evaluated by foreign professors, and aspire to an international audience. To cover both aspects – internal and external – several regulations were identified, as in the Czech Republic, requiring that doctoral dissertations included at least an abstract in the national language and/or in English. Another area of frequent concern for language policies was that of funding and valuing academic achievements. A good deal of the pressure to publish in English, already described, stemmed from practices attributed to national organisations, such as the systems used by the authorities to assess the impact of scientific research, which often give more value to publications in English. Timid initiatives were detected in this area in Finland and Catalonia aiming at reconsidering the value of publications in the local medium-sized languages. On a different level, the requirement to complete the application to raise funds from national authorities in English was detected even in societies in which the influence of English was comparatively low, as in the Czech Republic. In spite of the rhetoric about the appreciation of multilingualism, not many practical measures were recorded as trying to counterbalance these trends.[9]

Guaranteeing adequate language skills

Language policy efforts to guarantee that university members have the right linguistic abilities revolved around two different strategies: on the one hand, the linguistic requirements of the university members and, on the other, the provision of resources for language learning.

Linguistic requirements were found to be especially important for teaching staff. For instance, competence in Hebrew is explicitly required to work at Israeli universities, whereas in Finland a decree from the national government requires university teaching and research staff to master the language, Finnish or Swedish, which they are supposed to use for instruction. In other cases, proficiency in the official language is taken for granted to the extent that it is not mentioned in either university legislation or in job advertisements. In these cases, indirect clues such as the fact that the advertisement is published exclusively in a particular language may function as a clear index of the fact that this language is expected. Legal linguistic requirements for university staff may exist as a consequence of very general language legislation principles, which make them almost invisible at first glance. In the Catalan case, for instance, and until 1993, the requirement to be proficient in Castilian to work at a Catalan, Valencian or Balearic university had two main sources: On the one hand, since virtually all teaching staff was composed of civil servants, and civil servants were required to be Spanish nationals, they were subject to the regulation of Spain's 1978 Constitution, according to which all citizens must be proficient in Castilian (art. 3). On the other hand, a large percentage of the process to become a professor was to be done in Castilian, which guaranteed that only people highly proficient in that language would manage to gain a post. This situation changed when the right of nationals from other European Union countries to become civil servants was recognised. At that point, the duty to know Castilian had to be explicitly introduced.[10] On the contrary, it was not until 2010 that Catalonia's authorities required knowledge of Catalan for permanent positions in Catalonia.

Non-teaching staff and students were subject to less linguistic requirements. In the case of administration and support staff, requirements seem lower, less stringent and focused on the national languages. This is quite expectable, given that administration seems to function basically in the local languages, although competence in English seemed to be increasingly valued. On their side, students were not often explicitly obliged to know particular languages, although linguistic requirements were often part of the process to enter university. Moreover, competence in either the local language and/or an academic lingua franca often played some role in the acceptance of students into the university system or into some particular programmes. In many cases, the explicit linguistic requirements of students seem to be related to the dynamics of supply and demand.

The second strategy developed in the area of language competence was that of providing resources for language learning. Support for the teaching and learning of the local language by foreign students and staff was detected in several cases, such as the Danish and, very especially, the Catalan case. Most of the efforts detected in the area of language teaching and learning were connected with internationalisation, and very particularly, with English. Again, most measures seem to be taken at the level of university or even departments, making the strategy difficult to summarise. Whereas official documents tend to refer to the promotion of multilingualism, it is nevertheless English that takes the lion's share of these initiatives. Indeed, the low level of English proficiency of teaching staff is a recurrent complaint, and it is hardly surprising that several measures have been detected to increase this level. *Ad hoc* courses and other supportive actions are taken to increase this level, and in some places like Denmark, tests and certifications are being developed. Requirements and initiatives are less demanding for administrative staff. As far as students enrolled in English-medium courses are concerned, they are obviously expected to be proficient in this language, although no general measures seem to be taken to guarantee this proficiency. The fact that in many cases they are the payers is probably not a minor detail here.

Dealing with corpus-related needs

Corpus planning was not totally absent from university activities, although it played a secondary role in language policy activities. Preoccupation with the 'excessive' influx of English in the local languages was present in several of the cases, for example Israel and Denmark, whereas in Catalonia, this preoccupation could be detected but only second to the interference of Castilian on Catalan. Research in the Danish case suggests that the presence of loanwords and code-switching in actual teaching settings was smaller than expected. Nevertheless, a number of initiatives in the area of terminology were recorded. In Israel, the Israeli Office for Technological Terminology, which works to provide Hebrew equivalents for international terms, is deeply connected with some university sectors. In Catalonia, universities' linguistic services are active not only in producing a number of scientific terminological works for Catalan – an area where they enjoy the support of the official centre for terminology TERMCAT – but also in standardising English translations of local academic institutions and posts.

Corpus-related deficits were apparently alleged by some sources as a reason why African languages were kept away from higher education. But important as they may be, it is unclear to what extent they are a cause and/or a pretext to reproduce the current status quo. At least two of the languages reviewed in this volume, Hebrew and Catalan, only managed to overcome their scientific corpus deficits once the language was put to use in the higher education sphere. It was only then that professors and researchers ran into terminological and expressive problems, and sought a way to solve them, asking for help from professional language planners when it became possible.

Building consensus around higher education language policies

As with any other social institution, universities host different actors with different interests that transform into different, even contradictory discourses. Higher education institutions are faced not only with the challenge of developing more adequate policies, but they also need to develop discourses that legitimise their practices and therefore contribute to their functioning. In this respect, the higher education language policies reviewed in this volume are not always unanimously accepted. Whereas the need to internationalise has been gaining support, sectors insisting on the importance of local and national dimensions have by no means vanished. The primacy of English as the academic lingua franca is today less contested than a couple of decades ago, but the position it should occupy is far from agreed. Neither is the adequate position of other foreign languages a matter of unanimity. Debate and disagreement have also been reported in relation to the role of local languages in higher education, now and in the immediate future.

Most of these ideological debates seem to be neutralised by making reference to a set of ambiguous terms that allow for different interpretations. One of them is 'internationalisation' and another is 'multilingualism'. These terms may neutralise the conflict between actors with different linguistic ideologies, and both have proliferated in official documents. Nevertheless, several examples presented in the volume prove that these terms – and others like 'world languages' – are often used as euphemisms to refer basically to English (Saarinen, 2012: 168). For instance, the review of Finland's university language policy proved that, despite references to multilingualism:

> Only at the University of Helsinki the importance of publishing in foreign languages other than English was formulated on a more general level: *The University also believes in the importance of publishing scientific and other scholarly work in foreign languages other than English.* (University of Helsinki, 2007: 47) (Ylönen, this volume)

Not surprisingly, at the core of many of the ideological debates surrounding language choices in academic environments lies the classical question of *cui prodest*, i.e. who is profiting from each decision. In individual terms, it is obvious that local students and scholars may legitimately see that it is in their interest that a particular course is given in the language they feel more comfortable, whereas international students and mobile scholars may see it in their interest that it is given in English. From a collective perspective, the reduction in academic linguae francae facilitates access to innovations, but it is also true that achieving and retaining the status of lingua academica constitutes an enormous investment in cultural capital that can be enjoyed, as a hypercollective good, by any member of the language community without major barriers (de Swaan, 2001, 2010), not to speak of its value in terms of self-confidence and self-esteem. Losing this status would probably provoke not only an objective loss in cultural capital for the community affected, but also a devastating psychological effect on its perceived ethnolinguistic vitality. In these terms, it is hardly surprising that the debates between internationalisation and national approaches become heated and that they linger for a long time.

Four Sociolinguistic Paradoxes of the Internationalisation of Higher Education

The chapters in the current volume have allowed us to identify at least four paradoxes of internationalisation in higher education that should be taken into consideration when defining language policies in this field.

The first paradox, which Haberland and Preisler name the 'paradox of internationalization', is purely linguistic: the more languages that are present within a course, the easier it is for participants to end up adopting a lingua franca and working with just one language. In truth, this phenomenon is not exclusive to internationalisation and is to be witnessed in any sort of multilingual context, as proved by the linguistic evolution at South African universities. This seems to be the same trend that leads to the adoption of a single language of communication whenever a multilingual population has to interact, described by Shepard and Giles (2001) as linguistic convergence and as the Babel principle by Laponce (2006), and is derived from universal maxims and principles of politeness (Brown & Levinson, 1987; Leech, 1983).

A second paradox, the potential 'English overkill factor' described by Sherman in Chapter 4, is defined as 'excessive publication in English, but not in top-tier journals, and often not suitable in terms of either content or style (or both) for an English-speaking readership'. The result of this paradox is that papers that might have had a significant audience and impact if published in the national language end up passing unnoticed although published in the language that *a priori* guaranteed more diffusion.

A third paradox frequently evoked in this volume was what we may call 'state-induced anglicisation'. Several authors in this volume have pointed to the fact that the movement towards English is not always a market-driven phenomenon, but rather a consequence of state regulations. The recommendation, or even requirement, that applications to obtain national funding for research should be written in English, the adoption of criteria that favour English for the evaluation of scientific production and the requirement that a percentage of undergraduate programmes should be taught in English are clear examples of this third paradox.[11]

Finally, a fourth paradox arose, which can be described as the 'paradox of subsidised anglicisation'. In many respects, the adoption of English as the means of instruction is promoted essentially as a means to increase the funding sources for academic life. The paradox arises when the means to become and remain internationalised lie in obtaining public subsidies. A clear example of this paradox is provided by a decision made by some universities in Catalonia: in order to promote the use of English as the language of instruction, professors who volunteered to teach in English were offered extra bonuses – for instance, a reduction in their teaching assignment, free English language lessons and *ad hoc* support with the production of their materials, all of which implied, of course, a bewildering policy of positive discrimination in favour of English, the language *presumably* favoured by the market, with regard to Catalan, a much weaker language in market terms, and even Castilian.[12] The medium of instruction for postgraduate courses provides a second example of this paradox: one of the main practical arguments to opt for English as the means of instruction is a fund-raising one, since at least in theory this language will make courses accessible to a wider number of would-be students. The paradox arises when courses taught in English to attract external funding remain basically state funded and no clear measure of their return – be it in economic or in academic terms – is provided. The paradox, in fact, can be further complicated: Ylönen (this volume) evoked the quandary posed by the mismatch between the remarkable percentage of postgraduate courses taught in English in Finland versus the modest percentage of foreign students attracted from abroad. Gazzola (2012: 149) points out that this paradox is the consequence of adopting the number of foreign students attracted by universities as a criterion to evaluate their quality. But, as pointed out by some of the authors in the volume, this criterion is not necessarily related to quality – it may signal, for instance, lower tuition fees.

Conclusion

Language practices in higher education have evolved with time. For centuries, Latin guaranteed the communication of science and contributed to the mobility of scholars and students. In the last centuries, a growing number of vernacular languages were raised to the status of lingua academica, and a handful of languages competed for the status of academic lingua franca. This competition for the status of academic lingua franca came to a (provisional?) truce during the second half of the 20th century, when English took over this role and its competitors were relegated to a clear secondary position (Ammon, 2010).

But the hegemony of English as the language of international academic communication has not implied the demotion of the other academic languages and their ousting from university life. To date, these other languages have remained the main vehicles of university life in their respective societies. The comparison developed in this volume does not support the idea that medium-sized languages are rapidly disappearing from the area of higher education. Instead, we have identified a variety of arrangements which tend to favour complementary, non-diglossic distributions of languages, where language choices depend more on the (potential) interlocutors than on the presumed 'language domain'. These arrangements recall in many respects the 'principle of subsidiarity' which is so basic to the European Union, and which Bastardas (2012) proposes as the basis for sustainable multilingualism in complex societies. According to these arrangements, local linguae academicae should be used whenever it is feasible, i.e. whenever the interlocutors can be reasonably expected to be able to use them, whereas the academic lingua franca should only be used to overcome these limits. In practical terms, this means that although a great many publications, addressed as they are to the whole scientific community, are being produced in English, the other academic languages should not be absent from written or, very especially, oral communications. Two clues may be identified for the sustained maintenance of the local linguae academicae: on the one hand, speakers of these languages should find themselves in secure environments where they can use their languages because they are understood by everybody; otherwise, a lack of mutual intelligibility will promote the adoption of minimal common denominators, i.e. linguae francae. On the other hand, the use of each language should be significant *per se*. In Harder's words:

> (...) the university can choose to present itself in guises that include being a servant of the community at one end and being part of international academic life at the other. (Harder, 2009: 125)

One corollary can be inferred from these arrangements, and it is connected with the reason why language choices are made, at least in the contexts analysed in the current volume. Very briefly, the choice of either a local lingua academica or an international one is basically made on the basis of pragmatism. Local languages are not used because of their symbolic value (Cots *et al.*, 2012), but because speakers find it easier to use their language rather than a lingua franca. Linguae francae, on their side, are picked up when they simplify communication in multilingual settings. In other words, in the contexts described here, it would be wrong to assume that some languages are basically associated with 'identity' whereas others are basically associated with 'utility', because all the languages in the scene have their own utility, as well as their own identity associations.

Within this context, what are the prospects for the current linguae academicae? If the assumptions we have just made are right, one may venture to say that the maintenance of the status of lingua academica for all the languages reviewed here will be in danger only if their communities stop producing and reproducing the many social spaces where using the local language remains the most practical option. The steady weakening of Afrikaans as a lingua academica shows that such changes are not impossible, but the sharp contrast between the South African experience and the rest of the cases suggests that such a dramatic transformation would require major sociopolitical and demographic changes – a combination of massive change in ideological premises that downgrade the local languages, deep demographic transformations with huge population movements and fundamental changes in the power structure at the national scale – that do not seem probable in the near future for any of the societies analysed. Leaving aside this particular case, none of the other languages under study seems to be at risk of losing its status of lingua academica in the near future, and it is quite possible that the same conclusion may be extended to most of the linguae academicae in existence around the world today. The growing contexts in which English as an academic lingua franca is being used do not necessarily imply that the local linguae academicae will lose this status in the immediate future. Only if the distinction between these two roles became blurred, i.e. if the lingua franca was progressively adopted as the means of instruction in contexts where there was no objective need for it, would the status of lingua academica of the other languages be in real danger.

Will new languages rise to the status of lingua academica in the foreseeable future? Predictions in this field are even more difficult to make. In fact, not only Catalan, but a number of other languages such as Basque, Welsh, Kurdish and Faroese have (re)gained this status during the last decades. So, it is not at all impossible for the number of linguae academicae to grow in the near future, as more communities decide that it is to their benefit to introduce their languages into the highest spheres of knowledge and thought. But whereas the possibilities are there, the *de facto* requirements are also huge. On the one hand, market rules *per se* do not seem to favour the formidable effort that becoming a lingua academica seems to imply. On the other hand, the development of a fully fledged lingua academica has historically demanded the support of some sort of national ideology, one that regards as beneficial that the national language is expanded to its ultimate possibilities. Today, though, this sort of linguistic ideology does not seem prevalent among most language communities around the world. The promotion of new languages to the status of lingua academica is made more difficult by the discourse of the internationalisation of higher education. Ironically, many discourses about the benefits of multilingualism may turn out to be objective allies of linguistic homogenisation, because they help to legitimise the use of the lingua franca instead of the local languages. In fact, if we look at empirical data, it turns out that none of the countries that acceded to independence – either *de jure* or *de facto* – between 2000 and 2013 promoted a new language to the status of lingua academica.[13] Combined, these pressures make it difficult for the list of linguae academicae to increase substantially in the near future.

Higher education has been a multilingual sphere for centuries, and it seems that it will remain multilingual for at least some time to come. Whereas the role of academic lingua franca seems to be firmly occupied by English, a number of languages have retained their status of lingua academica and do not seem in imminent danger of losing it. Whether this select pool of languages will be reduced, transformed or enlarged in the years to come remains to be seen. One may only hope that, whatever decisions are made, they are made by the speakers themselves and in their interests. This volume only aspires to offer them a number of objective elements so that they can make their choices with due objectivity.

Notes

(1) Unless the contrary is stated, the references to particular cases made in this chapter derive from the previous chapters.
(2) See http://english.hi.is/.
(3) For Faroese and Sami, see Bull (2012), for Scottish Gaelic, see McLeod (2004).
(4) The same pattern is detectable in other contexts: in 2009, 25% of undergraduate programmes and 65% of master's programmes in Sweden were taught in English (Söderlunh, 2012: 90).
(5) The role and position of English as a language of instruction in postgraduate courses is a delicate issue. To fully understand it, it is necessary to pay attention not only to English-language programmes, but also to the programmes offered in other languages. In this respect, reports like Brenn-White and van Rest (2012: 9) about master's programmes in English in Europe, that point to a degree of anglicisation of postgraduate courses that is much deeper than the one portrayed in this volume – e.g. see sentences such as 'in the Benelux countries and Scandinavia, master's education has switched almost entirely to English language instruction' – might be underestimating the use of other languages in this sphere. This study in particular is based on a thorough analysis of an international website (StudyPortal http://www.mastersportal.eu/) which may be partially consulted in four languages, but has an obvious predominance of English information. To check the accuracy of this database, the author compared the data from StudyPortal with the data furnished by the Dutch-language website of one Flemish university (Vrije Universiteit Brussel [VUB]) in March 2013.

(6) According to StudyPortal, the VUB offered 40 masters, 39 in English and 1 in Dutch and French. But the analysis of the VUB's Dutch language website offered quite a different picture: 47 academic masters in Dutch and 24 in English (http://www.vub.ac.be/infoover/onderwijs/bama/m-opleidingen.html), plus 13 LLL masters in Dutch plus 9 in English (http://www.vub.ac.be/infoover/onderwijs/bama/mnm-opleidingen.html). The author also tried to find in StudyPortal the four masters that he had been teaching during the last 4–5 years (three in Catalan and one in English) in his own university (Universitat de Barcelona), but none was included in the databases. Although this is hardly more than anecdotal evidence, these results suggest that international websites like StudyPortal may be significantly biased towards English and cannot therefore be taken as a good indicator of the actual degree of anglicisation of European universities.
(6) The distinction between 'foreign', i.e. with a different passport, and 'alloglot', i.e. unable to speak the local language or languages, is very pertinent here.
(7) A total of 7623 in 2011. See http://www.idescat.cat/pub/?id=aec&n=762&t=2011&x=8&y=8.
(8) Cédric Klapisch's film 'L'auberge espagnol' (2002) tried to reproduce this situation.
(9) As a point of comparison, the Slovene Research Agency established the obligation that every research programme financed by the state must publish at least one expert article and one popular article in Slovene at least once a year in order to ensure the development of the Slovene terminology and the popularisation of science among the Slovene public (Bitenc, 2013: 70).
(10) Article 6 Royal Decree 800/1995, of 19 May, for regulating access to certain sectors of public administration of nationals of other member states of the European Union.
(11) Arzoz (2012: 249) furnishes further examples of how states actually penalise the use of medium-sized languages in terms of academic recognition. In this respect, Bordons and Gómez (2004), Gazzola (2012) and Hamel (2013) show that the decision of official agencies to adopt bibliometric criteria that are inherently language biased is pushing Italian and Spanish researchers to publish more in English.
(12) Kangas Christiansen (2009: 64) furnishes other examples of how the Danish state actually subsidises the use of English, and Gazzola (2012: 145) provides similar examples from Italy. In fact, the same paradox may appear in all countries where education is state funded.
(13) The countries that became independent and were accepted as member states of the United Nations during this period were Serbia, Montenegro, Tuvalu and South Sudan. In February 2013, the *de facto* independent territories with non-existent or limited international recognition were Somaliland, Nagorno-Karabakh, Pridnestrovian Moldavian Republic, Abkhazia, Taiwan, Kosovo, Palestine, Northern Cyprus, Sahrawi Democratic Republic and South Ossetia.

References

Ammon, U. (2010) World languages: Trends and futures. In N. Coupland (ed.) *The Handbook of Language and Globalisation* (pp. 101–122). Chichester: Wiley-Blackwell.

Arzoz, X. (ed.) (2012) *Bilingual Education in the Legal Context. Group Rights, State Policies and Globalisation*. Leiden/Boston: Martinus Neijhoff.

Bastardas-Boada, A. (2012) *Language and Identity Policies in the 'Glocal' Age. New Processes, Effects and Principles of Organization.* Barcelona: Institut d'Estudis Autonòmics, Generalitat de Catalunya.

Bitenc, M. (2013) Challenges facing Danish as a medium-sized language. In F.X. Vila (ed.) *Survival and Development of Language Communities: Prospects and Challenges* (pp. 58-80). Bristol: Multilingual Matters.

Bordons, M. and Gómez, I. (2004) Towards a single language in science? A Spanish view. *Serias* 17 (2). See http://www.adawis.de/admin/upload/navigation/data/English%20as%20a%20single%20language%20of%20Science%20-%20A%20Spanish%20view.pdf (accessed 27 July 2014).

Brenn-White, M. and van Rest, E. (2012) *English-Taught Master's Programs in Europe: New Findings on Supply and Demand.* New York: Institute of International Education. See http://www.iie.org/Research-and-Publications/Publications-and-Reports/IIEBookstore/English-Language-Masters-Briefing-Paper (accessed 2 October 2013).

Brown, P. and Levinson, S. (1987) *Politeness.* Cambridge: Cambridge University Press.

Bull, T. (2012) Against the mainstream: Universities with an alternative language policy. *International Journal of the Sociology of Language* 216, 55-73.

Cots, J.M., Lasagabaster, D. and Garrett, P. (2012) Multilingual policies and practices of universities in three bilingual regions in Europe. *International Journal of the Sociology of Language* 216, 7-32.

de Swaan, A. (2001) *Words of the World. The Global Language System.* Malden, MA: Polity Press.

de Swaan, A. (2010) Language systems. In N. Coupland (ed.) *The Handbook of Language and Globalisation* (pp. 55-76). Chichester: Wiley-Blackwell.

Gazzola, M. (2012) The linguistic implications of academic performance indicators: General trends and case study. *International Journal of the Sociology of Language* 216, 131-156.

Hamel, R. E. (2013) El campo de las ciencias y la educación superior entre el monopolio del inglés y el plurilingüismo: Elementos para una política del lenguaje en América Latina. *Trabalhos em Linguística Aplicada, No 52-2, 321-384, 2013. Universidad de Campinas,* 52(2), 321-384.

Harder, P. (2009) Parallel language use: a case for active social contruction. *Angles on the English-Speaking World* 9, 109-120.

Kangas Christiansen, M. (2009) The language of instruction at Danish universities. *Angles on the English Speaking World* 9, 58-67.

Laponce, J. (2006) *Loi de Babel et autres régularités des rapports entre langue et politique.* Lévis, Québec: Presses de l'Université Laval.

Leech, G.N. (1983) *Principles of Pragmatics.* London: Longman.

McLeod, W. (1994) Lessons from Gaelic - medium higher education in Scotland. In C. N. Pháiidin and D. u. Bhraonáin *University Education in Irish: Challenges and Perspectives. Conference Papers* (pp.43-51) Dublin: Fiontar; Dublin City University.

Milian-Massana, A. (ed.) (2012) *Language Law and Legal Challenges in Medium-Sized Language Communities: A Comparative Perspective.* Barcelona: Institut d'Estudis Autonòmics.

Ozolins, U. (2013) A small national language and its multilingual challenges: The case of Latvian. In F.X. Vila (ed.) *Survival and Development of Language Communities: Prospects and Challenges* (pp. 130-156). Bristol: Multilingual Matters.

Saarinen, T. (2012) Internationalization of Finnish higher education - is language an issue? *International Journal of the Sociology of Language* 216, 157-173.

Shepard, C. and Giles, H. (2001) Accommodation theory. In W.P. Robinson and H. Giles (eds) *The New Handbook of Language and Social Psychology* (pp. 33–56). Chichester: Wiley.

Skerrett, D.M. (2013) Challenges for the Estonian language: A poststructuralist perspective. In F.X. Vila (ed.) *Survival and Development of Language Communities: Prospects and Challenges* (pp. 105–129). Bristol: Multilingual Matters.

Söderlundh, H. (2012) Global policies and local norms: Sociolinguistic awareness and language choice at an international university. *International Journal of the Sociology of Language* 216, 87–109.

Vila, F.X. (2013) Challenges and opportunities for MSLCs in the 21st century: A (preliminary) synthesis. In F.X. Vila (ed.) *Survival and Development of Language Communities: Prospects and Challenges* (pp. 179–200). Bristol: Multilingual Matters.

Vila, F.X. and Bretxa, V. (2013) The analysis of medium-sized language communities. In F.X. Vila (ed.) *Survival and Development of Language Communities: Prospects and Challenges* (pp. 1–17). Bristol: Multilingual Matters.

Index

administrative purposes, 46, 67, 70, 71, 76, 169, 172, 187 [see also administration]
administrative staff, 8, 35, 52, 65, 84, 86, 116, 121, 127, 145, 161, 170, 178, 200
administration [university], 8, 25, 35, 67, 72, 75, 76, 86, 91, 95, 121, 145, 162, 167, 183, 187, 196 [see also administrative purposes]
Afrikaans, 11, 133, 134, 135, 136, 137, 138, 139, 140, 141, 142, 146, 147, 148, 149, 150, 151, 152, 155, 183, 184, 187, 190, 193, 195, 206
Alcón, E., 176, 179
Alexander, N., 135, 137, 149
Ammon, U., 2, 12, 16, 38, 39, 103, 129, 204, 208
Andorra, 153, 161
anglicisation, 5, 147, 203, 207, 208
Anglicism, 22
Arabic, 7, 15, 16, 104, 105, 112, 127, 130, 133, 151
Aracil, L.V, 36, 38
Armengol, L., 162, 174, 175, 179
Arzoz, X., 1, 3, 5, 12, 13, 155, 157, 159, 160, 179, 180, 186, 208
attitude, 20, 41, 62, 105, 115, 128, 162, 175, 176, 177
Australia, 82, 148, 151
Austria, 48
Azriel, S, 106, 107, 129

bachelor [BA], 25, 29, 45, 48, 51, 55, 79, 80, 81, 85, 92, 104, 118, 119 ,120, 121, 122, 123, 125, 128, 143, 144, 151, 188
Bacher, P., 18, 39
Bak, H.F., 26, 31, 39
Balearic Islands, 153, 154, 161, 165, 178, 199
Baltic, 7, 64, 75
Barkhuizen, G., 148, 149
Barraclough, F., 172, 179

Basque, 168, 206
Bastardas-Boada, A., 205, 209
Ben-Haim, Z., 112, 129
Beukes, A-M., 10, 132, 136, 139, 141, 142, 143, 145, 150
big language, 4, 17 [see also international language]
bilingual/bilingualism, 2, 12, 13, 23, 37, 39, 44, 64, 66, 67, 84, 91, 93, 94, 114, 118, 137, 150, 157, 158, 160, 170, 176, 186, 187, 190, 192, 194, 197, 209
Bitenc, M., 185, 208, 209
Björkman, B., 2, 13
Blaauw, J., 147, 150
Blau, J., 114, 129
Blommaert, J., 2, 13, 17, 39
Boix, E., 41, 175, 176, 179, 180
Bologna Process, 45, 175, 196
Bordons, M., 173, 179, 208, 209
Bornman, E., 149, 150
Brenn-White, M., 2, 13, 80, 96, 207
Bretxa, V., 4, 14, 180, 181, 210
Brown, P., 203, 209
Bull, T., 6, 13, 27, 39, 207, 209
Business School, 26, 29, 31, 39, 80, 92, 188

Castilian, 7, 153, 154, 156, 157, 158, 159, 160, 161, 164, 165, 166, 167, 168, 169, 170, 172, 173, 174, 175, 176, 177, 178, 186, 188, 189, 193, 198, 199, 200, 201, 204 [see also Spanish]
Catalan, 6, 11, 12, 36, 139, 153, 154, 155, 156, 157, 158, 159, 160, 161, 162, 163, 164, 165, 166, 167, 168, 169, 170, 171, 172, 173, 174, 175, 176, 177, 178, 179, 180, 183, 184, 186, 190, 193, 194, 195, 196, 198, 199, 200, 201, 204, 206, 208
Catalonia, 6, 11, 153, 154, 155, 156, 157, 158, 159, 160, 161, 163, 164, 165, 167, 168, 169, 171, 172, 173, 174, 175, 177, 178, 179, 180, 184, 185, 186, 188, 189,

190, 194, 195, 196, 197, 198, 199, 200, 201, 204
central language, 15, 16
Chinese, 4, 15, 16, 27, 37, 53, 58, 74, 75
Clemmensen, N., 39
CLIL, 2, 13, 112, 164
code-switching, 19, 21, 22, 23, 121, 201
commodification, 1, 3, 4, 195
common language, 10, 37, 154
complementary languages, 32, 38, 193
corpus planning, 112, 197, 201
Cots, J.M., 5, 13, 38, 179, 205, 209
Crystal, D., 37, 39
Czech, 6, 9, 43, 44, 45, 46, 47, 48, 49, 50, 51, 52, 53, 54, 55, 56, 57, 58, 59, 60, 61, 62, 63, 183, 185, 188, 189, 190, 191, 193, 194, 195, 196, 199
Czech Republic, 6, 9, 44, 45, 47, 48, 49, 51, 53, 55, 57, 59, 60, 61, 63, 195

Daavittila, T., 97
Danish, 6, 7, 8, 13, 14, 15, 16, 17, 18, 19, 20, 21, 22, 23, 24, 25, 27, 28, 29, 30, 31, 32, 33, 34, 35, 36, 37, 38, 39, 40, 41, 42, 60, 183, 185, 186, 188, 190, 193, 200, 201, 208, 209
Daryai-Hansen, P.G., 23, 38, 39
De Kadt, J., 137, 148,150
De Swaan, A., 2, 13, 15, 16, 17, 39, 181, 183, 202, 209
Denmark, 6, 7, 8, 14, 15, 17, 18, 19, 21, 23, 24, 25, 27, 28, 29, 30, 31, 34, 35, 37, 40, 41, 87, 185, 186, 190, 192, 194, 195, 196, 200, 201
department [university], 34, 38, 51, 52, 54, 55, 56, 59, 157, 169
diglossia/diglossic, 13, 18, 30, 32, 36, 38, 39, 205
discourse, 4, 5, 8, 9, 23, 58, 62, 65, 90, 91, 143, 174, 175, 190, 201, 207
dissertations, 2, 8, 65, 66, 88, 89, 90, 96, 110, 118, 190, 196, 198, 199 [see also thesis]
doctorate, 65, 80, 81 [see also Ph.D.]
Doiz, A., 2, 13
domain loss, 2, 9, 18, 36, 59, 60 [see also language domain]
dominant language, 105, 136, 197
Dovalil, V., 59, 61

Du Plessis, J.A, 137, 141, 142, 143, 150
Duchêne, A., 3, 4, 13
Dutch, 5, 45, 148, 207, 208

ecology of language, 7, 13, 17, 109, 113, 129, 130
educational institutions/sphere/system, 20, 23, 24, 28, 44, 105, 156, 160, 186, 201
English, 1, 2, 3, 4, 5, 6, 7, 8, 9, 10, 11, 12, 13, 14, 15, 16, 17, 18, 19, 20, 21, 22, 23, 24, 25, 26, 27, 28, 29, 30, 31, 32, 33, 34, 35, 36, 37, 38, 39, 40, 41, 42, 43, 44, 45, 46, 47, 48, 49, 50, 51, 52, 53, 54, 55, 56, 57, 58, 59, 60, 61, 62, 65, 69, 72, 73,74, 75, 76, 77, 78, 79, 80, 82, 83, 84, 85, 86, 87, 90, 91, 92, 93, 94, 95, 96, 98, 100, 103, 105, 107, 108, 109, 110, 111, 112, 113, 114, 115, 116, 117, 118, 119, 120, 121, 122, 123, 124, 125, 126, 127, 128, 129, 130, 131, 133, 134, 135, 136, 137, 138, 139, 140, 141, 142, 143, 145, 146, 147, 148, 149, 150, 153, 161, 162, 164, 165, 166, 167, 170, 171, 172, 173, 174, 175, 176, 177, 179, 181, 182, 183, 184, 185, 186, 187, 188, 189, 190, 191, 192, 193, 196, 198, 199, 200, 201, 202, 203, 204, 205, 206, 207, 208, 209
English-medium [instruction], 2, 3, 29, 49, 187, 188, 189, 200
Erasmus, 48, 49, 51, 171
Estonia, 185
Ethnologue, 15, 39
Eurobarometer, 15, 17, 18, 39
Europe, 1, 6, 10, 11, 13, 21, 31, 37, 41, 43, 49, 60, 62, 80, 96, 105, 149, 153, 170, 177, 180, 207, 209
European, 3, 11, 12, 14, 15, 16, 18, 27, 32, 38, 39, 41, 43, 47, 53, 54, 60, 62, 70, 74, 75, 79, 82, 100, 109, 153, 159, 160, 162, 166, 167, 170, 171, 172, 175, 177, 179, 188, 195, 200, 205, 208
European Union [EU], 15, 18, 19, 27, 31, 39, 47, 82, 170 171,175, 200, 205

Fabricius, H. 14, 18, 38, 39, 41, 42, 62
faculty, 32, 46, 50, 52, 54, 55, 57, 59, 60, 61, 104, 123, 125, 127, 161, 168, 169, 173, 175, 179

Faeroese, 185
Ferguson, G., 56, 62
Finland, 6, 9, 64, 65, 66, 67, 69, 70, 71, 73, 74, 76, 79, 80, 81, 82, 86, 87, 88, 89, 90, 91, 92, 93, 94, 95, 96, 97, 98, 99, 100, 101, 102, 105, 185, 186, 188, 190, 192, 193, 195, 196, 197, 198, 199, 202, 204
Finnish, 6, 9, 16, 42, 64, 65, 66, 67, 68, 69, 71, 72, 73, 74, 75, 76, 77, 78, 79, 80, 81, 82, 83, 84, 85, 86, 87, 88, 89, 90, 91, 92, 93, 94, 95, 96, 97, 98, 99, 100, 101, 102, 105, 155, 183, 185, 186, 190, 193, 195, 199, 209
Finnish sign language, 64
first language, 15, 18, 31, 33, 35, 43, 45, 73 [see also mother tongue]
Fishman, J., 35, 39, 131
Foley, A., 137, 150
Fonteyn, K., 100
foreign language, 9, 10, 19, 23, 28, 29, 31, 33, 38, 45, 47, 48, 49, 50, 51, 55, 56, 59, 69, 70, 72, 73, 74, 75, 75, 76, 78, 79, 80, 82, 83, 84, 85, 92, 93, 94, 95, 105, 108, 109, 110, 111, 112, 130, 136, 191, 193, 202
Fortanet-Gómez, I., 2, 13
France, 87, 153, 161
French, 15, 16, 20, 25, 28, 32, 36, 37, 41, 45, 47, 51, 53, 56, 58, 74, 75, 79, 87, 90, 105, 156, 167, 171, 176, 185, 193, 194, 208

Galicia, 168, 179
Garam, I., 79, 80, 81, 83, 97, 100
Garrett, P., 13, 209
Gazzola, M., 3, 13, 57, 62, 204, 208, 209
German, 7, 9, 15, 16, 18, 19, 20, 25, 28, 32, 36, 37, 38, 44, 45, 48, 49, 51, 52, 53, 56, 58, 59, 60, 61, 66, 74, 75, 79, 87, 89, 90, 103, 129, 171, 176, 185, 190, 191, 193
Germany, 15, 48, 49, 87
Giles, H, 203, 209
global language, 37 [see also world language]
globalisation, 1, 2, 4, 5, 6, 11, 39, 94, 109, 112, 128, 142, 154, 155, 162, 181, 182, 183, 195

Gómez, I., 173, 179, 208, 209
Gray, E., 149, 150
Greek, 16, 53, 75
Grové, N., 136, 151

Haarmann, H., 16, 39
Haberland, H., 1, 2, 3, 7, 12, 13, 14, 15, 16, 18, 24, 27, 34, 36, 39, 41, 42, 60, 62, 185, 186, 192, 203
Hakulinen, A., 92, 97
Hall, C., 91, 97, 131
Hamel, R.E., 3, 13, 28, 33, 34, 35, 40, 190, 208
Harder, P., 14, 30, 40, 41, 205, 209
Hatoss, A., 148, 151
Hauge, T., 32, 38, 40
Haugen, E., 2, 13
Hebrew, 10, 103, 104, 105, 106, 107, 108, 109, 110, 111, 112, 113, 114, 115, 116, 117, 118, 119, 120, 121, 123, 124, 125, 126, 127, 128, 129, 130, 131, 139, 155, 183, 184, 188, 190, 193, 195, 198, 199, 201
Heller, M., 3, 4, 13
Heltoft, L., 27, 40
Hill, L.B., 136, 151
Hilmarsson-Dunn, A.M., 17, 40
Hindi, 15, 53, 139
Hughes, R., 82, 84, 97
Hult, F.M., 109, 131
humanities, 8, 9, 33, 34, 44, 45, 50, 56, 57, 58, 59, 60, 75, 76, 80, 86, 127, 129, 130, 131, 147, 148, 149, 189, 190
Hungary, 17
hypercentral language, 2, 15, 181

Iceland, 7, 40, 185
identity, 22, 37, 62, 205
immigrant, 23, 73, 83, 148, 194
indigenous languages, 11, 132, 133, 148
international language, 24, 40, 62, 165, 184, 193 [see also world language]
internationalisation, 2, 3, 4, 5, 6, 9, 26, 29, 30, 33, 50, 57, 72, 74, 76, 79, 81, 82, 83, 84, 92, 93, 94, 95, 109, 160, 164, 166, 167, 169, 174, 181, 182, 192, 195, 196, 197, 200, 202, 203, 207
Irmay, S., 112, 130
isiNdebele, 134, 135
isiXhosa, 134, 135, 144

isiZulu, 134, 135, 145, 149
Israel, 6, 10, 103, 104, 105, 108, 111, 116, 117, 119, 127, 130, 131, 185, 188, 190, 193, 195, 196, 198, 201
Italian, 45, 75, 87, 171, 176, 194, 208

Jacobs, H., 91, 92, 97
Jacobsen, K.M., 39
Janse van Rensburg, H, 151
Jansen, J. 138, 151
Japanese, 15, 37, 53, 75
Jarvad, P., 33, 40
Jørgensen, J.N., 24, 36, 39, 40, 41
journal, 2, 49, 57, 58, 87, 88, 93, 118, 132, 147, 149, 173, 174, 190, 203

Kachru, B.B. 50, 62
Kangas Christiansen, M., 2, 13, 109, 130, 208, 209
Karelian, 64
Kaschula, R., 145, 151
Ketolainen, J., 92, 97
Kivelä, M., 66, 77, 78, 79, 83, 100
Kling, J., 32, 40
Klitgård, E., 14, 38
Kloss, H., 16, 40
Kolhinen, J, 100
Kopperi, M, 97
Korkala, S., 80, 97
Kuhlmann Madsen, J, 40
Kuteeva, M., 30, 40

language accommodation, 33
language hierarchies, 15, 41
language choice, 13, 14, 18, 24, 27, 28, 32, 35, 38, 58, 66, 88, 108, 110, 115, 117, 118, 121, 122, 123, 124, 125, 127, 160, 164, 166, 202, 210
language competence, 8, 9, 10, 29, 30, 33, 50, 52, 65, 68, 69, 73, 84, 85, 86, 95, 105, 111, 112, 167, 169, 200 [see also language proficiency]
language domain, 2, 8, 9, 18, 31, 35, 36, 39, 41, 47, 50, 57, 59, 60, 62, 64, 65, 93, 109, 118, 154, 157, 181, 189, 205 [see also domain loss]
language ideology, 8, 10, 17, 18, 23, 24, 40, 50, 62, 143, 174, 180 [see also linguistic ideology]

language knowledge, 53, 61 [see also language proficiency]
language management, 1, 2, 9, 10, 11, 43, 46, 48, 57, 58, 59, 62, 105, 106, 111, 112, 115, 116, 117, 118, 124, 128, 177, 184, 187, 198
language of accreditation, 55
language of instruction, 4, 9, 10, 25, 26, 43, 44, 47, 60, 65, 67, 68, 69, 76, 84, 105, 108, 119, 132, 133, 135, 139, 140, 141, 142, 146, 161, 164, 176, 177, 191, 204
language of science, 2, 3, 75, 129, 139, 144, 148, 151, 192, 198
language policy, 1, 2, 3, 6, 8, 9, 10, 11, 12, 13, 19, 24, 25, 27, 28, 29, 30, 31, 32, 38, 40, 42, 43, 44, 46, 64, 65, 66, 69, 70, 72, 73, 74, 75, 76, 82, 84, 91, 93, 94, 95, 97, 99,100, 105, 107, 109, 111, 114, 115, 117, 118, 132, 135, 136, 138, 147, 154, 155, 157, 158, 161, 162, 168, 176, 178, 184, 186, 187, 194, 195, 196, 199, 201, 202, 203, 209
language practices, 8, 9, 10, 24, 64, 65, 66, 67, 76, 86, 105 118, 121, 137, 143, 146, 149, 162, 170, 175, 181, 188, 189, 204 [see also language use]
language proficiency, 9, 26, 32, 48, 59, 68, 69, 70, 75, 84, 85, 86, 96, 112, 136, 145, 167, 170, 171, 186, 191, 192, 193, 199, 200 [see also language competence]
language regulation, 67, 101, 158
language repertoire, 18, 35, 73
language requirement, 52, 53, 84, 108, 169, 199, 200
language shift, 5, 188
language skills, 24, 32, 53, 78, 112, 114, 117, 135, 147, 161, 164, 197, 199
language use, 8, 9, 23, 25, 28, 30, 35, 55, 59, 65, 66, 77, 78, 90, 111, 113, 115, 160, 164, 177, 209 [see also language practices]
Laponce, J., 4, 13, 203, 209
Lasagabaster, D, 13, 209
Late, E., 13, 87, 98
Latin, 1, 14, 25, 27, 37, 38, 41, 44, 53, 75, 88, 105, 166, 173, 182, 183, 185, 190, 191, 194, 204

Lauridsen, K.M., 28, 40
lecturer, 10, 31, 40, 59, 86, 92, 103, 106, 107, 108, 109, 110, 111, 114, 115, 116, 117, 118, 119, 120, 121, 122, 123, 124, 125, 126, 127, 128
Leech, G.N, 203, 209
Levinson, S., 203, 209
lifelong learning, 8, 65, 82
lingua academica, 1, 2, 3, 4, 5, 6, 7, 9, 11, 12, 105, 127, 157, 181, 182, 183, 184, 185, 186, 187, 188, 189, 191, 193, 195, 197, 199, 201, 202, 203, 204, 205, 206, 207, 209
lingua franca, 2, 11, 16, 33, 37, 38, 39, 49, 73, 94, 128, 129, 166, 175, 176, 179, 181, 182, 184, 188, 191, 192, 193, 194, 197, 198, 200, 201, 202, 203, 204, 205, 206, 207
linguistic accreditation, 169, 173, 179
linguistic diversity, 37, 73, 174, 175
linguistic ideology, 106, 174, 192, 202, 206 [see also language ideology]
linguistic minorisation, 182
linguistic normalisation, 154, 184
linguistic practices [see language practices]
linguistic requirement [see language requirement]
linguistic right, 160
Linza, C, 100
Ljosland, R., 3, 13
Llurda, E.I., 179
local language, 37, 154, 190, 192, 197, 198, 200, 206, 208
Lønsmann, D., 18, 23, 38, 40
Luukka, M-R., 92, 98
Luxembourg, 18

Mac Mathúna, L., 16, 41
Madsen, M., 18, 34, 40, 41
Maegaard, M., 24, 41
Mahncke, H., 24, 41
Maiworm, F., 2, 14, 79, 100
Malay, 15, 148
Mancho-Barés, G., 179
Martel, Y., 113
Maseko, P., 145, 151
master [*programmes,* MA], 8, 13, 25, 26, 29, 33, 45, 48, 51, 65, 75, 79, 80, 81, 82, 84, 85, 92, 94, 96, 100, 108, 109, 110, 118, 119, 120, 121, 125, 126, 131, 146, 165, 166, 167, 176, 177, 188, 199, 207, 209
McLeod, W., 207, 209
media, 8, 19, 20, 21, 23, 38, 41, 47, 66, 91, 92, 96, 99, 120, 151
medium of instruction [see language of instruction]
medium-sized language, 1, 4, 5, 6, 7, 8, 11, 12, 13, 14, 17, 40, 43, 49, 58, 60, 61, 62, 103, 127, 129, 131, 149, 153, 181, 183, 184, 185, 187, 189, 192, 195, 199, 205, 208, 209, 210
medium-sized language community, 1, 3, 5, 6, 7, 9, 11, 13, 14, 59, 209, 210
Melichar, M., 50, 62
Michavila, F, 176, 179, 180
Miettinen, M., 86, 87, 98
Milian-Massana, A., 5, 13, 14, 209
minority languages, 16, 24, 64, 155, 157, 182, 195
mobility, 3, 32, 42, 47, 97, 142, 158, 161, 164, 166, 167, 170, 171, 175, 176, 192, 194, 204
Moed, H., 180
Mortensen, J., 1, 3, 12, 13, 14, 18, 27, 34, 38, 39, 41
mother tongue, 18, 24, 31, 35, 47, 60, 64, 91, 92 [see also first language]
Mouton, J, 147, 149, 151
multilingual/ multilingualism, 2, 8, 9, 11, 16, 17, 18, 24, 27, 31, 35, 36, 42, 43, 44, 46, 47, 59, 73, 79, 83, 87, 90, 136, 137, 139, 143, 145, 147, 150, 151, 160, 161, 162, 163, 167, 168, 171, 173, 175, 176, 177, 178, 181, 182, 185, 186, 191, 197, 199, 200, 202, 203, 205, 207, 209

Nábělková, M., 60, 62
Nadal, O., 156, 179
Namibia, 148
national language, 9, 60, 64, 65, 69, 72, 73, 76, 85, 90, 91, 93, 94, 95, 133, 196, 200
native speaker, 21, 46, 51, 54, 64, 157
natural sciences, 8, 33, 34, 75, 86, 92, 102, 110, 116, 130
Nekvapil, J., 46, 47, 59, 60, 61, 62

Neustupný, J.V., 46, 62
New Zealand, 148
Nikula, T., 42
Nogueira, A., 159, 168, 172, 179
non-native speaker, 46, 50, 54
Norway, 42, 87
Norwegian, 13, 17, 35
Nymark, J., 24, 41

official language, 47, 48, 64, 68, 85, 104, 135, 154, 156, 160, 164, 165, 168, 170, 174, 175, 177, 195, 199
Oliva, L., 157, 180
Ouane, A., 132, 151
Ozolins, U., 185, 209

Pabian, P., 50, 62
parallel language [use], 23, 30, 31, 32, 73, 74
Peeters, Y.J.D, 16, 41
Pennycook, A., 142, 151
Pérez-Llantada, C, 62
peripheral languages, 15
PhD, 8, 39, 40, 45, 65, 66, 88, 89, 90, 96, 108, 118, 119, 123, 125, 126, 127, 128, 131, 151, 188, 189, 190, 196
[see also doctorate]
Phillipson, R., 3, 14, 109, 130
Piech, K., 50, 62
Pienaar, M., 141, 150
Plo, R., 62
plurilingual/plurilingualism, 79, 83, 189, 191, 192, 1931
policymakers, 107, 182
Polish, 45
Pons, E., 11, 153, 157, 180
Portuguese, 15, 148
postgraduate course, 5, 8, 11, 188, 189, 204, 207
Potgieter, P.H, 150
Pöyhönen, S, 42
Preisler, B., 1, 2, 3, 7, 14, 15, 18, 20, 27, 32, 36, 38, 39, 40, 41, 42, 60, 62, 185, 186, 192, 203
Prendergast, C., 50, 62
preschool, 19, 103, 133, 178
prestige, 19, 20, 32, 179
primary school, 20, 134
private university, 45, 49, 165, 168, 178

professor, 3, 10, 29, 30, 104, 115, 126, 157, 168, 194, 198, 201, 204
public university, 45, 49, 50, 158, 159, 165, 168, 169, 178
Purser, L., 177, 180
Puuska, H-M., 86, 87, 98

Q-value, 16, 17

Radosevic, S., 50, 62
Ram, D., 10, 103, 105, 106, 107, 108, 115, 116, 131
Reinbothe, R., 90, 99
research, 2, 5, 6, 8, 9, 10, 11, 12, 13, 18, 25, 26, 28, 30, 33, 34, 36, 38, 41, 43, 44, 46, 49, 50, 52, 56, 57, 58, 59, 61, 62, 65, 66, 68, 69, 72, 74, 75, 76, 82, 83, 84, 86, 87, 88, 92, 93, 94, 95, 96, 97, 98, 99, 103, 104, 105, 107, 108, 109, 110, 111, 113, 115, 117, 118, 119, 121, 123, 127, 129, 131, 132, 133, 145, 146, 147, 148, 149, 150, 151, 158, 160, 161, 162, 167, 168, 171, 172, 173, 174, 176, 177, 178, 180, 183, 188, 189, 190, 192, 195, 199, 201, 203, 208
Risager, K., 15, 39, 41, 42, 62
Rokebrand, L, 142, 151
role of English, 4, 19, 72, 78, 94, 95, 188, 189
Romani, 64
Rosselló, C., 175, 176, 179
Russian, 4, 7, 15, 45, 49, 51, 53, 56, 58, 60, 74, 75, 87, 105, 193

Saarinen, T., 33, 42, 83, 99, 202, 209
Saarnisto, M., 92, 99
Sami, 64, 185, 207
Scandinavia, 8, 9, 17, 41, 207
Schiewe, J., 27, 42
school, 19, 20, 24, 33, 38, 44, 48, 85, 94, 104, 111, 112, 121, 134, 154, 178
School of Business [see Business School]
[scientific] publication, 3, 8, 9, 11, 12, 25, 33, 34, 36, 43, 57, 65, 66, 86, 87, 88, 93, 106, 126, 128, 129, 151, 189, 190, 191, 199, 205
Scottish Gaelic, 185
second language, 15, 30, 33, 37, 47, 74, 165, 186
secondary school, 20, 24, 44, 48, 178

Sesotho, 134, 135
Sesotho sa Leboa, 134, 135, 140, 143, 149
Setswana, 134, 135
Sevaldsen, J., 18, 42
Shepard, C., 203, 209
Sherman, T., 9, 43, 46, 47, 49, 62, 191, 203
Shohamy, E., 103, 104, 105, 106, 131
Sieglová, D., 49, 62
Sierra, J.M., 13
Siltala, A., 97
Simonsen, D.F., 36, 39, 42
Sintonen, K., 93, 99
siSwati, 134, 135
Skerret, D.M., 185, 209
Skutnabb-Kangas, T., 109, 130
Sloboda, M., 62, 63
Slovak, 7, 9, 44, 47, 48, 56, 57, 60, 61, 62, 189, 194
Slovene, 105, 208
Slovenia, 185
small language, 16, 38
Smit, F., 139, 151
social network, 32, 35, 54
social sciences, 9, 33, 34, 39, 44, 53, 57, 58, 59, 67, 75, 86, 87, 101, 102, 132, 147, 149, 167, 172, 189, 190, 209
sociolinguistic, 2, 7, 11, 28, 41, 44, 62, 141, 154, 165, 167, 172, 181, 182, 183, 186, 187, 210
Söderlundh, H., 2, 14, 210
Söderqvist, M., 100
South Africa, 6, 10, 132, 133, 134, 135, 136, 137, 138, 139, 141, 143, 145, 147, 148, 149, 150, 151, 183, 185, 187, 188, 197
South Sudan, 133
Spain, 153, 158, 159, 166, 168, 170, 172, 177, 199
Spanish, 4, 7, 15, 36, 37, 51, 53, 58, 74, 75, 87, 153, 154, 155, 158, 159, 167, 168, 170, 171, 172, 173, 175, 177, 179, 199, 208, 209 [see also Castilian]
speech community, 18
sphere of life, 2, 9
Spolsky, B., 103, 104, 105, 106, 109, 131
Stæhr, L.S., 32, 40
Starks, D., 151
status [of language], 4, 6, 9, 11, 16, 20, 21, 30, 39, 40, 47, 48, 59, 74, 93, 94, 95, 98, 104, 106, 107, 109, 111, 113, 114, 115, 116, 127, 128, 134, 138, 139, 145, 153, 154, 156, 158, 160, 164, 168, 169, 175, 176, 178, 181, 182, 183, 184, 185, 191, 193, 194, 196, 201, 202, 204, 206, 207
students, 3, 5, 8, 10, 19, 20, 21, 25, 26, 27, 29, 30, 31, 32, 33, 35, 45, 47, 48, 49, 50, 51, 52, 54, 55, 56, 59, 60, 61, 65, 66, 72, 73, 75, 76, 77, 78, 79, 80, 81, 82, 83, 85, 86, 91, 92, 94, 95, 96, 100, 104, 105, 106, 107, 108, 109, 110, 111, 114, 115, 117, 118, 119, 120, 121, 122, 123, 124, 125, 126, 127, 128, 129, 130, 131, 136, 137, 139, 141, 142, 143, 144, 145, 147, 149, 157, 158, 160, 161, 162, 164, 166, 167, 169, 170, 171, 175, 176, 177, 178, 184, 186, 187, 188, 189, 191, 192, 194, 196, 197, 198, 200, 202, 204
supercentral language, 15, 181
Swahili, 15, 37
Sweden, 64, 87, 92, 207
Swedish, 6, 9, 16, 17, 30, 31, 35, 42, 47, 64, 65, 67, 68, 69, 72, 73, 74, 76, 77, 78, 79, 84, 85, 86, 87, 88, 89, 90, 91, 92, 93, 94, 95, 96, 97, 99, 100, 101, 105, 185, 186, 190, 193, 199

teacher, 19, 25, 26, 29, 31, 32, 33, 45, 48, 49, 56, 70, 84, 104, 168, 169, 170, 178, 184, 191, 198
terminology, 107, 108, 157, 164, 174, 198, 201, 208
The Netherlands, 18, 49, 79, 87, 92
Thelander, M., 36, 42
thesis, 39, 40, 55, 109, 110, 119, 120, 124, 151, 173 [see also dissertation]
Tijssen, R., 180
Tollefson, J.W., 105, 131, 158, 180
trilingual, 172
Tshivenda, 134, 135
Tsu, A., 158, 180
Tsuda, Y., 109, 131
Tsui, A.B.M., 105, 131

United Kingdom [UK], 60, 61, 82, 87
undergraduate, 9, 65, 79, 108, 139, 140, 143, 145, 146, 151, 165, 166, 167, 175, 177, 187, 188, 189, 198, 203, 207

United States [USA], 39, 82, 87, 90, 108
university sphere, 44, 45, 46, 47, 185

Vainio, V., 66, 77, 100
Valencia, 153, 154, 161, 165, 178
Valencian, 154, 199
   [see also Catalan]
Välimaa, J., 80, 100
Van Coller, H.P., 142, 152
Van den Heuvel, E, 100
Van der Walt, C., 2, 14
Van Leeuwen, T., 172, 180
Van Raan, A., 180
Van Rest, E., 2, 13, 80, 96, 207
Vänskä, A., 91, 92, 100
vehicular language, 66 [see also language of instruction]
Vehkanen, M., 97
vernacularisation, 17, 18
Vernet, J., 158, 180
Vila, F.X., 1, 4, 5, 14, 40, 61, 62, 63, 127, 131, 154, 172, 176, 180, 181, 184, 194, 209, 210
Vinent, A., 157, 180

Visser, M., 180
Vivanco Cervero, V., 3, 14

Wächter, B., 2, 14, 79, 100
Wagner, P., 62
Wandall, J, 39
Webb, V., 137, 148, 150, 152
Wee, L., 15, 42
Willmers, M., 149, 150
Wolff, J.U., 100
Woolard, K.A., 174, 176, 180
working language, 177, 197
world language, 17, 37, 52, 53, 56, 58
   [see also international language]

Xitsonga, 134, 135

Yle, 91, 92, 93, 100
Ylönen, S., 9, 64, 66, 77, 78, 79, 83, 95, 100, 186, 202, 204
young, 18, 19, 20, 21, 23, 24, 78, 92, 116, 143, 175, 186, 193
youth culture, 8, 20, 21, 22, 38

Zeevaert, L., 17, 35, 42
Zinger, P, 109, 131

For Product Safety Concerns and Information please contact our EU Authorised Representative:

Easy Access System Europe

Mustamäe tee 50

10621 Tallinn

Estonia

gpsr.requests@easproject.com